Alexander Williams is a cartoonist and animator whose film credits include *Who Framed Roger Rabbit?, The Lion King, The Iron Giant,* the last three *Harry Potter* films and *The Chronicles of Narnia*. He has worked for many studios including Disney, DreamWorks, Fox, Warner Bros and Sony.

Alex is Head of Animation at Escape Studios in London, and the founder of the online animation school www.animationapprentice.org. He also draws the weekly cartoon strip *Queen's Counsel* which has appeared in the law pages of The Times since 1993, and has published many books.

Nick Reid is a former investment manager living in Edinburgh. He first met Alex whilst they were both working in Tokyo in 2002. Back in the UK, Nick and Alex collaborated together on the book *'101 Uses for a Useless Banker'*, published in 2009 in the aftermath of the Financial Crash. Around the same time Nick started contributing cartoons for Queen's Counsel in The Times.

For a Few Guineas More

The Legal Year in Cartoons

For a Few Guineas More

The Legal Year in Cartoons

Alex Steuart Williams

Nick Reid

Law Brief Publishing

Published 2019 by Law Brief Publishing, an imprint of Law Brief Publishing Ltd
30 The Parks
Minehead
Somerset
TA24 8BT

www.lawbriefpublishing.com

Paperback: 978-1-912687-56-5

Dedicated to my wife Sarah, who writes many, many jokes for Queen's Counsel. Or, as she would put it – just the funny ones.

PREFACE

It has been 26 years since the *Queen's Counsel* cartoon first graced the law pages of The Times; the strip began its life in October 1993 when the newspaper was still a broadsheet, the ink came off on your fingers, and newspapers were still the main way people got their news, fake or otherwise.

The law section was a titan; it occupied a princely 12 pages of the paper, packed with advertising, and was pretty much compulsory reading for both solicitors and barristers. If a candidate was asked, during a law interview, the question "what newspaper do you read?" there was only one answer – *The Times*. Since the internet, all that has changed, but *The Times* remains the only UK newspaper that makes a serious attempt to cover the law.

Meanwhile, Sir Geoffrey Bentwood QC has remained Head of Chambers at No 4 Lawn Buildings in the Outer Temple for an impressive 26 years, stoutly resisting (but not *too* much) the inevitable changes brought about by technology, women (gasp) and even chaps with ear-rings, not all of whom went to public school and wear proper tailoring. Some even have – Heaven forbid – beards, but this sort of thing is not to be encouraged. Real barristers shave daily.

Sir Geoffrey's young junior Edward Longwind struggles to take silk (ie become a Queen's Counsel himself) – failing every year that he tries, and now grumbles about being too "pale, male and stale" ever to make the grade. Quentin Crawley is the perpetual pupil barrister, endlessly hoping to get taken on in Chambers, but never successful, and Helena Goodwood continues to try – mostly unsuccessfully – to make the legal world a better place.

At the firm of Loophole and Fillibuster, Richard Loophole continues to enrich himself, mostly at his clients' expense, and yet his client, the end-lessly unsuccessful litigant, Mr Sprocket, always seems to return for further punishment.

Curiously, none of the characters have aged much over the years, unlike their creator. They have, however, blossomed into colour. Quentin is ginger, and the bar itself is a kind of muddy grey-ish brown, but the books on the shelves (now sadly redundant – all research is done online) are a rather charming shade of green.

Alexander Steuart Williams
October 2019

ACKNOWLEDGEMENTS

Queen's Counsel has been in The Times for over 25 years, and a lot of people have helped keep it alive. Thanks are due to former Times art editor David Driver for taking a chance on the strip back in 1993, and to law editor Frances Gibb to putting up with it for a quarter of a century and nurturing it – especially in the early years. My old friend (and best man) Graham Defries was my early collaborator and I'd never have got the strip off the ground without him. Jonathan Ames took over the legal reins from Frances at The Times in 2018 and has been a stalwart champion ever since. In the early 2000s Mark Furber sent in lots of great ideas – I miss his emails. Today, my co-author Nick Reid writes lots of the jokes and, but for his energy and elbow grease, this book would never have seen the light of day. And thanks to Sarah Crowther, my wife, collaborator and long-suffering editor.

CONTENTS

THE CHARACTERS

4 Lawn Buildings

1   2   3   4   5

1. Derek Hardman

Head clerk at 4 Lawn Buildings – and the power behind the throne. Publicly defers to the barristers in his chambers, but behind the scenes he deftly controls their careers.

2. Helena Fairchild

Junior barrister and human rights lawyer. Went into law to make a better world, but found to her disappointment that villains pay better than the angels. Wrestles with her conscience – and tries to do the right thing.

3. Quentin Crawley

Pupil barrister and all-round dogsbody. Desperate to win a tenancy. Hopeless in court – and lives in permanent terror that someone in chambers will notice.

4. Edward Longwind

Junior barrister and understudy to Sir Geoffrey, to whose levels of prosperity and pomposity Edward can only aspire. Thoroughly cynical and jaded. Desperate to take silk and add those magic letters "QC" to his name.

5. Sir Geoffrey Bentwood QC

Senior barrister, silk, part-time judge and Master of the Universe. Even his children call him "your honour". Longs to be promoted to the High Court so he can retire in comfort, splendour and ermine.

Fillibuster & Loophole

6   7   8

6. Richard Loophole

Senior partner at Fillibuster & Loophole. Legal fat cat, chief beneficiary of the fountain of cash that rises to the top of big law firms. Long ago forgot anything he learned at law school; delegates all the hard bits to his associates. Plays a lot of golf.

7. Rachel Underwood

Extremely bright and able associate solicitor; permanently on the verge of quitting her oppressive job. Works absurdly long hours. She is (in theory) entitled to holiday but can rarely take it. The firm promises to make her partner "some day". Her friends say she has Stockholm Syndrome.

8. Arthur Greybinder

Tax partner. Reads HM Revenue reports for fun. Motto: "the Code is Lord". A workaholic who is only vaguely aware of a family he has at home.

Judges & Clients

9   10

9. His Honour Judge Humphrey Barnacle

Formerly Head of Chambers at 4 Lawn Buildings, now put out to pasture in the courts. Hopelessly out of touch, and far more interested in gardening than the finer points of law and evidence.

10. Nigel Sprocket

The endlessly unlucky litigant whose lawyers will not rest until they have spent all of his money.

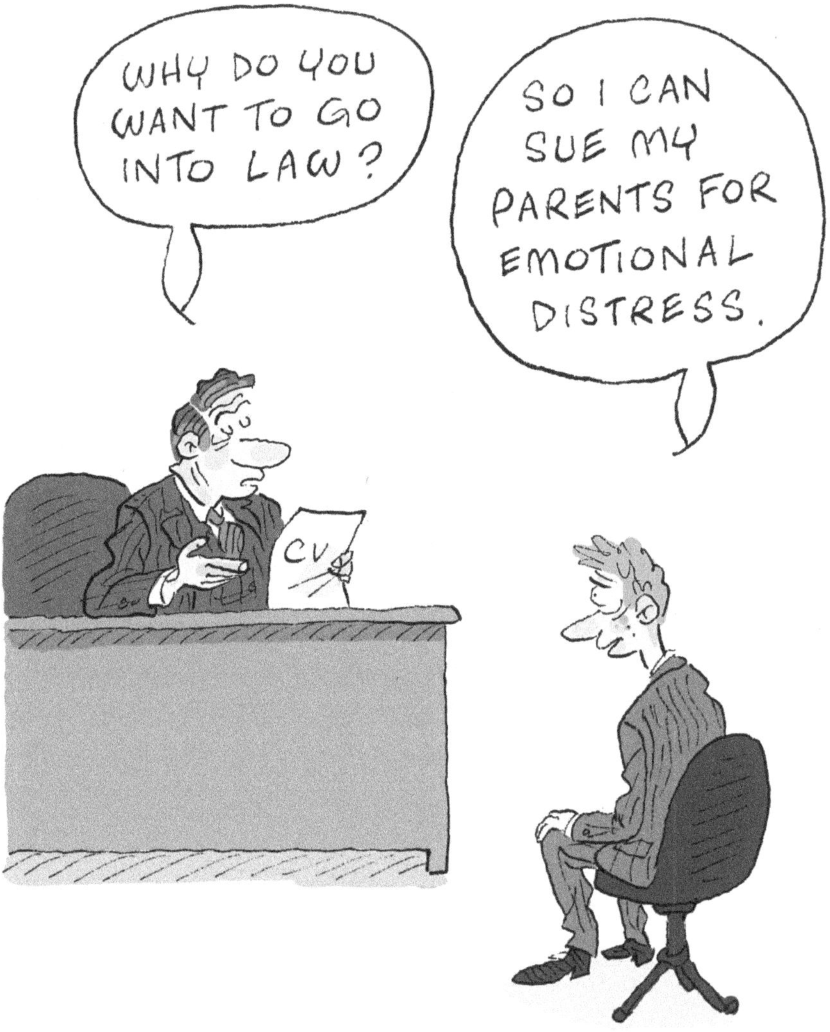
WHY DO YOU WANT TO GO INTO LAW?
SO I CAN SUE MY PARENTS FOR EMOTIONAL DISTRESS.
CV

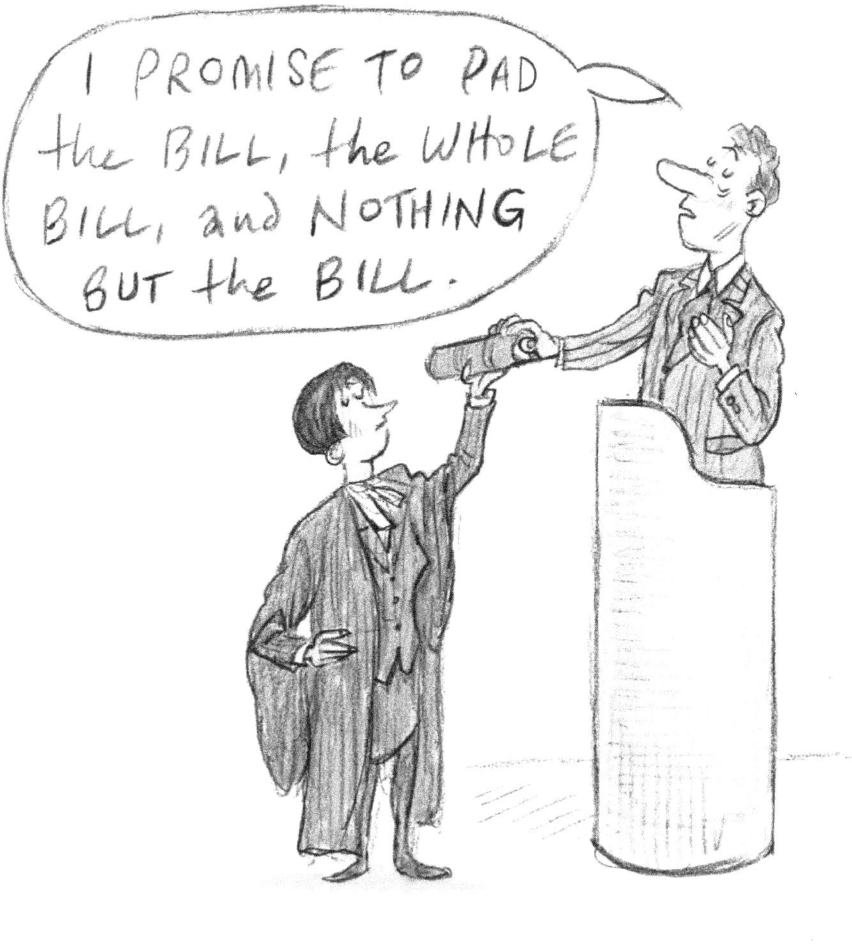
I PROMISE TO PAD the BILL, the WHOLE BILL, and NOTHING BUT the BILL.

MICHAELMAS TERM
October to December

The legal year commences at the beginning of October with a reception known as the Lord Chancellor's breakfast in the medieval splendour of Westminster hall.

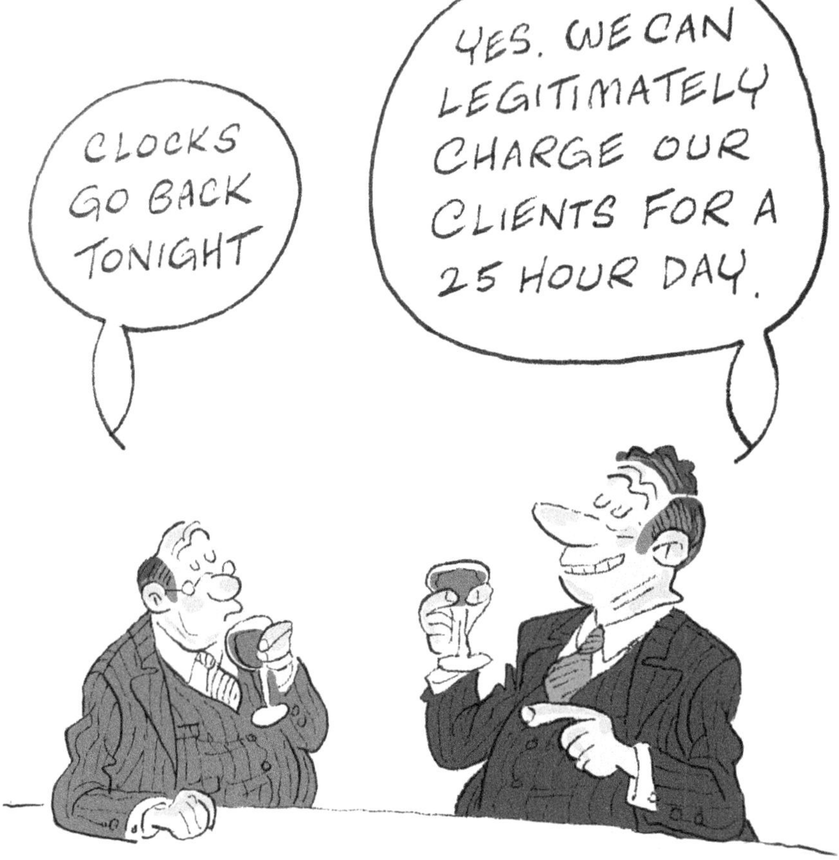
CLOCKS GO BACK TONIGHT
YES. WE CAN LEGITIMATELY CHARGE OUR CLIENTS FOR A 25 HOUR DAY.

WE BARRISTERS GET CRITICISED FOR OUR OLD-FASHIONED WIGS AND GOWNS
BUT IT ISN'T AN AFFECTATION. THE ANONYMITY IT PROVIDES US IS CRUCIAL!
IT HIGHLIGHTS THAT IT IS THE LAW THAT IS IMPORTANT, AND NOT THE EGO OF THE LAWYER.
I CAN SEE DISCRETION IS TERRIBLY IMPORTANT TO YOU, SIR GEOFFREY...
QC 1

YOU KNOW, I DID ACTUALLY READ "A BRIEF HISTORY OF TIME"
STEPHEN HAWKING DEAD
IT'S A FASCINATING ACCOUNT OF HOW CONCEPTS LIKE TIME ARE REALLY RELATIVE.
IT'S COME IN VERY USEFUL AT WORK.
YOU'VE BILLED ME FOR 26 HOURS' WORK LAST TUESDAY.
FUNNY YOU SHOULD MENTION THAT...
BILL

AS A NEW PUPIL IN CHAMBERS, I MUST WARN YOU TO WATCH OUT FOR SIR GEOFFREY.
HE MAY EXPECT YOU TO PERFORM CERTAIN, ER... FAVOURS.
YOU MAY EVEN HAVE TO, UM, MASSAGE HIS...
...EGO
SO, WHAT DID YOU THINK OF MY PERFORMANCE IN COURT TODAY?
OH, YOU WERE WONDERFUL, SIR GEOFFREY.

I HEAR THAT RACHEL MAY BE LEAVING THE FIRM.
WHAT?! HOW COULD SHE?!
WHY?
TO JOIN A BIG INSURANCE COMPANY.
WHAT TREACHERY! I'LL NEVER SPEAK TO HER AGAIN!
...ONE THAT SENDS US LOTS OF WORK...
ER...
ONE OF OUR BIGGEST CLIENTS...
RACHEL! I HEAR YOU'RE LEAVING US! IT'S TIME I TOOK YOU OUT FOR AN EXCELLENT LUNCH...

RICHARD HAS BECOME INSUFFERABLE SINCE HE BECAME "LAWYER OF THE WEEK"!
CHECK OUT THIS BIT ABOUT "MY MANAGEMENT PHILOSOPHY".
HE SAYS HE HAS AN "OPEN DOOR POLICY TOWARDS JUNIORS"
WELL... DOES HE?
ERM... SORT OF...
RICHARD, HERE'S YOUR SKINNY LATTE, GOLF CLUBS, AND DRY CLEANING...
AH, COME IN, THE DOOR'S OPEN...

I SEE THAT BERNARD HAS BEEN MADE HEAD OF DISPUTE RESOLUTION AT HIS MAGIC CIRCLE FIRM.
"DISPUTES"? ISN'T THAT WHAT WE USED TO CALL LITIGATION?
EXACTLY.
SO WHAT'S THE DIFFERENCE?
... A SMOOTHER MANNER AND A 30% HIKE IN FEES I THINK.

IT'S A BIT OF A PAIN, THIS 5p CHARGE FOR A PLASTIC BAG.
5p
WELL, I'VE GOT MY OWN RATHER STYLISH ROBUST CARRIER.
BEEP!
YOU MEAN... ONE OF THOSE BAGS FOR LIFE?
NO... A 19TH CENTURY HORSE HAIR WIG!

AWFUL NEWS ABOUT OLD BINKY GETTING CAUGHT WATCHING THOSE VIDEOS AT WORK.
YES
SO HUMILIATING FOR A SENIOR JUDGE.
POOR CHAP – HE'LL NEVER LIVE IT DOWN.
... CUTE KITTEN VIDEOS ON YOU TUBE ... A MAN OF HIS AGE!

I'M BEING SENT ON A TRAINING COURSE TO LEARN "EMOJI"
WHAT'S THAT?
A LANGUAGE. NOWADAYS, DEFENDANTS TEXT EACH OTHER IN SYMBOLS
WHY CAN'T THEY USE ENGLISH LIKE THE REST OF US?
INDEED!
...VOS AUTEM OMNINO RECTA, OLD CHAP*
NOLO CONTENDERE** !!
*YOU'RE RIGHT **EXACTLY

1ST XI CRICKET AT UNI, 5 HANDICAP GOLFER, GRADE 8 CELLO...
PUPILLAGE INTERVIEWS DO NOT DISTURB
CV
CV
YOU'RE JUST THE SORT OF TALENTED CANDIDATE THAT CHAMBERS IS LOOKING FOR.
CV
CV
I'D RECOMMEND EBAY FOR THE CELLO, AND GUM-TREE FOR THE GOLF CLUBS AND CRICKET BAT.
...YOU WON'T BE NEEDING ANY OF THEM FROM SEPTEMBER...

YET ANOTHER UK COMPANY BLAMES ITS POOR RESULTS ON BREXIT!
RBS BOSS BLAMES BREXIT
EVEN MPs COMPLAIN THEY CAN'T DEBATE REAL ISSUES DUE TO BREXIT!
...BREXIT IS JUST A POOR EXCUSE FOR FAILURE!
ER... I WAS WONDERING IF THERE MIGHT BE A CHANCE OF A PAY RISE...?
SORRY, WE'D LOVE TO, BUT WITH ALL THIS BREXIT UNCERTAINTY...

YOU LOOK AWFUL. CLEAN YOUR SHOES AND BRUSH YOUR HAIR!
DO UP YOUR TOP BUTTON! STRAIGHTEN YOUR TIE!
?
MUM, IT'S ME GOING BACK TO SCHOOL, NOT DAD!
WELL, HE'LL NEVER MAKE PARTNER THIS YEAR IF HE DOESN'T SMARTEN UP!

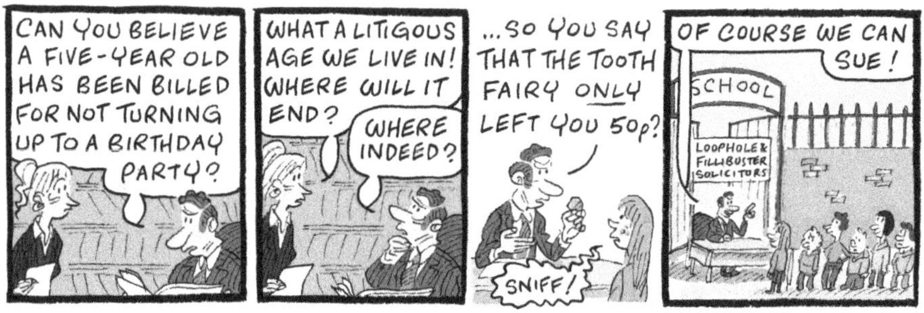
CAN YOU BELIEVE A FIVE-YEAR OLD HAS BEEN BILLED FOR NOT TURNING UP TO A BIRTHDAY PARTY?
WHAT A LITIGOUS AGE WE LIVE IN! WHERE WILL IT END?
WHERE INDEED?
...SO YOU SAY THAT THE TOOTH FAIRY ONLY LEFT YOU 50p?
SNIFF!
OF COURSE WE CAN SUE!
SCHOOL
LOOPHOLE & FILLIBUSTER SOLICITORS

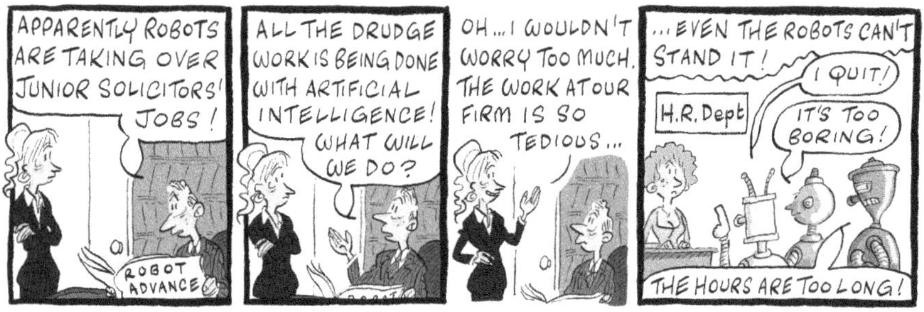
APPARENTLY ROBOTS ARE TAKING OVER JUNIOR SOLICITORS' JOBS!
ROBOT ADVANCE
ALL THE DRUDGE WORK IS BEING DONE WITH ARTIFICIAL INTELLIGENCE!
WHAT WILL WE DO?
OH...I WOULDN'T WORRY TOO MUCH. THE WORK AT OUR FIRM IS SO TEDIOUS...
...EVEN THE ROBOTS CAN'T STAND IT!
I QUIT!
IT'S TOO BORING!
H.R. Dept
THE HOURS ARE TOO LONG!

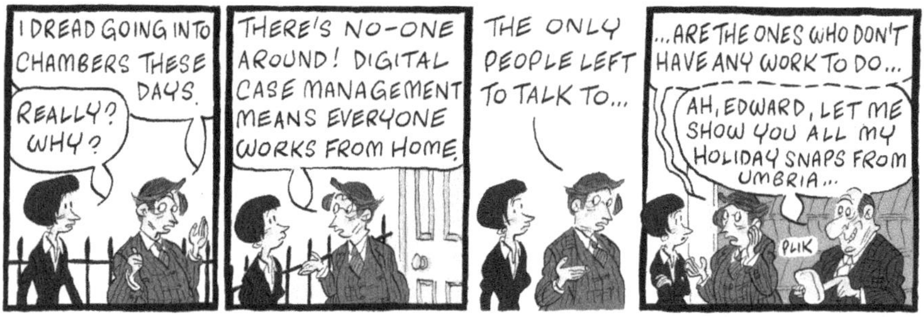
I DREAD GOING INTO CHAMBERS THESE DAYS.
REALLY? WHY?
THERE'S NO-ONE AROUND! DIGITAL CASE MANAGEMENT MEANS EVERYONE WORKS FROM HOME.
THE ONLY PEOPLE LEFT TO TALK TO...
...ARE THE ONES WHO DON'T HAVE ANY WORK TO DO...
AH, EDWARD, LET ME SHOW YOU ALL MY HOLIDAY SNAPS FROM UMBRIA...
PLIK

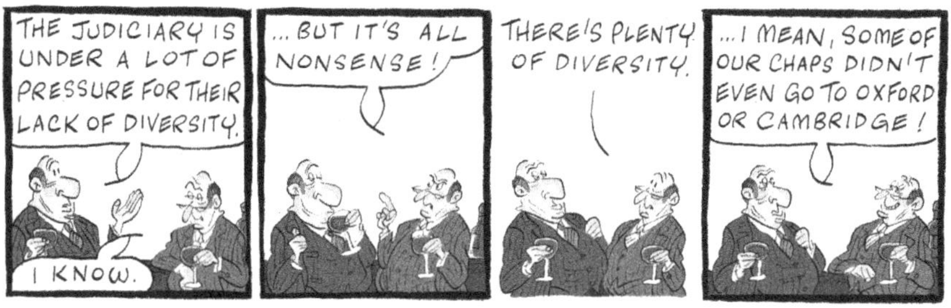
THE JUDICIARY IS UNDER A LOT OF PRESSURE FOR THEIR LACK OF DIVERSITY.
I KNOW.
...BUT IT'S ALL NONSENSE!
THERE'S PLENTY OF DIVERSITY.
...I MEAN, SOME OF OUR CHAPS DIDN'T EVEN GO TO OXFORD OR CAMBRIDGE!

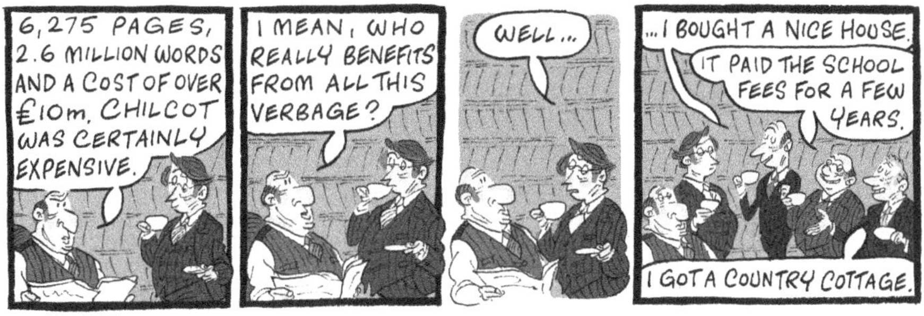
6,275 PAGES, 2.6 MILLION WORDS AND A COST OF OVER £10m, CHILCOT WAS CERTAINLY EXPENSIVE.
I MEAN, WHO REALLY BENEFITS FROM ALL THIS VERBAGE?
WELL...
...I BOUGHT A NICE HOUSE.
IT PAID THE SCHOOL FEES FOR A FEW YEARS.
I GOT A COUNTRY COTTAGE.

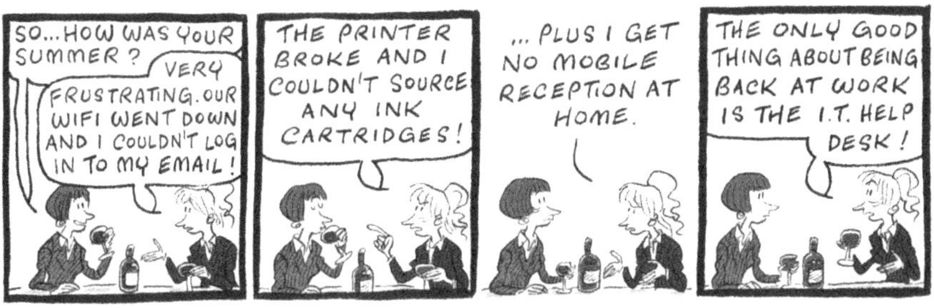
SO...HOW WAS YOUR SUMMER?
VERY FRUSTRATING. OUR WIFI WENT DOWN AND I COULDN'T LOG IN TO MY EMAIL!
THE PRINTER BROKE AND I COULDN'T SOURCE ANY INK CARTRIDGES!
...PLUS I GET NO MOBILE RECEPTION AT HOME.
THE ONLY GOOD THING ABOUT BEING BACK AT WORK IS THE I.T. HELP DESK!

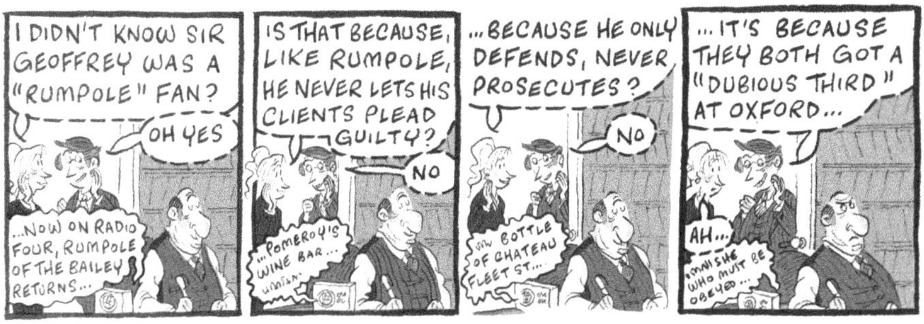
I DIDN'T KNOW SIR GEOFFREY WAS A "RUMPOLE" FAN?
OH YES
...NOW ON RADIO FOUR, RUMPOLE OF THE BAILEY RETURNS...
IS THAT BECAUSE, LIKE RUMPOLE, HE NEVER LETS HIS CLIENTS PLEAD GUILTY?
NO
...POMEROY'S WINE BAR...
...BECAUSE HE ONLY DEFENDS, NEVER PROSECUTES?
NO
...BOTTLE OF CHATEAU FLEET ST...
...IT'S BECAUSE THEY BOTH GOT A "DUBIOUS THIRD" AT OXFORD...
AH...
SHE WHO MUST BE OBEYED...

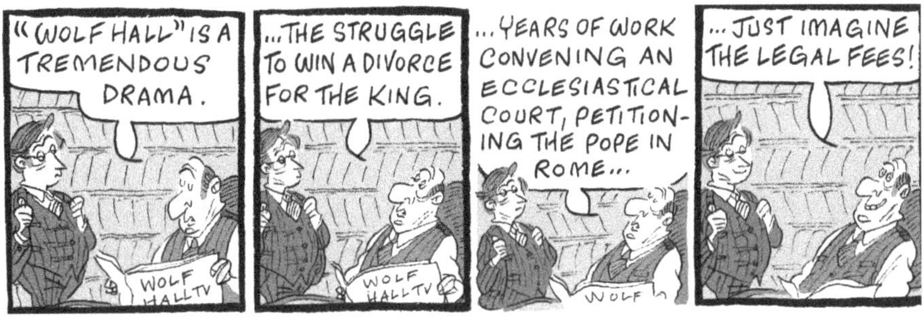
"WOLF HALL" IS A TREMENDOUS DRAMA.
WOLF HALL TV
...THE STRUGGLE TO WIN A DIVORCE FOR THE KING.
WOLF HALL TV
...YEARS OF WORK CONVENING AN ECCLESIASTICAL COURT, PETITIONING THE POPE IN ROME...
WOLF
...JUST IMAGINE THE LEGAL FEES!

THIS US SUPREME COURT CONFIRMATION IS SO BRUTAL: CULTURE WAR, THE #ME TOO MOVEMENT...
KAVANAUGH
WE DO THINGS SO MUCH BETTER OVER HERE.
KAVANAUGH
AH... BALLIOL AND THE ATHENAEUM...
CV
CV
ME TOO! WELCOME ABOARD!
CV
CV

TECHNOLOGY HAS TRANSFORMED THE WAY WE WORK IN FAMILY LAW.
IN PARTICULAR, BEING ABLE TO TALK TO A CHILD OVER A WEB LINK
YOU MEAN, IN THE COURTS?
NOT THE COURTS!
...AT HOME! I WORK SUCH LONG HOURS, IT'S THE ONLY WAY I GET TO SEE MY DAUGHTER...
ONCE UPON A TIME, THERE LIVED A PRINCESS...

SO TELL ME YOUR VIEW OF THE CASE.
ER... I BELIEVE...
NO!
PRIESTS "BELIEVE". TRY AGAIN.
ER... IN MY JUDGMENT...
WHAT?! ARE YOU A JUDGE?!
ER... NO... I FEEL...
BARRISTERS NEVER "FEEL"!
I THINK...
DON'T "THINK"!
UM... IN MY LEARNED OPINION...
THAT'S BETTER.

I ALWAYS SAID THESE FANCY ESOTERIC CURRENCIES WOULD NEVER CATCH ON.
BITCOIN SLIDE
FAR MORE SENSIBLE TO STICK TO GOOD OLD POUNDS STERLING.
BITCOIN
RING! RING!
AH, SIR GEOFFREY, YOUR FEE IS £750 AN HOUR?
ER... GUINEAS, IF YOU DON'T MIND...

SO WHAT MADE YOU WANT TO BE A JUDGE, HUMPHREY?
TO HELP THE UNFORTUNATE!
INDEED?
YES, THE POOR, THE DOWNTRODDEN. THOSE POOR CREATURES WHO NEVER GET A BREAK!
YOU MEAN... VICTIMS OF CRIME?
OH NO!
PUPIL BARRISTERS! ... RELEASED INTO COURT FOR THE FIRST TIME
ER... YOUR HONOUR... I MEAN, M'LUD...
TREMBLE
NOW, MR CRAWLEY, TAKE A DEEP BREATH AND START AGAIN...

AS A SOLICITOR, I HARDLY EVER USE BARRISTERS ANY MORE. WE CAN DO EVERYTHING THEY CAN!
YES, BUT...
I STILL FIND THEM USEFUL.
FOR WHAT? ADVOCACY?
NO...
-ADVISING THE CLIENT.
BUT CAN'T YOU DO THAT JUST AS WELL?
OF COURSE!
...BUT SOMEONE HAS TO BREAK THE BAD NEWS TO THE CLIENT ABOUT HOW RUBBISH THEIR CASE REALLY IS...
...AND I DON'T WANT IT TO BE ME!

THE TRICK WITH HANDLING CLIENTS, RACHEL, IS TO KNOW THE LAW BACK TO FRONT.
MASTER THE FACTS! BE SURE YOU KNOW THEIR NEEDS INSIDE OUT!
AND THEN, ONCE YOU'VE DONE ALL THAT...
... TELL THEM EXACTLY WHAT THEY WANT TO HEAR.

THESE UNEXPLAINED WEALTH ORDERS, OR "UWOs", ARE WORRYING A LOT OF OUR RUSSIAN CLIENTS.
IT'S NOT JUST DODGY RUSSIANS WHO SHOULD BE WORRIED.
THERE ARE OTHERS WHO MAY HAVE SOME EXPLAINING TO DO...
SON, WHERE DID YOU GET THOSE FANCY TRAINERS?
ER... WITH MY POCKET MONEY?
UWO

LAWSCHOOL: DAY ONE
STUDENTS, YOU MUST PREPARE YOURSELF FOR MONTHS OF HARD WORK.
YOUR ROAD WILL NOT BE AN EASY ONE, AND MANY OF YOU WILL FAIL YOUR EXAMS.
... UNLESS, OF COURSE...
... YOU BUY A FULL SET OF MY LAW BOOKS. I'LL BE SIGNING COPIES AFTER THE LECTURE...

WHAT SCARY COSTUME SHALL I WEAR FOR HALLOWE'EN? WITCH? VAMPIRE? GHOST?
NO.
MAYBE I'LL GO AS JEREMY CORBYN, OR AS HARVEY WEINSTEIN...
... MAYBE NOT...
I KNOW... I'LL GO AS SOMETHING REALLY SCARY...
... MYSELF!
OH NO... IT'S A... LAWYER!!
GRRR!
AAHHH!!!

WHAT DID THE KIDS PICK FOR THEIR HALLOWE'EN COSTUMES THIS YEAR?
OH, SOMETHING REALLY SCARY.
ZOMBIES?
NO
WERE-WOLVES...
NO
... MUCH SCARIER THAN THAT...
LIKE WHAT?
... MEMBERS OF THE BAR STANDARDS BOARD.
HAVE YOU MET YOUR DIVERSITY TARGETS YET?
WHAT ABOUT YOUR CPD POINTS?
YIKES!
AAAARRGHH!!

IT'S AWFUL, THIS GHASTLY AMERICAN CUSTOM THAT EVERY-ONE HAS ADOPTED
... DRESSED UP IN GOD KNOWS WHAT FANCY DRESS FOR HALLOWE'EN PARTIES.
I MEAN, REALLY, GROWN ADULTS SHOULD KNOW BETTER...
NOW... WHERE DID I PUT MY 18TH CENTURY HORSEHAIR WIG?

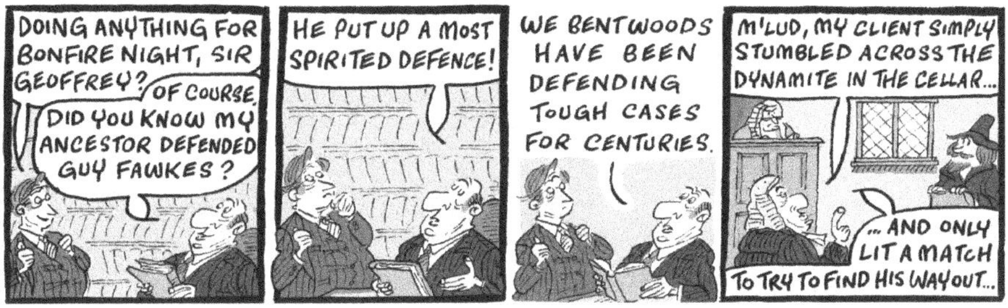
DOING ANYTHING FOR BONFIRE NIGHT, SIR GEOFFREY?
OF COURSE. DID YOU KNOW MY ANCESTOR DEFENDED GUY FAWKES?
HE PUT UP A MOST SPIRITED DEFENCE!
WE BENTWOODS HAVE BEEN DEFENDING TOUGH CASES FOR CENTURIES.
M'LUD, MY CLIENT SIMPLY STUMBLED ACROSS THE DYNAMITE IN THE CELLAR...
... AND ONLY LIT A MATCH TO TRY TO FIND HIS WAY OUT...

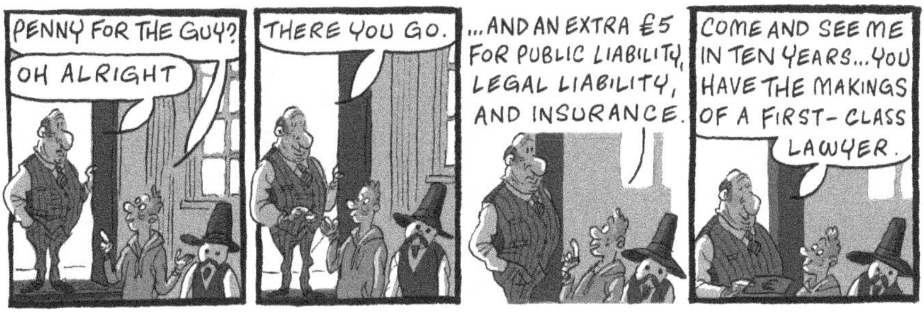
PENNY FOR THE GUY?
OH ALRIGHT
THERE YOU GO.
...AND AN EXTRA £5 FOR PUBLIC LIABILITY, LEGAL LIABILITY, AND INSURANCE.
COME AND SEE ME IN TEN YEARS...YOU HAVE THE MAKINGS OF A FIRST-CLASS LAWYER.

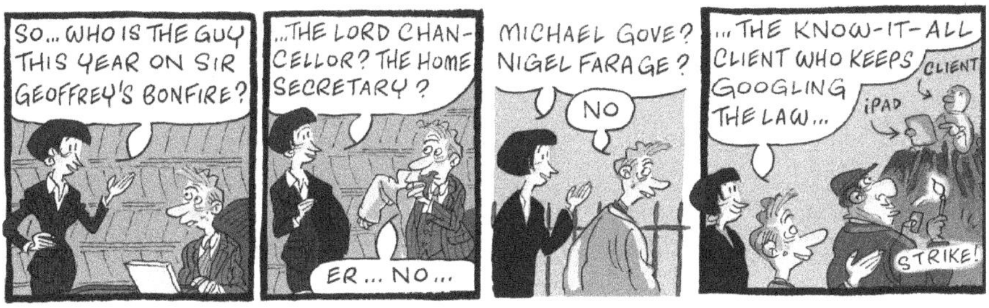
SO... WHO IS THE GUY THIS YEAR ON SIR GEOFFREY'S BONFIRE?
...THE LORD CHAN-CELLOR? THE HOME SECRETARY?
ER ... NO ...
MICHAEL GOVE? NIGEL FARAGE?
NO
... THE KNOW-IT-ALL CLIENT WHO KEEPS GOOGLING THE LAW...
CLIENT
iPAD
STRIKE!

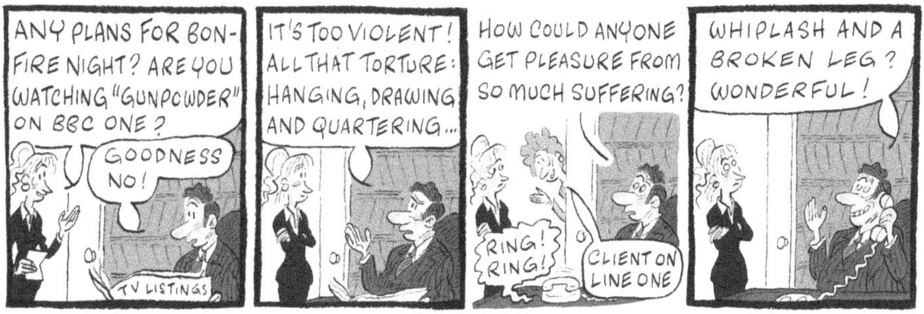
ANY PLANS FOR BON-FIRE NIGHT? ARE YOU WATCHING "GUNPOWDER" ON BBC ONE?
GOODNESS NO!
TV LISTINGS
IT'S TOO VIOLENT! ALL THAT TORTURE: HANGING, DRAWING AND QUARTERING...
HOW COULD ANYONE GET PLEASURE FROM SO MUCH SUFFERING?
RING! RING!
CLIENT ON LINE ONE
WHIPLASH AND A BROKEN LEG? WONDERFUL!

I CAN'T DECIDE WHICH SIDE SHOULD WIN. SHOULD WE FIND ON THE BASIS OF THE FACTS?
...OR ON THE BASIS OF THE LAW?
...OR BOTH? WHAT DO YOU THINK?
WELL...
...LET'S FIND AGAINST THE BARRISTER WITH THE GHASTLY "MOVEMBER" MOUSTACHE...
QUITE RIGHT

YES... £250 A MONTH ON WIG MAINTENANCE... AND £400 ON GOWN DRY-CLEANING...
GOSH... I HAD NO IDEA LIFE AS A BARRISTER COULD BE SO EXPENSIVE!
SILVER BUTTONS: £300...
WELL, AT THIS TIME OF YEAR IT IS...
...£550...
SIR GEOFFREY IS DOING HIS TAX RETURN...
GOLD BRAID, £350, VINTAGE CLARET FOR CLIENTS, £1,750...

I REMEMBER MY GRANDFATHER TELLING ME OF THE DREADFUL ARTILLERY BARRAGES IN THE WAR...
ARMISTICE DAY
...HE SUFFERED PERMANENT HEARING LOSS.
ARMISTICE DAY
...THOUGH IT CAME IN HANDY WHEN HE BECAME HEAD OF CHAMBERS.
ARMISTICE DAY
EXCUSE ME SIR, BUT WE JUNIORS ARE VERY OVER-WORKED AND UNDERPAID...
EH? WHAT'S THAT? CAN'T HEAR YOU...

RACHEL, I'M AFRAID I'LL NEED YOU TO DO THIS EMERGENCY APPLICATION FOR MONDAY.
BUT I'M SWAMPED!
I KNOW...
IT CAN'T BE HELPED. THERE IS JUST SO MUCH TO DO AT THIS TIME OF YEAR!
EVERYTHING'S SO BUSY... I'M OVERWHELMED!
...THERE ARE CAROL CONCERTS, SHOPPING TO BE DONE, PARTIES, AND CLIENT LUNCHES
HIC!

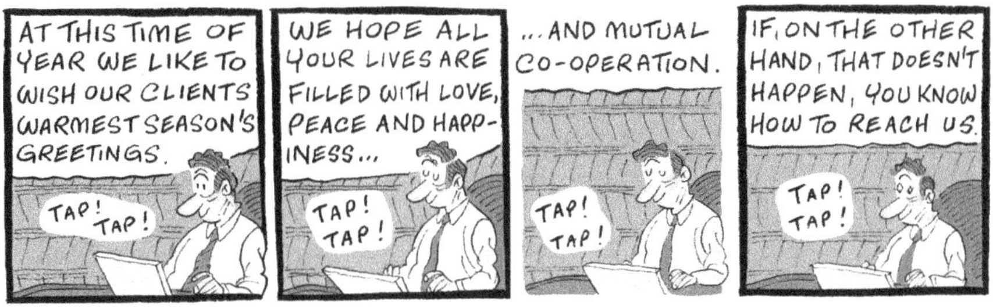
AT THIS TIME OF YEAR WE LIKE TO WISH OUR CLIENTS WARMEST SEASON'S GREETINGS.
TAP! TAP!
WE HOPE ALL YOUR LIVES ARE FILLED WITH LOVE, PEACE AND HAPPINESS...
TAP! TAP!
...AND MUTUAL CO-OPERATION.
TAP! TAP!
IF, ON THE OTHER HAND, THAT DOESN'T HAPPEN, YOU KNOW HOW TO REACH US.
TAP! TAP!

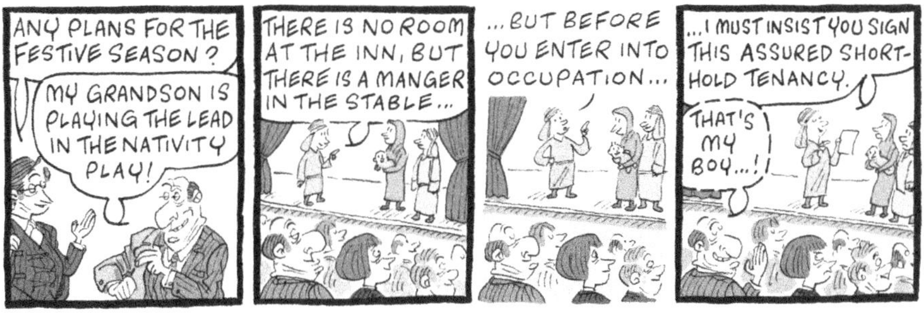
ANY PLANS FOR THE FESTIVE SEASON?
MY GRANDSON IS PLAYING THE LEAD IN THE NATIVITY PLAY!
THERE IS NO ROOM AT THE INN, BUT THERE IS A MANGER IN THE STABLE...
...BUT BEFORE YOU ENTER INTO OCCUPATION...
...I MUST INSIST YOU SIGN THIS ASSURED SHORT-HOLD TENANCY.
THAT'S MY BOY...!

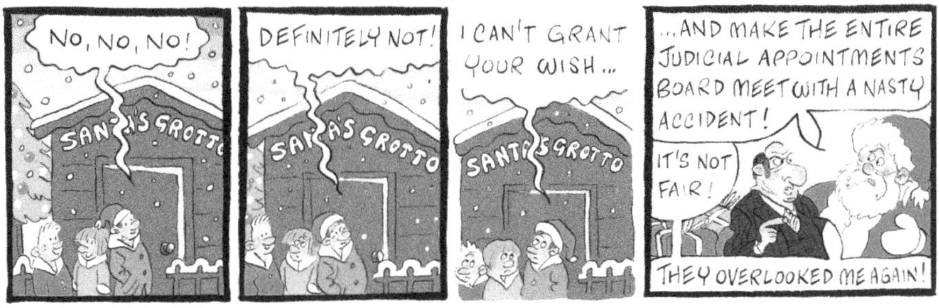
NO, NO, NO!
SANTA'S GROTTO
DEFINITELY NOT!
SANTA'S GROTTO
I CAN'T GRANT YOUR WISH...
SANTA'S GROTTO
...AND MAKE THE ENTIRE JUDICIAL APPOINTMENTS BOARD MEET WITH A NASTY ACCIDENT!
IT'S NOT FAIR!
THEY OVERLOOKED ME AGAIN!

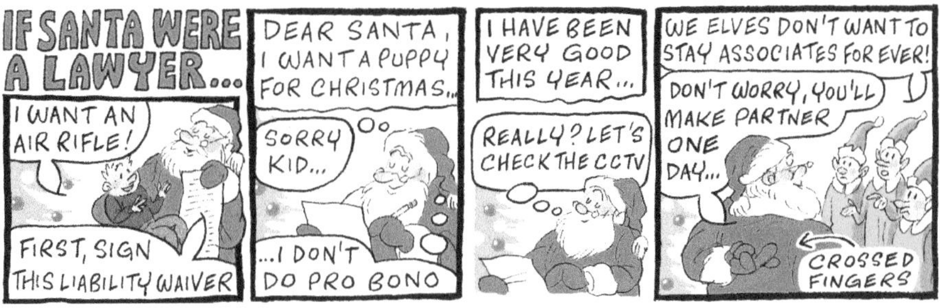
IF SANTA WERE A LAWYER...
I WANT AN AIR RIFLE!
FIRST, SIGN THIS LIABILITY WAIVER
DEAR SANTA, I WANT A PUPPY FOR CHRISTMAS...
SORRY KID...
...I DON'T DO PRO BONO
I HAVE BEEN VERY GOOD THIS YEAR...
REALLY? LET'S CHECK THE CCTV
WE ELVES DON'T WANT TO STAY ASSOCIATES FOR EVER!
DON'T WORRY, YOU'LL MAKE PARTNER ONE DAY...
CROSSED FINGERS

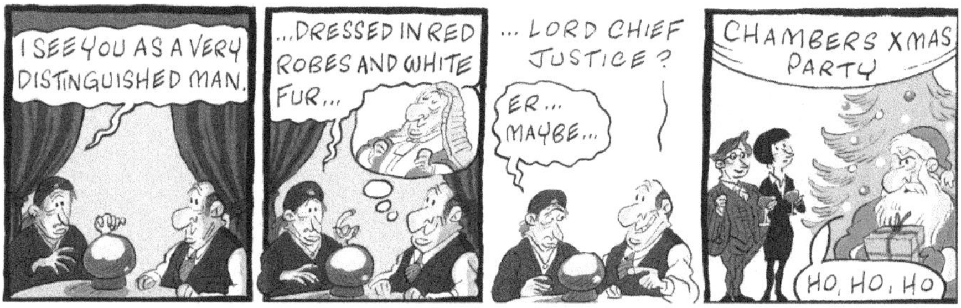
I SEE YOU AS A VERY DISTINGUISHED MAN.
...DRESSED IN RED ROBES AND WHITE FUR...
... LORD CHIEF JUSTICE ?
ER... MAYBE...
CHAMBERS XMAS PARTY
HO, HO, HO

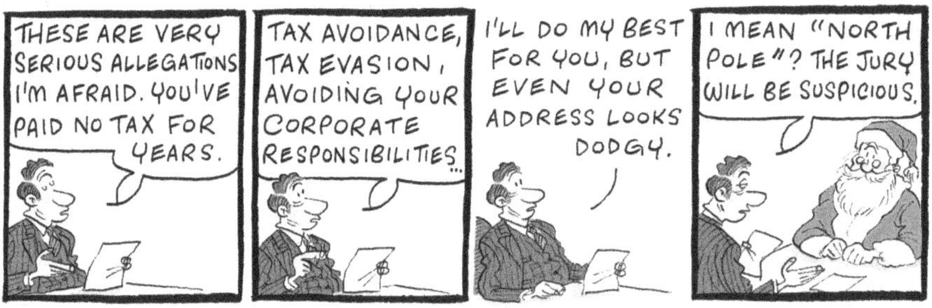
THESE ARE VERY SERIOUS ALLEGATIONS I'M AFRAID. YOU'VE PAID NO TAX FOR YEARS.
TAX AVOIDANCE, TAX EVASION, AVOIDING YOUR CORPORATE RESPONSIBILITIES...
I'LL DO MY BEST FOR YOU, BUT EVEN YOUR ADDRESS LOOKS DODGY.
I MEAN "NORTH POLE"? THE JURY WILL BE SUSPICIOUS.

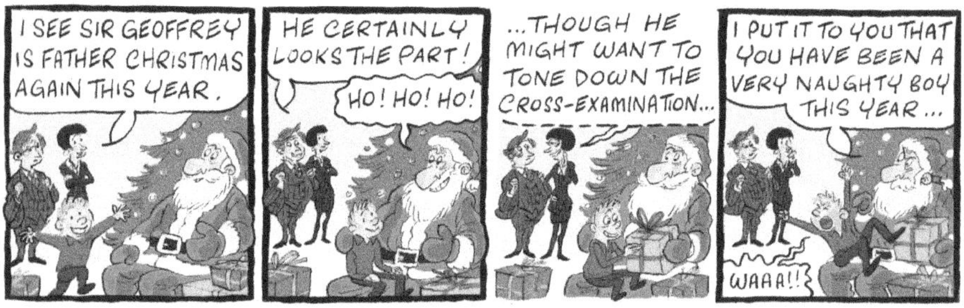
I SEE SIR GEOFFREY IS FATHER CHRISTMAS AGAIN THIS YEAR.
HE CERTAINLY LOOKS THE PART!
HO! HO! HO!
...THOUGH HE MIGHT WANT TO TONE DOWN THE CROSS-EXAMINATION...
I PUT IT TO YOU THAT YOU HAVE BEEN A VERY NAUGHTY BOY THIS YEAR...
WAAA!!

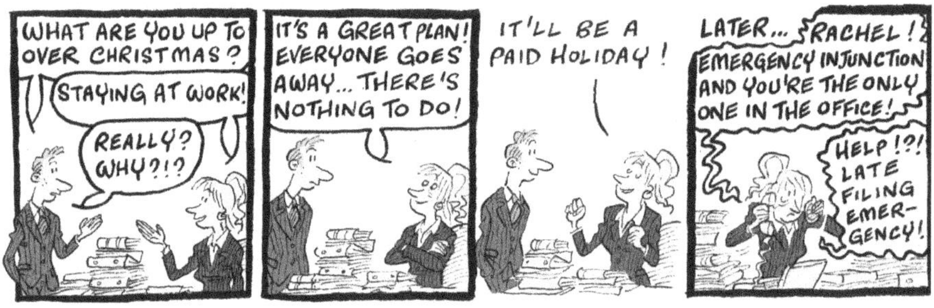
WHAT ARE YOU UP TO OVER CHRISTMAS?
STAYING AT WORK!
REALLY? WHY?!?
IT'S A GREAT PLAN! EVERYONE GOES AWAY... THERE'S NOTHING TO DO!
IT'LL BE A PAID HOLIDAY!
LATER...
RACHEL! EMERGENCY INJUNCTION AND YOU'RE THE ONLY ONE IN THE OFFICE!
HELP!?! LATE FILING EMERGENCY!

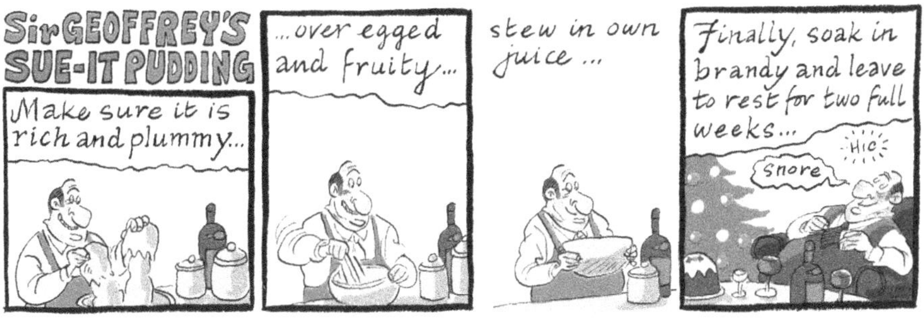
Sir GEOFFREY'S SUE-IT PUDDING
Make sure it is rich and plummy...
...over egged and fruity...
stew in own juice ...
Finally, soak in brandy and leave to rest for two full weeks...
Snore
HIC

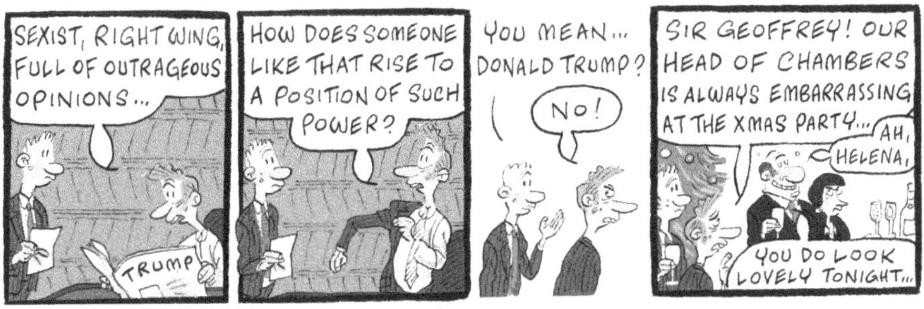
SEXIST, RIGHT WING, FULL OF OUTRAGEOUS OPINIONS...
TRUMP
HOW DOES SOMEONE LIKE THAT RISE TO A POSITION OF SUCH POWER?
YOU MEAN... DONALD TRUMP?
NO!
SIR GEOFFREY! OUR HEAD OF CHAMBERS IS ALWAYS EMBARRASSING AT THE XMAS PARTY...
AH, HELENA,
YOU DO LOOK LOVELY TONIGHT...

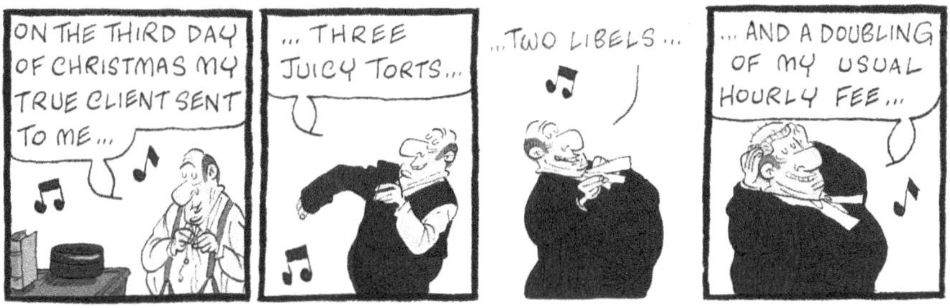
ON THE THIRD DAY OF CHRISTMAS MY TRUE CLIENT SENT TO ME...
... THREE JUICY TORTS...
...TWO LIBELS...
... AND A DOUBLING OF MY USUAL HOURLY FEE...

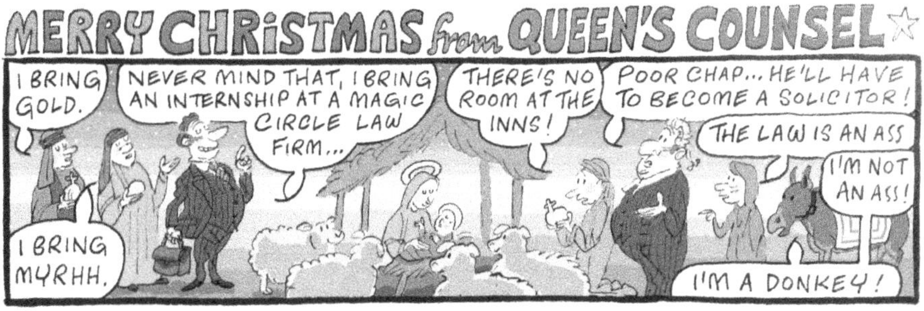
MERRY CHRISTMAS from QUEEN'S COUNSEL
I BRING GOLD.
I BRING MYRHH.
NEVER MIND THAT, I BRING AN INTERNSHIP AT A MAGIC CIRCLE LAW FIRM...
THERE'S NO ROOM AT THE INNS!
POOR CHAP... HE'LL HAVE TO BECOME A SOLICITOR!
THE LAW IS AN ASS
I'M NOT AN ASS!
I'M A DONKEY!

FINALLY, THE END OF THE DAY... NO MORE LAW !
WAP!
NO MORE GORDIAN KNOTS OF LEGAL PROBLEMS TO UNTANGLE.
TIME TO PARTY!
SO YOU'RE A LAWYER? CAN YOU HELP ME WITH MY MOTHER'S WILL?
MIND IF I BOTHER YOU ABOUT A GARDEN FENCE?
I GOT A SPEEDING TICKET. HOW CAN I GET OFF?

During the festive season, we are offering all our clients 20% off divorce proceedings...

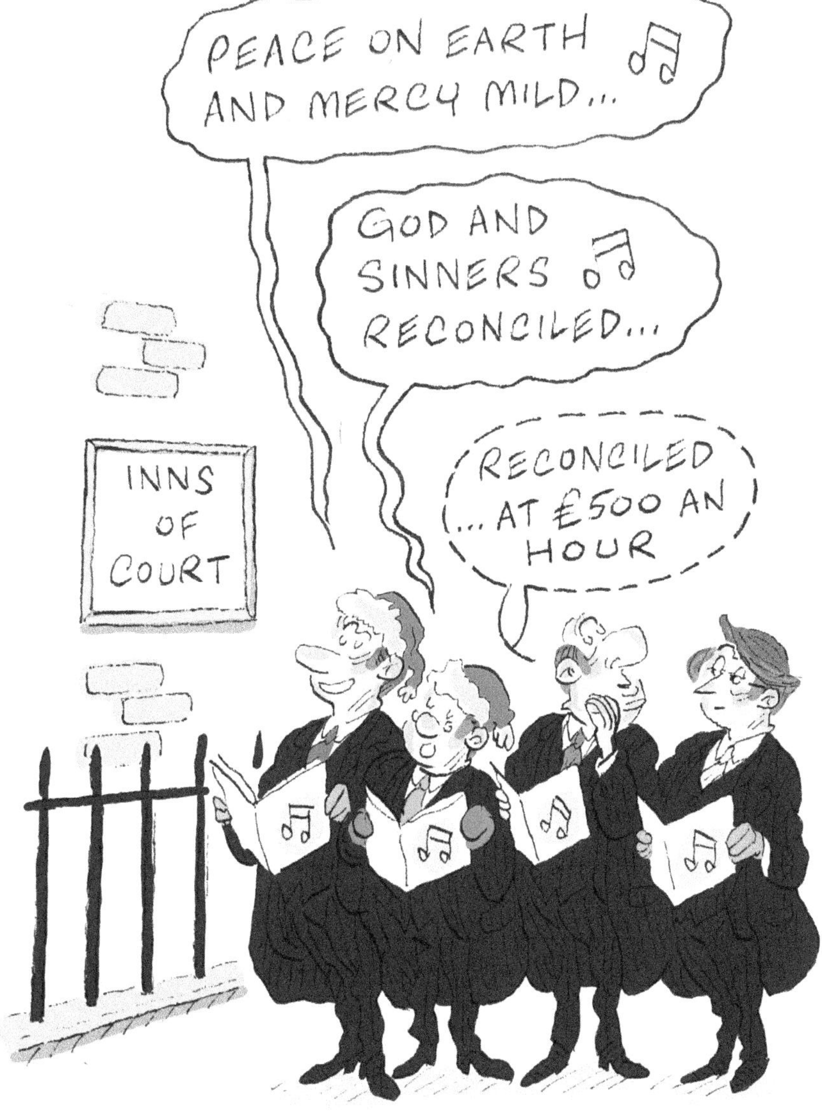
PEACE ON EARTH AND MERCY MILD...
GOD AND SINNERS RECONCILED...
RECONCILED ...AT £500 AN HOUR
INNS OF COURT

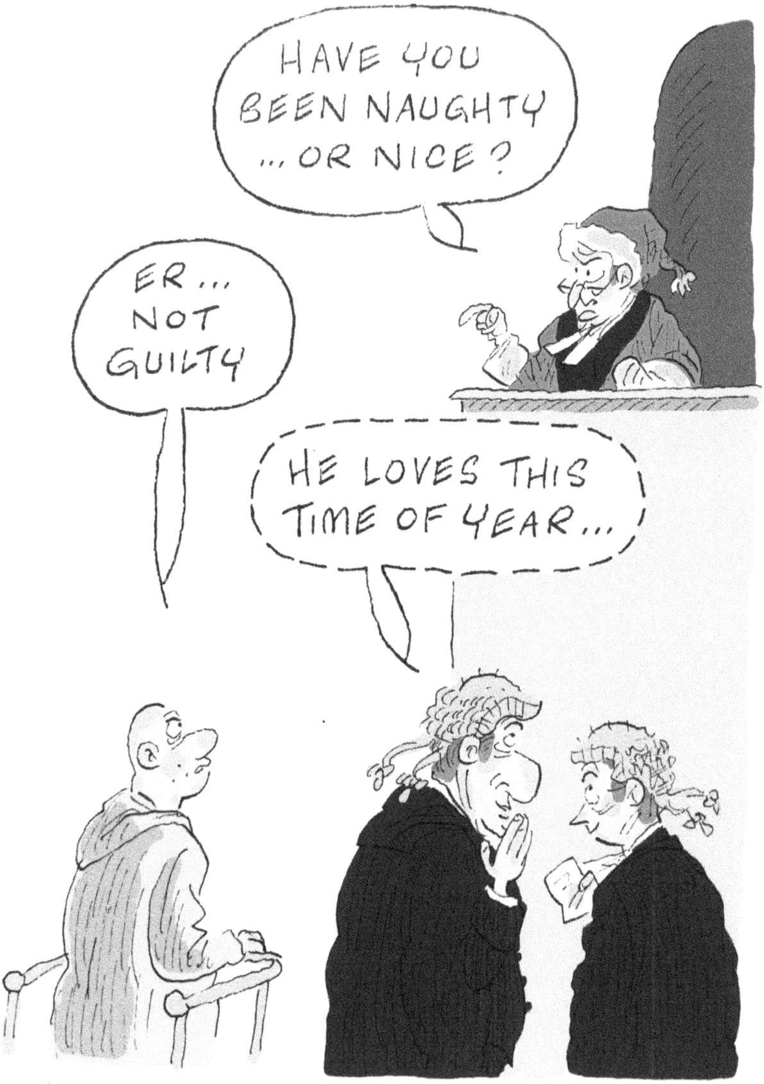
HAVE YOU BEEN NAUGHTY ... OR NICE?
ER... NOT GUILTY
HE LOVES THIS TIME OF YEAR...

HILARY TERM
January to April

Named after Hilary of Poitiers, the patron saint of lawyers, Hilary from hilaris, the Latin word for happy.

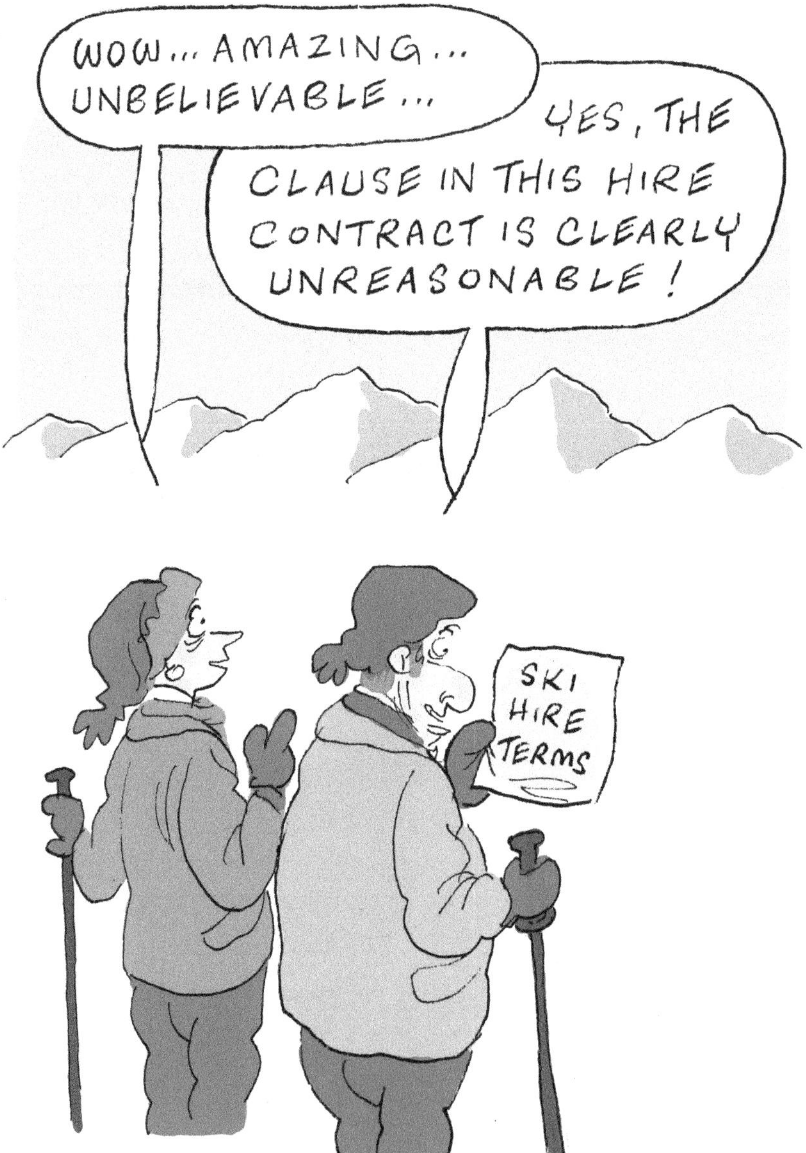
WOW... AMAZING... UNBELIEVABLE...
YES, THE CLAUSE IN THIS HIRE CONTRACT IS CLEARLY UNREASONABLE!
SKI HIRE TERMS

ANY NEW YEAR'S RESOLUTIONS, SIR GEOFFREY?
YES. LADY BENTWOOD AND I HAVE JOINED "DRY JANUARY."
WHAT!?
REALLY? NO BOOZE FOR A MONTH?
EXACTLY. EVERY NIGHT WE DRINK FIZZY WATER OR GRAPE JUICE WITH DINNER.
IT'S ALL ABOUT HAVING A GROWN-UP CONVERSATION WITH ALCOHOL.
BUT HOW DO YOU COPE?
... BY GETTING COMPLETELY SOZZLED AT LUNCH TIME, OBVIOUSLY.

SORRY RACHEL I JUST CAN'T GET IN TODAY ... SNOWED IN COMPLETELY.
... YOU'LL HAVE TO HOLD THE FORT
... BUT I'LL BE WORKING FROM HOME ALL DAY ...
... ALONG WITH MY TEAM ...
WHAT ARE YOU WORKING ON?
OH, A BIG PROJECT ...
... A FREEZING INJUNCTION.

ANY RESOLUTIONS THIS YEAR?
I'VE PROMISED THE WIFE I'LL GIVE UP WHISKY FOR THE NEW YEAR.
HOW WILL YOU COPE?
OH, I'LL MANAGE.
FORTUNATELY, THE LEGAL NEW YEAR DOESN'T START UNTIL OCTOBER,
WINK!
... BY WHICH TIME SHE'LL HAVE FORGOTTEN.
TWO MORE LARGE MALTS, PLEASE!

THE QUEEN'S COUNSEL SYSTEM IS OUTMODED AND OUTDATED. IT'S JUST AN EXCUSE TO CHARGE HUGE FEES!
... ARCHAIC, ELITIST AND A CONSPIRACY AGAINST THE PUBLIC!
THE WHOLE THING SHOULD BE ABOLISHED.
... SO YOU GOT TURNED DOWN AGAIN THEN?
HOW DID YOU KNOW?

WELCOME BACK TO WORK, EVERYONE!
NOW, WE KNOW HOW STRESSFUL FAMILY LIFE CAN BE OVER CHRISTMAS.
...TERRIBLE WEATHER, AWFUL ROWS...
...TIME TO TURN IT ALL INTO NEW BUSINESS!
AND, AS YOU KNOW, WE EXPECT TO SEE A 20% INCREASE IN BILLINGS THIS MONTH...
DIVORCE
SOLICITORS

DID YOU KNOW, DEREK, THAT 2015 IS THE 800th ANNIVERSARY OF MAGNA CARTA?
...THE BEDROCK OF ENGLISH LIBERTIES!
"NO FREED MAN SHALL BE IMPRISONED EXCEPT BY LAWFUL JUDGMENT OF HIS PEERS."
RING RING!
"TO NO-ONE WILL WE SELL, OR DELAY JUSTICE!"
HELLO?
4 LAWN BUILDINGS...
SIR GEOFFREY'S FEE IS £10,000 A DAY WITH A £50,000 RETAINER.
COUGH!

I SEE THAT MARINA WHEELER QC IS TO DIVORCE BORIS.
YES.
BORIS DIVORCE
COULDN'T STAND A POMPOUS, EGOTISTICAL CHAP...
BORIS DIVORCE
...CONSTANTLY SPOUTING LATIN.
I EXPECT SHE GETS ENOUGH OF THAT AT WORK...
A PRIORI, EX POST FACTO...
AD INFINITUM...

IT'S A DISGRACE WHAT'S BEING DONE IN OUR NAME!
YES, HUMILIATING INTERROGATIONS
CIA TORTURE ROW
...SHUT UP IN A DARK SOULLESS ROOM FOR HOUR AFTER HOUR...
CIA TORTURE ROW
I REMEMBER MY OWN PUPILLAGE INTERVIEW WAS PRETTY BRUTAL.
CIA TORTURE ROW
SO, YOUNG MAN, I SEE YOU ONLY GOT A 2:1 FROM A REDBRICK UNIVERSITY...
CV

I HATE THIS "DRY JANUARY", IT'S NO FUN AT ALL!
POOR YOU!
IT'S ONLY TEMPORARY.
WELL, IT DOESN'T FEEL THAT WAY.
THERE'S ONLY ONE THING FOR IT – A REALLY BIG DRINK!
?
I THOUGHT "DRY JANUARY" MEANT SIR GEOFFREY WASN'T DRINKING!
HIC!
NO, IT'S HIS WORK THAT'S DRIED UP... NO BRIEFS SINCE DECEMBER!

TONIGHT AT OUR ANNUAL AWARDS CEREMONY, I PRESENT OUR FIRM'S HIGHEST AWARD.
IT'S THE AWARD FOR "MOST HOURS BILLED"
UNFORTUNATELY, THE WINNER CAN'T BE HERE TONIGHT.
...AS HE IS STILL AT THE OFFICE.

A LOT OF THE HOSTESSES EMPLOYED AT THIS INFAMOUS PRESIDENTS CLUB DINNER WERE LAW STUDENTS.
DINNER SCANDAL
...BRIGHT YOUNG WOMEN, PANDERING TO BOORISH MIDDLE AGED MEN!
SCANDAL
... ALL FOR A MEASLY £20 AN HOUR AND A TAXI HOME AT 2 AM!
SCANDAL
THEY SOUND PERFECT!
I KNOW... I'VE HIRED FOUR OF THEM ALREADY...
PLIK PLIK

MICHAEL GOVE SAYS TOP LAW FIRMS NEED TO DO MORE PRO BONO WORK.
GOVE SAVAGES LAWYERS
TROUBLE IS... WE DON'T DO PRACTICAL STUFF LIKE FAMILY LAW AND GARDEN FENCE DISPUTES.
WE'LL HAVE TO THINK OF A WAY TO BE USEFUL...
LAW CENTRE
NOW... I CAN DO YOU A NICE CONTRACT FOR A CONVERTIBLE DEBENTURE OR A CREDIT DEFAULT SWAP...

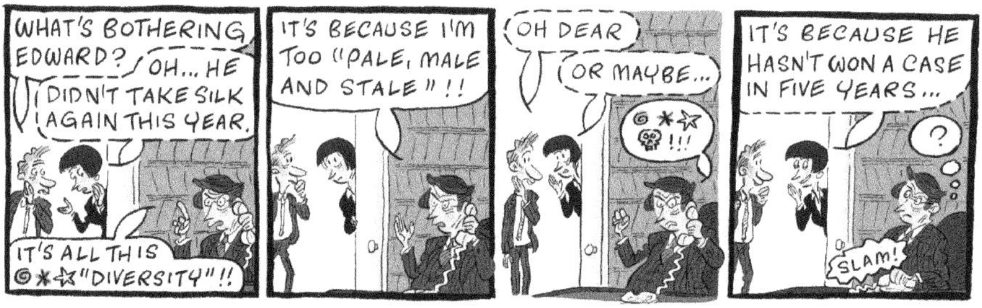
WHAT'S BOTHERING EDWARD?
OH... HE DIDN'T TAKE SILK AGAIN THIS YEAR.
IT'S ALL THIS ☹✱✫ "DIVERSITY"!!
IT'S BECAUSE I'M TOO "PALE, MALE AND STALE"!!
OH DEAR
OR MAYBE...
☹✱✫ ☠ !!!
IT'S BECAUSE HE HASN'T WON A CASE IN FIVE YEARS...
?
SLAM!

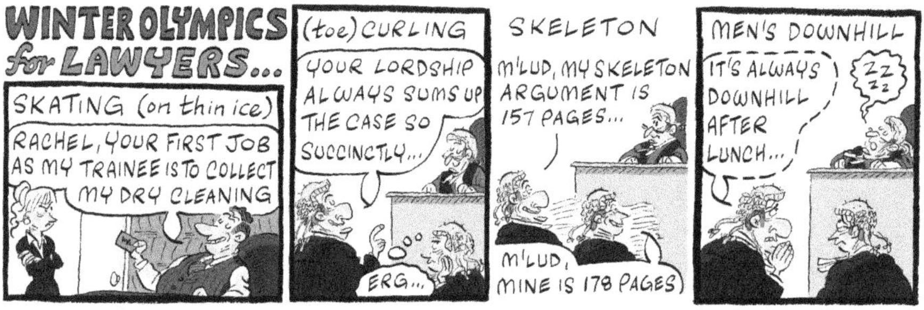
WINTER OLYMPICS for LAWYERS...
SKATING (on thin ice)
RACHEL, YOUR FIRST JOB AS MY TRAINEE IS TO COLLECT MY DRY CLEANING
(toe) CURLING
YOUR LORDSHIP ALWAYS SUMS UP THE CASE SO SUCCINCTLY...
ERG...
SKELETON
M'LUD, MY SKELETON ARGUMENT IS 157 PAGES...
M'LUD, MINE IS 178 PAGES
MEN'S DOWNHILL
IT'S ALWAYS DOWNHILL AFTER LUNCH...
Z Z Z

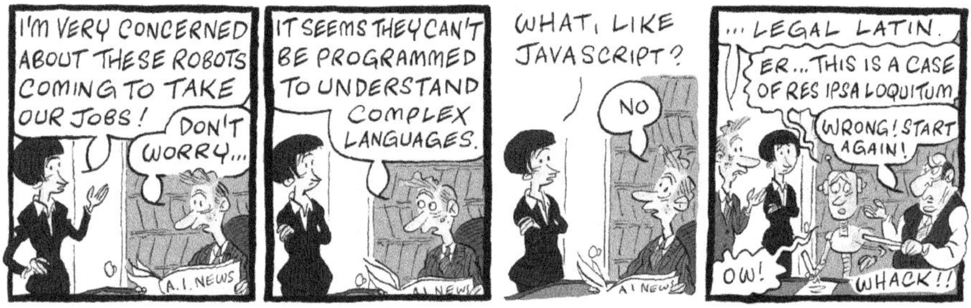
I'M VERY CONCERNED ABOUT THESE ROBOTS COMING TO TAKE OUR JOBS!
DON'T WORRY...
A.I. NEWS
IT SEEMS THEY CAN'T BE PROGRAMMED TO UNDERSTAND COMPLEX LANGUAGES.
WHAT, LIKE JAVASCRIPT?
NO
... LEGAL LATIN.
ER... THIS IS A CASE OF RES IPSA LOQUITUM
WRONG! START AGAIN!
OW!
WHACK!!

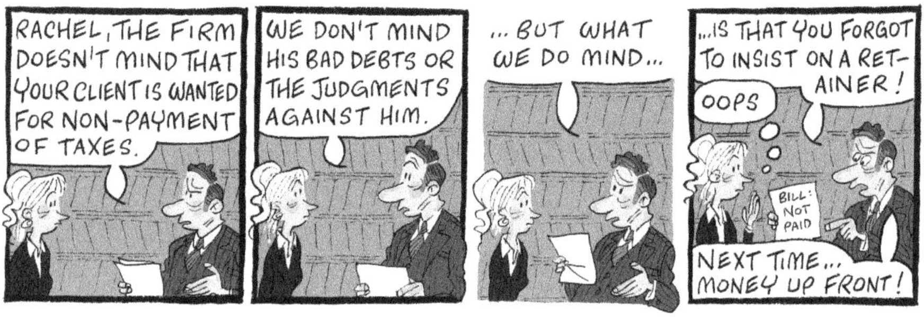
RACHEL, THE FIRM DOESN'T MIND THAT YOUR CLIENT IS WANTED FOR NON-PAYMENT OF TAXES.
WE DON'T MIND HIS BAD DEBTS OR THE JUDGMENTS AGAINST HIM.
... BUT WHAT WE DO MIND...
...IS THAT YOU FORGOT TO INSIST ON A RET-AINER!
OOPS
BILL: NOT PAID
NEXT TIME... MONEY UP FRONT!

ANOTHER SENIOR ASSOCIATE HAS LEFT THE FIRM... WHO IS GOING TO DO ALL OUR WORK FOR US?
WELL...
JUST GET ANOTHER ASSOCIATE!
BUT THERE AREN'T ANY! THEY'VE ALL GONE!
WELL, GET ONE OF THE NEW TRAINEES TO DO IT THEN!
REALLY?
AH, MR SPROCKET, FOXLEY HERE WILL BE WORKING ON YOUR CASE...
DON'T TELL HIM YOU'RE ONLY TWO WEEKS QUALIFIED...

A GREAT CHARACTER... SUCH A HUGE INSPIRATION TO ME!
ATTICUS FINCH AUTHOR DIES
AS A LAWYER I'VE ALWAYS TRIED TO FOLLOW HIS EXAMPLE.
ATTICUS FINCH? FIGHTING FOR TRUTH AND JUSTICE?
GOODNESS ME, NO!
RUMPOLE! A BOTTLE OF CHATEAU FLEET ST, OLD DARLING!
EL VINO

HOW DID THE CLIENT CONFERENCE GO?
WELL, I DID ALL THE WORK, ASKED THE QUESTIONS, KNEW THE LAW, TOOK A NOTE...
RICHARD HARDLY DID ANYTHING! HE DOESN'T KNOW A THING ABOUT THE CASE!
TSK!
I MEAN... WHAT IS IT THAT THE PARTNERS DO EXACTLY?
BEATS ME!
OH, GOOD SHOT!
THWOK!

I CAN'T BELIEVE THAT A JOURNALIST HAS COME UP WITH A LIST OF THE "HOTTEST BARRISTERS"
I MEAN, HOW LOW CAN JOURNALISTIC ETHICS SINK?
THIS LIST... IT'S ABSOLUTELY DEGRADING AND INSULTING!
LEFT YOU OFF IT, DID SHE?
I'M WAY BETTER LOOKING THAN THIS LOT!

OF COURSE, I WAS APPROACHED BY A FUNNY RUSSIAN CHAP BACK IN MY OXFORD DAYS
RUSSIA SPY ROW
I OFTEN WONDER WHAT IT SAYS ON MY FILE.
RUSSIA
POMPOUS, INDISCREET, UNPRINCIPLED.
... HE'S NO USE TO US, BUT HE'D MAKE A FINE ENGLISH BARRISTER

OH LOOK, THERE'S BRIAN, TONY AND CHARLIE...
?
BAFTAs 2018
DARLING, I NEVER KNEW YOU WERE A FILM BUFF.
I'M NOT
BAFTAs 2018
I HAVEN'T BEEN TO THE CINEMA FOR YEARS.
THEN HOW DO YOU...
2018
... THEY'RE ALL SEXUAL HARRASSMENT CLIENTS.
BAFTAs

ALL THESE ALLEGATIONS OF ABUSE MAKE ME GLAD WE DON'T HAVE THESE PROBLEMS AT THE BAR.
WEINSTEIN APOLOGY
BACK IN THE 1970s 1980s AND 1990s NO ONE WAS MOLESTING WOMEN IN OUR CHAMBERS!
ER... ACTUALLY, THAT'S PROBABLY BECAUSE...
... THERE WEREN'T ANY.
OOPS... I FORGOT...

CARILLION IS A MASSIVE AND HUGELY COMPLEX CORPORATE BANKRUPTCY.
CONTENTIOUS ISSUES OF STATE OWNERSHIP, LIABILITY, AND BIG PENSION DEFICITS.
IT'S DREADFUL!
OH, I KNOW...
I'LL BARELY HAVE TIME FOR A WEEK'S SKIING!
BANKRUPTCY LAWYERS
HEAD OF INSOLVENCY

VALENTINE GIFTS FOR LAWYERS
HMV AND JESSOPS GIFT CARD*
HMV £100
JESSOPS £200
* INSOLVENCY SPECIALISTS ONLY.
ROMANTIC DINNER FOR ONE, "AL DESKO"
SIGH
SINGLE MILK CHOCOLATE TRUFFLE*
* DEEMED TO BE A PERMISSIBLE GIFT UNDER SECTIONS 1-5 OF THE BRIBERY ACT, 2010
"BROKEN HEART" BOX OF CHOCS*
* FOR DIVORCE LAWYERS ONLY.

WE WOULD LIKE TO WISH ALL OUR CLIENTS A VERY HAPPY ST. VALENTINE'S DAY...
TAP! TAP!
...AND, AS A SPECIAL GESTURE...
TAP! TAP!
...WE'D LIKE TO OFFER ALL OUR CLIENTS...
TAP! TAP! TAP!
...A SEASONAL DISCOUNT ON ALL PRE-NUPS, DIVORCE ADVICE, AND CHILD CUSTODY PROCEEDINGS
TAP! TAP!

ANY PLANS FOR VALENTINE'S DAY?
OH, A ROMANTIC NIGHT IN, I THINK.
SOMETHING MY PARTNER AND I BOTH LOVE DOING.
...HAVING A NICE CHAT...
...ENJOYING OUR FAVOURITE FOOD...
ie WORKING LATE AT THE OFFICE AND EATING TAKE OUT PIZZA.
YOU OK HUN?
...BE HERE FOR A COUPLE OF HOURS YET...
...HOME BY MIDNIGHT...

A MYSTERIOUS VALENTINE! ANY IDEA WHO IT'S FROM?
NO
HMM... LET'S CHECK THE HANDWRITING...
OH YES, IT'S FROM MY BOYFRIEND.
YOUR BOY-FRIEND?
WE'RE BOTH OVER-WORKED LAWYERS. I SEE HIM SO SELDOM I TEND TO FORGET I HAVE ONE!

HOW DISGUSTING! WHAT HORRID THINGS MEN SAY ABOUT WOMEN!
TRUMP IN SEXISM ROW
MEN DON'T REALLY TALK LIKE THAT IN LOCKER ROOMS, DO THEY?
WELL ...
... NOT THE ONES AROUND HERE, CERTAINLY.
SO I REPLIED ... "DE MINIMIS NON CURAT LEX!"
... CORPUS DELICTI, OLD CHAP!
NUDGE

WHAT SHOULD WE DO WITH ALL THESE OLD LAW BOOKS – NOW THAT THE LAW REPORTS HAVE GONE ONLINE?
... AND WHAT ABOUT THESE NOW-OBSOLETE BOOKSHELVES?
HMM ... I THINK I HAVE AN IDEA.
... WINE RACKS! HAVE ANOTHER GLASS OF CHATEAU MARGAUX!
HIC!

GOOD NEWS THAT JUDGES' RETIREMENT AGE MAY BE RAISED TO 75!
EH? SURELY YOU'RE LOOKING FORWARD TO A REST?
CLINK!
NOT REALLY, NO.
... BECAUSE YOU'D MISS THE CAMARADERIE OF THE BENCH?
NO
ER ... THE INTELLECTUAL CHALLENGE?
NO
I'M AFRAID THERE'S A LONG LIST OF JOBS WAITING FOR ME AT HOME ...
HUMPHREY! GET TO WORK!
... I THINK I'M BETTER OFF STAYING AT THE OFFICE!

THE FEES CHARGED BY THE COMMERCIAL BAR THESE DAYS ARE A DISGRACE!
I WON'T ALLOW COSTS LIKE THIS! THIS APPLICATION IS DENIED!
SOMETHING MUST BE DONE ... AND I INTEND TO DO IT!
SUCH AS?
... SUCH AS CALL THE CLERKS AT MY OLD CHAMBERS AND SEE IF THEY'LL TAKE ME BACK!
AH, DEREK, GOT ANY BRIEFS FOR ME?

ANOTHER HIGH-PROFILE CELEBRITY DIVORCE?
YES. AND IT CAN BE VERY HARD ON THE LAWYERS INVOLVED.
BRAD AND ANGELINA SPLIT
THERE IS A HUGE AMOUNT OF MEDIA SCRUTINY!
YOU DON'T MEAN...
YES!
SIR GEOFFREY'S HAD HIS WIG AND GOWN DRY-CLEANED FOR THE FIRST TIME IN 20 YEARS!
GLEAM!

I WAS APPROACHED BY AN ODD RUSSIAN CHAP BACK IN MY OXFORD DAYS.
CORBYN SPY SCANDAL
DID THEY MAKE YOU AN OFFER?
YES.
...BUT YOU TURNED THEM DOWN?
OH NO!
CORBYN
...THEY COULDN'T AFFORD MY FEES.
CORBYN

YOU'VE BEEN WORKING HARD LATELY RACHEL AND I THINK YOU SHOULD HAVE A FEW DAYS OFF.
I'LL DO ALL THE HEAVY LIFTING ON THE CASE. YOU TAKE IT EASY.
IN FACT, WHY DON'T YOU GO HOME EARLY TODAY?
REALLY?
NO. APRIL FOOL! IT NEED IT ALL DONE BY MONDAY MORNING.

I CAN'T BELIEVE HE CALLED THEM "FANTASTICALLY CORRUPT"
VERY EMBARRASSING
PM IN NIGERIA ROW
WELL, A FEW GLASSES OF WINE... IT OFTEN HAPPENS
REALLY?
TO DAVID CAMERON?
NO! TO SIR GEOFFREY!
HE'S ALWAYS GETTING SLOSHED AT CHAMBERS' PARTIES AND BEING INDISCREET ABOUT CLIENTS
WHOOPS
HIC!
OF COURSE, THE OLD BOY'S AS GUILTY AS SIN...

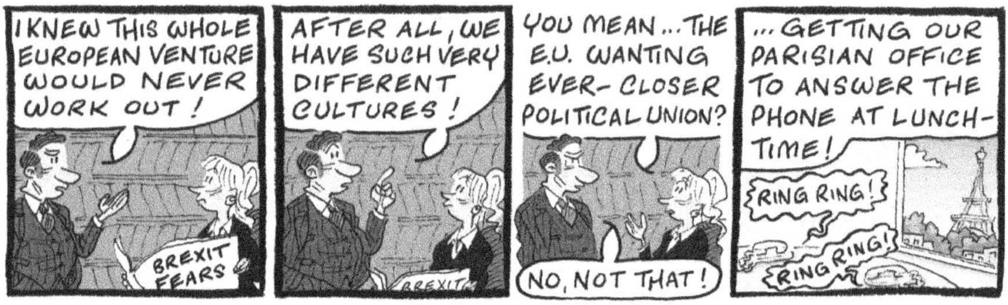
I KNEW THIS WHOLE EUROPEAN VENTURE WOULD NEVER WORK OUT!
BREXIT FEARS
AFTER ALL, WE HAVE SUCH VERY DIFFERENT CULTURES!
BREXIT
YOU MEAN ... THE E.U. WANTING EVER-CLOSER POLITICAL UNION?
NO, NOT THAT!
... GETTING OUR PARISIAN OFFICE TO ANSWER THE PHONE AT LUNCH-TIME!
RING RING!
RING RING!

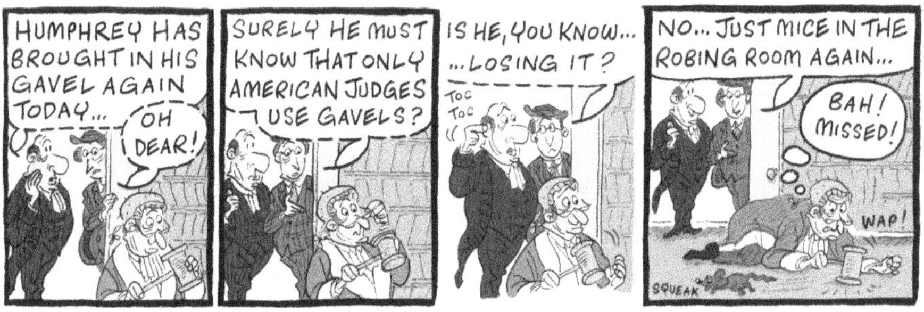
HUMPHREY HAS BROUGHT IN HIS GAVEL AGAIN TODAY...
OH DEAR!
SURELY HE MUST KNOW THAT ONLY AMERICAN JUDGES USE GAVELS?
IS HE, YOU KNOW... ...LOSING IT?
TOC TOC
NO... JUST MICE IN THE ROBING ROOM AGAIN...
BAH! MISSED!
WAP!
SQUEAK

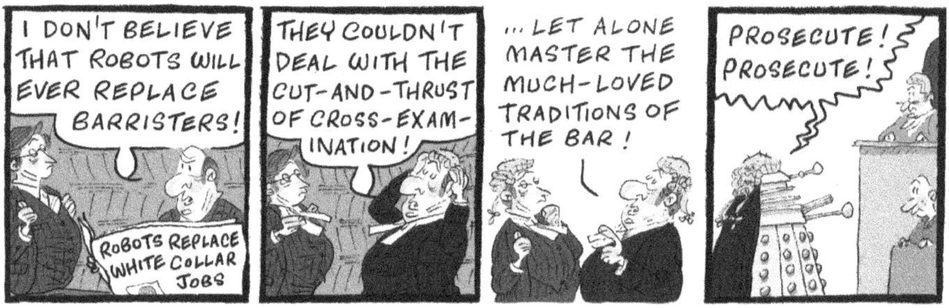
I DON'T BELIEVE THAT ROBOTS WILL EVER REPLACE BARRISTERS!
ROBOTS REPLACE WHITE COLLAR JOBS
THEY COULDN'T DEAL WITH THE CUT-AND-THRUST OF CROSS-EXAMINATION!
... LET ALONE MASTER THE MUCH-LOVED TRADITIONS OF THE BAR!
PROSECUTE! PROSECUTE!

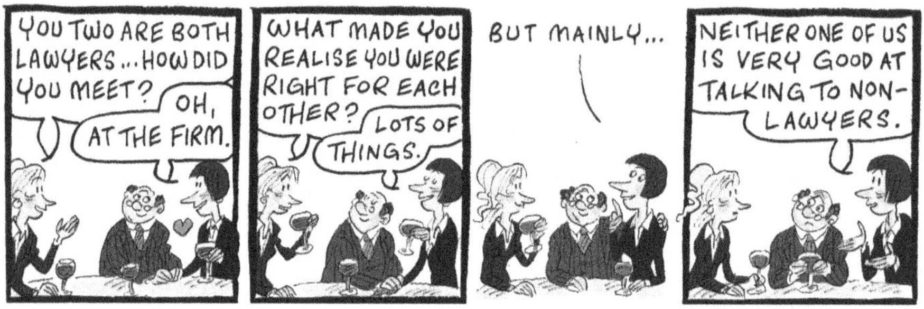
YOU TWO ARE BOTH LAWYERS... HOW DID YOU MEET?
OH, AT THE FIRM.
WHAT MADE YOU REALISE YOU WERE RIGHT FOR EACH OTHER?
LOTS OF THINGS.
BUT MAINLY...
NEITHER ONE OF US IS VERY GOOD AT TALKING TO NON-LAWYERS.

I CAN'T BELIEVE JEREMY CORBYN IS LIKELY TO BE THE NEXT LABOUR LEADER!
HE'S STUCK IN THE PAST! NATIONALISATION, RE-OPENING COAL MINES...
HOW DOES SUCH A DINOSAUR STILL EXIST?
I SUGGEST, YOUNG MAN, YOU BEGIN WITH ARMORY-V-DELAMIRIE (1722)...

IN CHAMBERS TODAY I COULDN'T UNDERSTAND A WORD THAT ANYONE SAID!
AH...
...SIR GEOFFREY TALKING IN INCOMPREHENSIBLE LEGAL LATIN AGAIN?
NO... IT'S THE NEW SUMMER INTERNS!
YO, SIR G HASHTAG, REALLY BURNED THAT POSSE!
??
PLIK
...AND YOUR FACE, YO.

NO, NO, NOT THAT WAY! DON'T TAKE THE EMBANKMENT!
LISTEN, YOU BLITHERING IDIOT, TAKE THE NEXT LEFT!
DON'T YOU KNOW WHO I AM? I'M A VERY SENIOR QC!
GEOFFREY, WE'VE BEEN MARRIED FOR 30 YEARS. OF COURSE I KNOW WHO YOU ARE. NOW BE QUIET AND LET ME DRIVE.
HMF!

ALL THIS MONEY AND CORRUPTION IS RUINING FOOTBALL
YES
FIFA
FIFA MUST BE REFORMED!
NOT FIFA!
WHAT THEN?
THE INTER-CHAMBERS FIVE-A-SIDE CHAMPIONSHIP!
FIFA
HERE'S £5K IN CASH... AND IF ANYONE ASKS... YOU'RE OUR NEW JUNIOR CLERK!

WELCOME BACK TO WORK, RACHEL, AND CONGRATULATIONS ON YOUR BABY.
THANKS!
NOW I SEE YOU'VE APPLIED FOR A FLEXIBLE WORK SCHEDULE
YES
WELL, OF COURSE, THE FIRM CAN BE VERY FLEXIBLE.
...YOU CAN WORK ANY SIXTEEN HOURS IN THE DAY YOU WANT!

WHY DO THESE ENQUIRIES TAKE SO LONG?
WELL, HUNDREDS OF HOURS OF TESTIMONY...
CHILCOT DELAY
THOUSANDS OF PAGES OF EVIDENCE...YOU NEED A TOP QC TO MANAGE IT!
HM
CHILCOT
ISN'T SIR GEOFFREY WORKING ON ONE?
I THINK SO
CHILCOT
OH NO, I THINK I'VE JUST DELETED THE WHOLE FILE AGAIN...
HELP! IT SUPPORT!

CAN YOU BELIEVE THIS COUPLE WHO SPENT £1m ON THEIR DIVORCE?
SHOCKING!
£1m DIVORCE
OF THEIR TOTAL ASSETS OF £3m, ONE THIRD WENT TO THE LAWYERS!
£1m
THE JUDGE DESCRIBED IT AS "MADNESS".
SO IT IS
£1m
...THE LAST DIVORCE I DID – WE GOT HALF THEIR ASSETS!

ALL THIS TALK OF LEAVING THE EURO-PEAN COURT OF HUMAN RIGHTS IS A DISGRACE!
QUITE RIGHT!
TORIES TO PULL OUT
THE UNIVERSAL DECLARATION OF HUMAN RIGHTS IS ONE OF OUR FINEST ACHIEVEMENTS.
IT'S A SHOCKING ATTACK ON OUR BASIC LIBERTIES!
ER, WELL, ACTUALLY, HELENA...
I WAS REALLY JUST HOPING TO GET A JOB THERE ONE DAY. THEY HAVE THE MOST FABULOUS FOIE GRAS IN STRASBOURG

WHAT A FINE JUDGE WE HAD TODAY.
I THOUGHT HE WAS USELESS!
HE CUT STRAIGHT THROUGH TO THE NUB OF THE CASE.
CONFUSED, AND CONFUSING.
RIGHT ON THE LAW AND THE FACTS.
WRONG ON BOTH.
LET ME GUESS...
YOU LOST...
...AND YOU WON
HOW CAN YOU TELL?

SO HOW'S LIFE?
STRESSFUL. LOTS OF SCREAMING AND CRYING.
IT'S ALL ABOUT PLEASING SOMEONE WHO CAN'T BE PLEASED AND WHO THROWS ENDLESS TANTRUMS
WAA!
...AND SHOVELLING A GREAT DEAL OF POOP.
TOUGH BEING A MUM, EH?
NO, BEING A MUM IS FINE. IT'S MY CLIENTS I CAN'T COPE WITH.
GURGLE

TO MAKE PARTNER AT THE FIRM YOU HAVE TO GO ON "BUSINESS DEVELOPMENT COURSES" AND LEARN "LEADERSHIP SKILLS."
BUT THE ONLY ASSOCIATES WHO HAVE THE TIME TO DO THIS NONSENSE ARE THE ONES WHO AREN'T THAT GOOD - AND NO-ONE WANTS TO WORK WITH
... SO WHAT'S THE SOLUTION?
I NEED TO GET WORSE AT MY JOB.

WEST END SHOWS for LAWYERS
ONE MAN, THREE GUVNORS
WORK ON MY CASE!
NO MINE!
NO, MINE!
The Judas Kiss
THANKS FOR ALL YOUR HARD WORK
MWAH!
MWAH!
...YOU WILL BE REWARDED!
THE LYIN' KING
DON'T WORRY, YOU WILL MAKE PARTNER SOME DAY.
THE BOOK OF MOREON
MORE ON THIS FILE PLEASE!
MORE ON THIS CASE!
MORE ON MINE!

THE ROYAL COURTS OF JUSTICE: OBSCURE LANGUAGE, PETTIFOGGING ARGUMENTS, INTERMINABLE PROCEDURES...
RCJ
NO WONDER SIR GEOFFREY IS IN HIS ELEMENT!
I HOPE HE'S NOT LIKE THAT AT HOME!
ER...
IT'S SIMPLE, MY DEAR, LET ME EXPLAIN: BACKSTOP... CANADA PLUS... ARTICLE 50... NORWAY OPTION...
...DRONE...

THERE'S TALK OF GETTING RID OF THESE NDA GAGGING ORDERS.
PHILIP GREEN ROW
PEOPLE SAY THAT NDAs ONLY BENEFIT THE WEALTHY!
...LIKE FOOTBALL STARS, RETAIL TYCOONS, AND CELEBRITIES?
NO
..., LIKE US, OBVIOUSLY.
NDA BRIEF FOR YOU, SIR.
THANKYOU, DEREK.

I FEEL SORRY FOR THESE NAIVE YOUNGSTERS.
ISIS BRIDES
...SUCKED INTO A HEARTLESS ORGANISATION BY RUTHLESS PROPAGANDA!
...WHICH BLEEDS THEM DRY AND RUINS THEIR LIVES!
...YOU MEAN... ISIS?
NO, LAW FIRMS. THESE POOR TRAINEES HAVE NO IDEA WHAT THEY'RE IN FOR.
RACHEL HERE IS NOW ON HER 2ND ALL-NIGHTER...

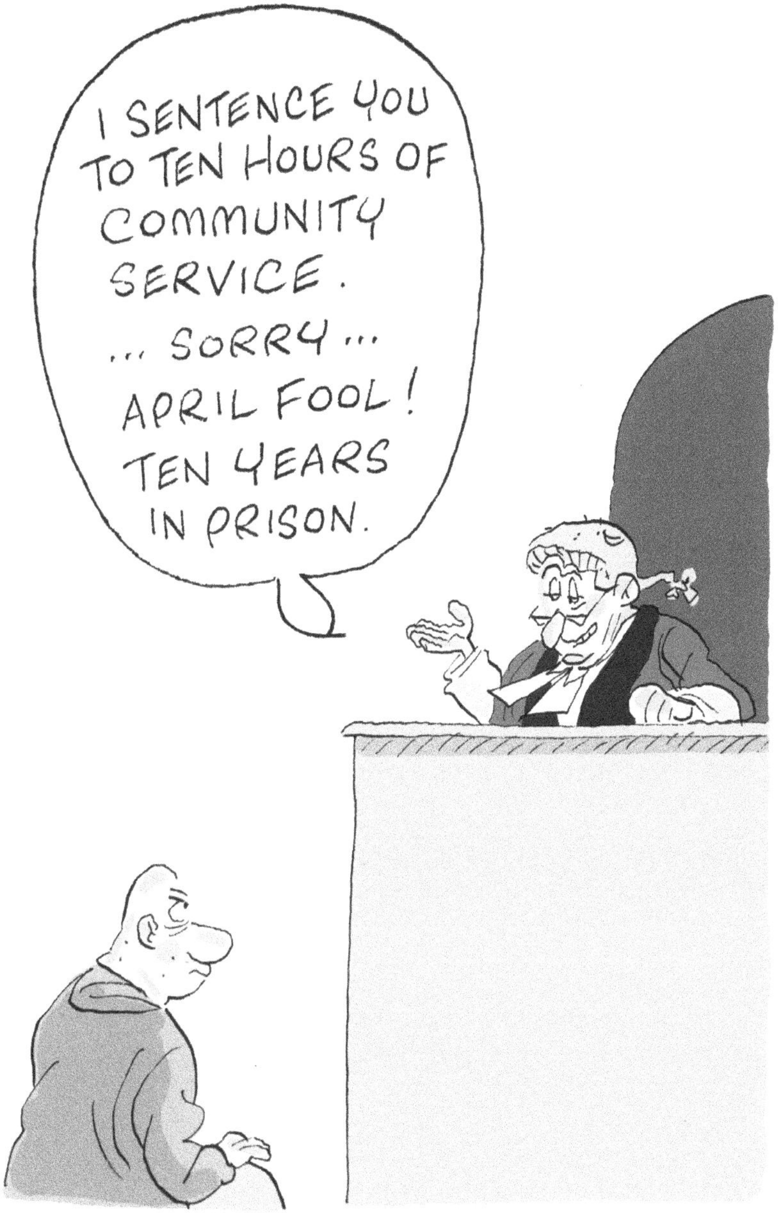
I SENTENCE YOU TO TEN HOURS OF COMMUNITY SERVICE. ... SORRY ... APRIL FOOL! TEN YEARS IN PRISON.

EASTER TERM
April to May

The Christian celebration of the resurrection of Jesus preceded by Lent, a 40 day period of fasting and abstinence.

6 AM MAY MORNING
OXFORD UNIVERSITY

6 AM, MAY MORNING
TEN YEARS LATER

CUTS TO LEGAL AID MEAN THAT WE JUNIOR BARRISTERS BARELY GET PAID FOR OUR WORK!

ON STRIKE

ON STRIKE

LUCKILY, WE HAVE THE SUPPORT OF SENIOR MEMBERS OF CHAMBERS.

...THOUGH I'M NOT SURE THEIR CONTRIBUTION IS ALWAYS THAT HELPFUL.

ON STRIKE

...GLASS OF FIZZ AND A CUCUMBER SANDWICH, GENTLEMEN?

ON STRIKE

ON STRIKE

FORTNUMS

GOOD TO SEE UBER WIN ITS APPEAL AGAINST TFL

IT'S BECOME AN INTEGRAL PART OF LONDON LIFE.

SO CONVENIENT AND EASY TO USE.

PLIK PLIK

...PLUS IT'S THE ONLY JOB MY USELESS SON SEEMS ABLE TO GET...

WHERE TO, DAD?

MEGHAN MARKLE WAS GREAT AS A PARALEGAL IN THE TV SERIES "SUITS"

YES.

SHE MADE ME REALLY WANT TO BE A LAWYER!

...THE DESIGNER CLOTHES, THE STRETCH LIMOS, THE GLAMOROUS COCKTAIL PARTIES...

WHEREAS THE REALITY IS DULL BUSINESS SUITS, THE NORTHERN LINE IN RUSH HOUR, AND DRINKS AFTER WORK WITH BRIAN FROM I.T.

BREXIT MEANS BREXIT, SAYS PM...

TYPICAL SLIPPERY POLITICIANS, WHAT DOES THAT EVEN MEAN?

THEY DELIBERATELY USE OBFUSCATORY LANGUAGE! IT'S A DISGRACE!

RING! RING!

CLIENT ON LINE ONE, RICHARD.

OK.

AH, MR SPROCKET, THE ANSWER TO YOUR CASE IS "ACTORI INCUMBIT PROBATIO."

...UNLIKE LAWYERS...

BREXIT IS THE MOST IMPORTANT DECISION WE HAVE FACED FOR DECADES.
IT'S DISGRACEFUL THAT MANY OF OUR POLITICIANS HAVEN'T EVEN READ THE FULL DOCUMENT!
KNOCK! KNOCK!
CORBYN ROW
ER... 3,000 PAGES TO READ FOR TOMORROW'S TRIAL, SIR GEOFFREY...
AH...
...JUST GIVE ME A BRIEF OUTLINE.

BEING A SECRETARY IN A LAW FIRM MUST HAVE CHANGED A LOT OVER THE YEARS.
YES.
I BET SHORTHAND ISN'T MUCH USE ANY MORE!
WELL...
...YOU'D BE SURPRISED!
KNOCK! KNOCK!
HI CHERYL, I'D LIKE A GRANDE, ICED, SUGAR FREE VANILLA LATTE WITH SOYA MILK, PLEASE.
NO PROBLEM
SCRIBBLE

IN THIS LIST OF TOP 50 COMPANIES IN THE UK TO WORK FOR, THERE ISN'T A SINGLE LAW FIRM!
WELL...
TOP 50 FIRMS
THE HOURS ARE LONG, ASSOCIATES OFTEN WORK WEEK-ENDS, AND THE DEADLINES ARE STRESSFUL!
INTERESTING.
...PERHAPS YOU COULD WRITE A REPORT?
...HAVE IT DONE FIRST THING MONDAY MORNING

I DON'T GET THESE SUPER INJUNCTION CASES. THE COURTS MUZZLE THE PRESS, BUT NOT THE INTERNET.
INDEED.
A SIMPLE GOOGLE SEARCH REVEALS THE NAMES OF THE CELEBRITIES CAUGHT UP IN SCANDAL!
YES.
HOW CAN THE LAW BE SO OUT OF TOUCH?
LET'S FIND OUT
...AND WHAT IS THIS "INTERNET" SIR GEOFFREY?
AH... I SEE...

THESE PROPOSED REFORMS FROM THE SOLICITORS' REGULATION AUTHORITY ARE INTERESTING...
OH?
SRA NEWS
SOLICITORS WILL BE ABLE TO PRACTISE FROM WITHIN BANKS, ESTATE AGENTS, OR EVEN SHOPS.
SRA
SUPERMARKET
WHERE IS LEGAL SERVICES?
AISLE 12, NEXT TO THE FROZEN PEAS.
SIX YEARS OF LEGAL TRAINING AND IT'S COME TO THIS...

WHAT DO YOU MAKE OF CAMERAS BEING ALLOWED IN COURT?
IT'S AN ABSOLUTE DISGRACE!
TV COVERAGE IS ALL ABOUT SOUND BITES AND MERE SENSATIONALISM!
IT TRIVIALISES JUSTICE AND MISREPRESENTS THE PROCESS!
I TAKE IT NO-ONE HAS FILMED YOU THEN?
NOT EVEN ON SOMEONE'S iPHONE!

WHAT ABOUT THIS CANDIDATE, THEN?
JUDICIAL SELECTION COMMITTEE
NO ENTRY
FAMOUSLY GRUMPY!
...EASILY IRRITATED, PARTIALLY DEAF...
...AND NO SENSE OF HUMOUR.
I SEE.
...PERFECT FOR THE JOB, THEN.
EXACTLY.

WHY IS THIS CASE DRAGGING ON SO LONG? IS IT THE COMPLEXITY OF THE LAW?
ER...NO...
IS IT DELAYING TACTICS BY THE OTHER SIDE?
NO
THEN WHAT'S THE HOLD-UP?
I'LL SHOW YOU...
ZZZZ

THESE PEOPLE DON'T EVEN BELIEVE IN EVOLUTION!
TORY-DUP ALLIANCE
THEY THINK THE WORLD WAS CREATED 6,000 YEARS AGO!
... AND THEY'RE RATHER KEEN ON THE DEATH PENALTY!
... WORKING WITH A TEXAS LAW FIRM HAS ITS CULTURAL DIFFICULTIES...
SHAKE

WHAT I CAN'T BEAR ABOUT THESE FOOTBALLERS IS HOW MUCH THEY GET PAID!
EURO 2016
... JUST BECAUSE A PLAYER IS A SO-CALLED "STAR STRIKER" THEY COMMAND AN ABSURD FEE!
IT WAS NEVER LIKE THIS IN MY DAY!
... BUT DEREK, HOW CAN SIR GEOFFREY JUSTIFY SUCH AN ENORMOUS FEE?
CLERKS ROOM
THINK OF HIM AS OUR "STAR STRIKER"

HAPPY BIRTHDAY SWEETIE ... I GOT YOU A HAMSTER!
YAY!
WHAT DOES IT DO?
HE GOES ROUND AND ROUND ALL DAY, GOING NOWHERE
WHIRRR
JUST LIKE YOU, MUMMY!
RACHEL, I NEED THESE DRAFTED BY TOMORROW
YOUR CLIENT IS WAITING ON LINE TWO...
RING RING!

MY FIRST DAY IN COURT, AND I HAVEN'T GOT A CLUE WHAT I'M DOING...
I FEEL LIKE SUCH A FRAUD...
... LIKE I'M JUST WAITING TO BE FOUND OUT...
... I WONDER IF I'M THE ONLY ONE WHO FEELS THIS WAY...

IT'S QUITE RIGHT OF LORD NEUBERGER TO SPEAK OUT ABOUT MEDIA ATTACKS ON THE JUDICIARY.
INDEED.
AN INDEPENDENT JUDICIARY IS THE CORNERSTONE OF OUR LIBERTIES!
THE MEDIA MUST NOT BE ALLOWED TO UNDERMINE THE RULE OF LAW!
... LIKE THIS STORY ABOUT POOR OLD BINKY'S AFFAIR WITH THE NANNY!
CHORTLE!

I CAN'T BELIEVE GEORGE OSBORNE IS TO BE EDITOR OF THE "EVENING STANDARD"!
"SIX JOBS" GEORGE
HE'S GOT PLENTY OF JOBS ALREADY!
NO ONE CAN BE IN MULTIPLE PLACES AT ONCE!
ER... SIR GEOFFREY, YOU'RE TRIPLE-BOOKED IN COURT TODAY.
EDWARD, YOU TAKE ONE BRIEF, AND YOUR PUPIL CAN HAVE THE OTHER...
IT'S "3 FEES" SIR GEOFFREY...

I SEE THEY NEED A PAY RISE TO RECRUIT MORE JUDGES!
JUDICIAL RECRUITMENT CRISIS
IT'S A FUNNY OLD BUSINESS, LAW: WE PUPIL BARRISTERS LIVE LIKE CHURCH MICE!
...BUT A TOP QC LIKE SIR GEOFFREY WON'T GET OUT OF BED FOR LESS THAN £10,000 A DAY!
... GUINEAS, DEAR BOY, 10,000 GUINEAS...

FIRST BREXIT, AND NOW THIS! IT'S JUST ALL BAD NEWS THESE DAYS.
OH, IT'S NOT ALL BAD.
TRUMP WINS
REALLY? WHAT'S GOOD ABOUT IT?
AS A DIVORCE LAWYER, I'VE NEVER BEEN BUSIER!
HOW'S THAT?
WELL...
TRUMP
I CAN'T BELIEVE YOU VOTED FOR BREXIT!
I CAN'T BELIEVE YOU WANTED HILLARY!
I'M FILING FOR DIVORCE!
I'M FILING FIRST!

ALL THIS SCURRILOUS GOSSIP ABOUT THE PM REMINDS ME OF MY OWN DAYS AT OXFORD.
CAMERON OXFORD ROW
...STRANGE RITUALS, EXOTIC COSTUMES, ALL THE EXUBERANCE OF YOUTH...
SO YOU WERE IN THE PIERS GAVESTON SOCIETY THEN?
OH NO!
...THE LAW SOCIETY MOOT CLUB...
BLAH BLAH

LAWYERS MUST USE SOCIAL MEDIA TO CONNECT PROFESSIONALLY THESE DAYS.
CLICK!
...BUT SOME OF THESE PHOTOS ARE A BIT MIS-LEADING!
LOOK AT SIR GEOFFREY'S PHOTO! - IT DOESN'T LOOK VERY RECENT!
...HE HASN'T HAD THIS MUCH HAIR SINCE THE 1970s!
LINKEDIN

I RATHER SYMPATHISE WITH THESE POOR UBER DRIVERS WHO ARE SUING FOR PROPER CONTRACTS.
UBER LITIGATION
AFTER ALL, THEY HAVE NO CLEAR WORKING HOURS, AND NO IDEA OF WHEN THE NEXT CLIENT WILL CALL
...NO PAID HOLIDAYS, AND NO SICKNESS BENEFIT.
UBER
JUST LIKE BEING A PUPIL IN YOUR CHAMBERS, THEN.
UBER

I BLAME THE LENDERS. THESE PEOPLE WERE NEVER LIKELY TO REPAY THEIR DEBTS
DEBT CRISIS
IT WAS IRRESP-ONSIBLE TO LEND THEM MONEY!
YES
...THE GREEKS WERE NEVER A GOOD CREDIT RISK
NOT THE GREEKS!
WHO THEN?
...PUPIL BARRISTERS! THEY'LL NEVER PAY OFF THEIR STUDENT LOANS ON LEGAL AID FEES!
YOUR BRIEF, MR CRAWLEY. £15 AND NO EXPENSES.

RACHEL, DRAFT THIS PLEADING FOR ME PLEASE.
BUT I HAVE PLANS TONIGHT...
SORRY... IT'S URGENT.
...AND I'LL NEED YOU TO WORK OVER THE WEEKEND ON THIS DEFENCE...
PLUS, I NEED YOU TO STAY LATE TO DRAFT MY SPEECH FOR TOMORROW'S SEMINAR.
ON WHAT?
"SUPPORTING WOMEN IN THE WORKPLACE"

THE MORE ONE READS ABOUT THIS NON-DOM STUFF, THE MORE SILLY IT LOOKS!
YES.
NON DOM TAX
IMAGINE BEING ABLE TO BE A NON-DOM JUST BECAUSE YOUR FATHER WAS ONE!
WHERE ELSE DOES ONE SEE SUCH BLATANT NEPOTISM?
...ANY NEPHEW OF OUR HEAD OF CHAMBERS IS WELCOME HERE, YOUNG MAN...

THERE ARE SO MANY LEGAL ERRORS IN THIS DRAMA!
REALLY?
BROAD-CHURCH
...MISTAKES IN PROCEDURE, NO KNOWLEDGE OF THE POLICE AND CRIMINAL EVIDENCE ACT...
BROAD
I JUST CAN'T IMAGINE WHERE THEY ARE GETTING THEIR KNOWLEDGE OF THE LAW FROM!
SO, SIR GEOFFREY, YOUR USUAL FEE AS LEGAL ADVISOR FOR THE NEXT SERIES?
€

ALL THAT EXPENSE, AND ALL THOSE GREAT INTELLECTS INVOLVED.
COMET LANDER LOST
AND AFTER ALL THAT EFFORT, IT JUST GOES INTO HIBERNATION MODE AND SHUTS DOWN!
YOU MEAN, THE PHILAE COMET LANDER?
NO...
... SIR GEOFFREY, AFTER ONE OF HIS JUDICIAL LUNCHES.
HIC!
ZZZZ

IT'S VERY WORRYING, THIS PLAGUE THAT IS THREATENING OUR SHORES.
EPIDEMIC THREAT
THESE THINGS START SMALL, BUT BEFORE YOU KNOW IT THEY'RE OUT OF CONTROL!
YOU MEAN EBOLA?
NO... MUCH WORSE THAN THAT!
AMERICAN LAW FIRMS, COMING OVER HERE... PINCHING OUR CLIENTS!
US FIRMS EXPAND IN U.K.

I OPPOSE MANDATORY RETIREMENT AGES FOR JUDGES. AFTER ALL, I'M NEARLY 90 AND STILL GOING STRONG!
HOW DO YOU MANAGE IT?
WELL, I GET UP AT 6AM AND HAVE A FULL ENGLISH BREAKFAST.
THEN I CHECK THE OBITUARY NOTICES IN THE PAPER.
IF I'M NOT THERE I GO TO WORK!

YOU LOOK DREADFUL CRAWLEY: SHABBY, OFF-THE-PEG SUIT, SLIP-ON SHOES... YOU NEED TO SHAPE UP!
... SINGLE-CUFF SHIRT... SOUP-STAINED TIE... I MEAN, LOOK AT YOU!
IF YOU'RE NOT CAREFUL, PEOPLE WILL START TO THINK YOU'RE A... A...
... SOLICITOR!

the LEAVING SPEECH
I'D JUST LIKE TO SAY WHAT FUN IT'S BEEN WORKING AT THE FIRM.
BARELY ENDURABLE MISERY.
I'VE MADE SO MANY FRIENDS HERE
... BACK-STABBING CUT-THROATS.
I'LL MISS YOU ALL.
NOT FOR ONE SECOND
... AND I'LL BE SURE TO KEEP IN TOUCH
... SO YOU'LL KNOW WHEN I MAKE PARTNER AT MY NEW FIRM...

SO I FINALLY STOOD UP TO THE CLERKS! TWO WEEKS AGO I REALLY TOLD THEM WHO'S BOSS!
OH?
I SAID "NO MORE CRAPPY BRIEFS FOR LOW PAY. JUST SEND ME THE GOOD STUFF!"
GOOD FOR YOU
AND DID IT WORK?
ABSOLUTELY!
SINCE THEN THEY HAVEN'T SENT ME A SINGLE BRIEF!

WHAT'S WRONG WITH SIR GEOFFREY?
IT'S THE SYRIA REFUGEE CRISIS!
THREE FORMER LAW LORDS AND 100 QCs HAVE WRITTEN TO THE GOVERNMENT IN PROTEST.
HE OBJECTS TO THEIR POLITICS?
OH NO!
...HE WASN'T ASKED TO SIGN!
OH
NOT IMPORTANT ENOUGH! IS THAT IT?

TAX LAWYERS READ THE BOTTOM LINE
LITIGATORS READ THE FINE PRINT
ACADEMIC LAWYERS READ BETWEEN THE LINES.
MEDIA LAWYERS ONLY READ THE HEADLINES.

SO... DID YOU JOIN THE PROTEST AGAINST THE GOVERNMENT'S CUTS TO LEGAL AID?
OH YES. I WAS THERE.
IF THE CUTS GO AHEAD...
...HOW WILL CITIZENS GET ACCESS TO JUSTICE? HOW WILL THEY HAVE FREEDOM OF CHOICE?
HOW WILL THEY HAVE THE RIGHT TO A FAIR TRIAL?
BUT MOST OF ALL...
...HOW WILL I PAY THE SCHOOL FEES?

IT'S GOOD TO SEE A TRADITIONAL INSTITUTION LIKE THE MONARCHY RE-INVENTING ITSELF FOR THE 21ST CENTURY.
ROYAL WEDDING
MEGHAN MARKLE, AS A DIVORCED MIXED-RACE AMERICAN ACTRESS, IS A BREATH OF FRESH AIR!
...THERE ARE LESSONS FOR US IN THE LEGAL PROFESSION, I THINK.
...JUST AS SOON AS YOU'VE GIVEN MY GODSON A PUPILLAGE IN YOUR CHAMBERS, OF COURSE.

SIR GEOFFREY, AS YOUR INSTRUCTING SOLICITOR, I MUST INSIST YOU RAISE YOUR FEES!
EH?
WHY?
YOU'RE NOT CHARGING ENOUGH!
WELL, ER... I'M GLAD YOU'RE SO CONCERNED FOR MY WELFARE...
NO NO... IT'S NOT THAT!
OH?
YOU'RE MAKING ME LOOK BAD IN FRONT OF MY CLIENTS!
... YOU'RE MAKING ME LOOK EXPENSIVE!

IS IT TRUE YOU'RE RUNNING IN THE LONDON MARATHON?
YES... YOU CAN DONATE AT MY JUSTGIVING PAGE
TAP TAP
RAISING MONEY FOR CHARITY? THAT'S NICE OF YOU!
WELL, ACTUALLY...
I JUST WANT TO BEAT THOSE B*ST*RDS IN ESTATES AND TRUSTS.

UPSET ABOUT THE UBER BAN?
NOT AT ALL. I'VE BEEN INSTRUCTED ON THE LITIGATION.
REALLY?
WELL, I COULDN'T SAY NO. "CAB RANK RULE", YOU KNOW.
HM... NOT REALLY YOUR AREA, IS IT?
THERE'S NO NEED FOR "THE KNOWLEDGE"
... AND IT'S "SURGE PRICING" ALL THE WAY...

ELITIST, HARD TO GET INTO, AND TOO MUCH LATIN. THAT'S WHAT PEOPLE THINK OF US!
OH, I DON'T KNOW...
...THE BAR IS SO MUCH MORE DEMOCRATIC THESE DAYS!
NOT THE BAR!
...THE CHELSEA FLOWER SHOW! AHH... ROSA DAMASCENA SEMPER-FLORENS... DELICIOUS!
SNIFF!

THE QUESTION BEFORE US IS HOW TO DECIDE OUR PLACE IN EUROPE.
WE'VE BEEN DEBATING THIS FOR MONTHS!
IT IS TIME TO MAKE A DECISION!
FINE
HERE ARE THE BROCHURES. WILL IT BE TUSCANY THIS YEAR OR THE DORDOGNE?
IT'S SO HARD TO DECIDE!

FINALLY, THE END OF THE DAY... NO MORE LAW!
WAP!
NO MORE GORDIAN KNOTS OF LEGAL PROBLEMS TO UNTANGLE.
TIME TO PARTY!
SO YOU'RE A LAWYER? CAN YOU HELP ME WITH MY MOTHER'S WILL?
MIND IF I BOTHER YOU ABOUT A GARDEN FENCE?
I GOT A SPEEDING TICKET. HOW CAN I GET OFF?

~~CHELSEA~~
Lawyers' FLOWER SHOW
CONVULVULUS LAWYERUS (common bindweed)
VENUS FLY TRAP
CLIENT
LAW FIRM
TRIFFID (BARRISTERUS SILKUS CARNIVOROUS)
TAKES OUT OPPONENTS AT FIFTY YARDS.
PILE OF DEAD WOOD
RARELY, IF EVER, REMOVED FROM LAW FIRMS.

AN EASTER PERFORMANCE OF HANDEL'S MESSIAH BY THE INNS OF COURT CHOIR IS ALWAYS A GAMBLE.
TONIGHT! HUGE CHOIR!
... BECAUSE THE SINGING CAN BE HIT-AND-MISS?
NO, IT'S NOT THAT.
THE REAL PROBLEM IS...
... WHETHER ANY OF THEM CAN GET OFF WORK ON TIME...
EMPTY SPACE
NO SHOW

RETIREMENT PARTY
SO, HUMPHREY, WHAT WILL YOU MISS MOST ABOUT BEING A JUDGE?
OH...
...THE CUT AND THRUST OF ADVOCACY, THE ADMINISTRATION OF JUSTICE...
...THE SENSE OF PUBLIC SERVICE... BUT MAINLY, THE FACT THAT...
... NO-ONE WILL EVER LAUGH AT YOUR JOKES AGAIN?
!!

SO, DID YOU TELL RICHARD YOU WANT TO LEAVE THE FIRM?
YES... HE SAID I COULDN'T GO!
APPARENTLY I'M "PART OF THE FURNITURE" AROUND HERE.
THAT'S NICE.
SORT OF LIKE THE EXPENSIVE CHIPPENDALE CHAIRS IN THE CONFERENCE ROOM?
NO
... MORE LIKE THE PUNCH BAG IN THE GYM.

CLIENT ON LINE ONE, RACHEL!
I'VE GOT ANOTHER ONE ON LINE TWO!
RING!
YES... WE'RE WORKING ON YOUR CASE NOW
!?!
TOMORROW, I PROMISE, YES!
YES, BY MONDAY, DEFINITELY!
!?!!
THE TROUBLE WITH KEEPING CLIENTS HAPPY...
...IS THAT I NEVER GET A CHANCE TO GET ANY ACTUAL WORK DONE.
RING! RING!
RING! RING!
WHERE IS THAT CLIENT REPORT?

EVEN THOUGH NOTHING HAS BEEN DECIDED YET, ALL THESE VOTES SHOW THAT DEMOCRACY DOES WORK.
BREXIT CRISIS
SOONER OR LATER OUR ELECTED REPRESENTATIVES WILL SURELY PRODUCE THE RIGHT RESULT.
JUST LIKE OUR GREAT JURY SYSTEM.
RIGHT – WE'VE BEEN HERE FOR HOURS AND WE CAN'T AGREE... HEADS OR TAILS?
HEADS... NO, TAILS.
ROCK, PAPER, SCISSORS.
JURY ROOM
DO NOT DISTURB
EENIE MEENIE...

HOW DID YOU DO IN THE LONDON MARATHON?
I DID IT IN 5 HOURS AND 10 MINUTES.
I DID IT IN 4 HOURS AND 45 MINUTES
IMPRESSIVE.
I RAN IT IN 12 HOURS AND 15 MINUTES.
I THOUGHT RICHARD RAN IT IN UNDER 5 HOURS?
HE DID.
...HE LIKES TO PAD HIS TIME SHEETS WITH A FEW EXTRA HOURS.

TIMES ARE CHANGING. MY LAW FIRM IS MUCH MORE SUPPORTIVE OF WOMEN THESE DAYS.
...RETURNING TO WORK AFTER MY MATERNITY LEAVE, THEY LET ME WORK A 4-DAY WEEK.
SO YOU WORK 4 DAYS AND GET PAID FOR 5 ?
NO
I WORK FOR 5 DAYS AND GET PAID FOR 4.

WE HOLD TO THE HIGHEST ETHICAL STANDARDS IN THESE CHAMBERS.
CV
SO WE MUST ASK YOU IF THERE IS ANYTHING IN YOUR YOUNGER DAYS WHOSE DISCLOSURE MIGHT EMBARRASS US.
WELL, ER...
...AT UNIVERSITY I DID DABBLE WITH, ER...
...THE IDEA OF BECOMING A SOLICITOR.

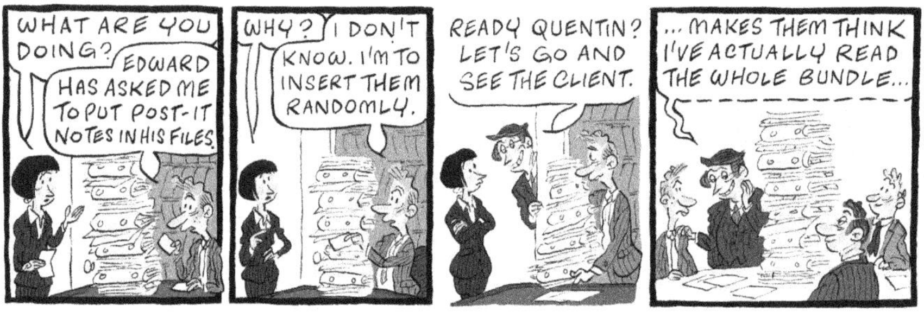
WHAT ARE YOU DOING?
EDWARD HAS ASKED ME TO PUT POST-IT NOTES IN HIS FILES.
WHY?
I DON'T KNOW. I'M TO INSERT THEM RANDOMLY.
READY QUENTIN? LET'S GO AND SEE THE CLIENT.
... MAKES THEM THINK I'VE ACTUALLY READ THE WHOLE BUNDLE...

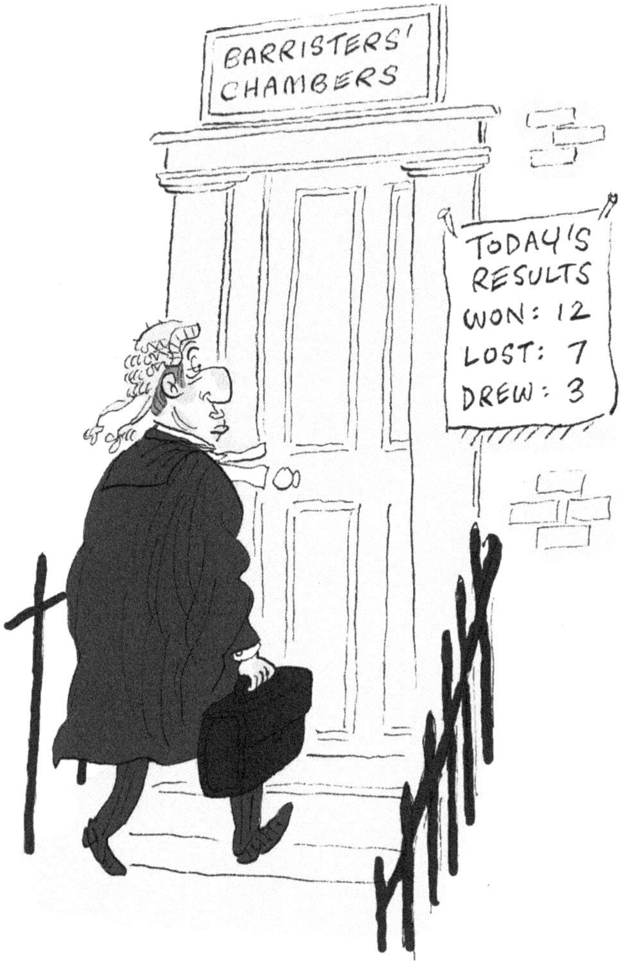
BARRISTERS' CHAMBERS
TODAY'S RESULTS
WON: 12
LOST: 7
DREW: 3

TRINITY TERM
June to July

Named after Trinity Sunday, the first Sunday after Pentecost and the 8th Sunday after Easter.

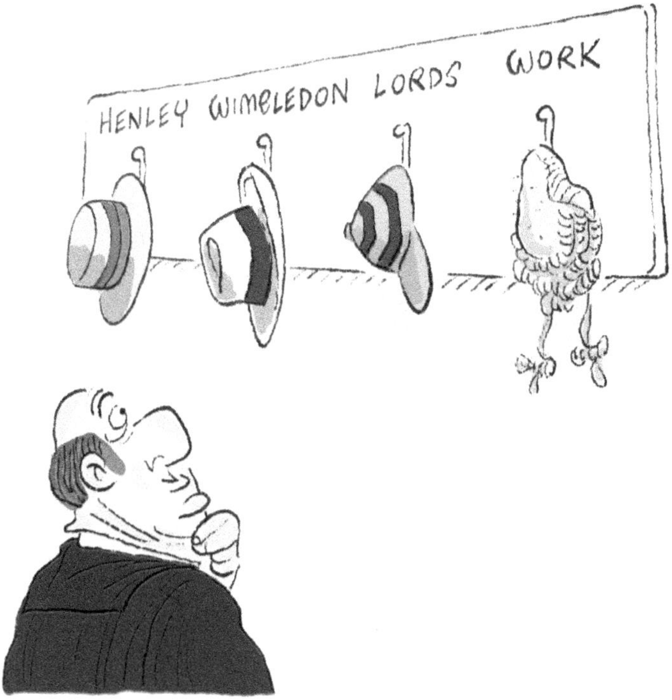
HENLEY WIMBLEDON LORDS WORK

NO, I'M AFRAID SIR GEOFFREY IS VERY BUSY RIGHT NOW.
HIS DIARY IS COMPLETELY FULL.
NO, SORRY, WE CAN'T SQUEEZE YOU IN.
HMM... LET'S SEE... CHELSEA FLOWER SHOW, GLYNDEBOURNE, THEN WIMBLEDON AND HENLEY REGATTA...

YES... PANAMA... FROM MY PRIVATE BANK ACCOUNT...
ALL VERY HUSH-HUSH... TOP SECRET...
... AND DON'T TELL THE WIFE!
GEOFFREY, YOU LOOK ABSURD
NONSENSE! A PANAMA HAT IS JUST THE THING FOR THE SUMMER SEASON...

TO OUR NEWEST PUPILS, I SUGGEST YOU ALL EMBRACE THE SPIRIT OF OUR NATION'S RECENT OLYMPIC SUCCESS.
YOU MEAN... HARD WORK AND LONG HOURS?
NO
ER... RUTHLESS PROFESSIONALISM?
NO
LOTTERY FUNDING. THE PAY HERE FOR PUPILS IS DREADFUL.

I CAN'T BELIEVE WE'RE GOING THROUGH THIS AGAIN
ELECTION
WE HAD THIS LAST YEAR AND THE YEAR BEFORE!
YOU MEAN... ANOTHER ELECTION?
NO!
RING! RING!
... OUR CLIENTS! WANTING SUMMER INTERNSHIPS FOR THEIR CHILDREN...

WHERE IS SIR GEOFFREY? I CAN'T FIND HIM ANY-WHERE!
OH... HE'S ENTERTAINING CLIENTS AT "THE SEASON"
RING! RING!
WHERE ARE YOU... GARSINGTON, QUEEN'S OR ROYAL ASCOT?
NONE OF THE ABOVE!
...SO WHERE THEN?
WELL, ACTUALLY OLD CHAP...
...NOWADAYS MY CLIENTS ARE ONLY INTERESTED IN GLASTONBURY...

GLYNDEBOURNE
THIS OPERA IS VERY LONG, ISN'T IT?
YOU'D THINK THE CONDUCTOR MIGHT PICK UP THE PACE A BIT!
...WELL, I HEAR HE WAS A LAWYER IN A FORMER LIFE!
REALLY? WHAT MAKES YOU SAY THAT?
...HE OBVIOUSLY CHARGES BY THE HOUR!

WHAT'S YOUR SON UP TO OVER THE SUMMER?
JAMIE? HE'S GOT A JOB AT A PLANT NURSERY.
SOUNDS TRICKY, ALL THOSE LATIN BOTANICAL NAMES.
ODDLY, HE SEEMS VERY USED TO ALL THAT.
MY LATEST CASE, JAMIE, TURNS ON THE PRINCIPLE OF RES IPSA LOQUITUR...

THESE POLITICIANS ALL MAKE PROMISES THEY CAN'T POSSIBLY KEEP!
POLLING
I DON'T KNOW WHO TO VOTE FOR. THEY'RE ALL SO DISHONEST!
I MEAN... WHAT SORT OF PERSON MAKES SUCH EXTRAVAGANT CLAIMS?
AH, MR SPROCKET, YOUR CASE LOOKS VERY STRONG TO ME... AND I'M SURE WE'LL WIN HANDS DOWN...

THERE HAS BEEN A MASSIVE COCK-UP ON THIS CASE. WHO IS RESPONSIBLE?
NOT ME.
I HANDED THE DRAFTING TO AN ASSOCIATE.
IT WAS NOTHING TO DO WITH ME. I GAVE IT TO MY JUNIOR.
... AND I PASSED IT ON TO ONE OF OUR TRAINEES.
WELL IT WASN'T MY FAULT!
I GAVE IT TO OUR SUMMER INTERN!
SHAME

MY ADVICE IS TO BAT IT RIGHT BACK AT THEM
HIT THEM WITH A VOLLEY OF LETTERS!
IF THAT DOESN'T WORK, WE'LL SERVE...
... AT WHICH POINT IT WILL BE GAME SET AND MATCH.
WIMBLEDON FINAL

I DON'T KNOW... IT JUST SEEMS ODD... A GROUP OF ELDERLY WHITE MEN SELECTING THEIR NEW LEADER IN SECRET.
ROME
CLOSED DOORS, NO WOMEN, AND EXCOMMUNICATION FOR BREAKING THE SILENCE!
WELL...
ROME
...I SUPPOSE THE PROCESS OF ELECTING A NEW POPE COULD BE MORE OPEN.
NO... NOT THE POPE!
THE ELECTION OF A NEW SENIOR PARTNER!
KEEP OUT
DO NOT DISTURB

FROM NOW ON, WE'RE GOING TO GIVE AWAY OUR LEGAL SERVICES FOR FREE.
WHAT!?!
IT'S OUR NEW BUSINESS STRATEGY...
INSTEAD, WE WILL ONLY CHARGE FOR ANCILLARY SERVICES LIKE PAPER, PENS, CHAIRS...
AIR CONDITIONING, HEAT, COFFEE, PAPER CLIPS, AND PRINTER INK. I ESTIMATE WE WILL DOUBLE REVENUES AND PROFITS
WHAT'S WITH RICHARD'S BIG IDEA?
OH... HE WENT ON HOLIDAY WITH RYAN AIR...

MR SPROCKET, SIR GEOFFREY WILL EXPLAIN YOUR CASE TO YOU...
...AS I HAVEN'T READ THE PAPERS...
!
...BUT I'VE HARDLY LOOKED AT THIS...
ER... I THINK I'LL LET MY JUNIOR OPEN THIS ONE...
WHAT? NOT ME... !?!
ER... ACTUALLY...
...THE PERSON WITH THE BEST GRASP OF THE DETAIL...
...IS MY PUPIL, CRAWLEY. HE'LL EXPLAIN IT ALL WON'T YOU?
ER, UM...
HELP!

WHAT DO YOU MAKE OF THE NEW JACKSON REFORMS?
EH?
YOU KNOW, THE NEW RULES ON DBAs
...CHANGES TO CFAs, CPRs AND QOCs
...AND CMCs
SO WHAT DO YOU THINK?
WTF!

HOW TO SUCCEED AT THE BAR
WHAT CAN I DO? MY CASE IS ON IN A MINUTE AND MY CLIENT IS A NO-SHOW.
ER, HELLO.
I'M FOR THE OTHER SIDE.
...WE'D LIKE AN ADJOURNMENT.
WHAT?!
YAY!
AT THIS LATE STAGE?
YOU'LL HAVE TO PAY OUR COSTS!
OK
...ON AN INDEMNITY BASIS!
AGREED.
THANKS FOR BEING SO REASONABLE!
...DON'T MENTION IT.

DISGRACEFUL BEHAVIOUR FROM THESE UKIP POLITICIANS!
UKIP PUNCHUP
BRAWLING IS NOT A GENTLEMAN'S WAY TO SETTLE A DISPUTE!
UKIP PUNCHUP
THERE ARE MUCH BETTER WAYS TO SORT THESE THINGS OUT!
UKIP
...WITH EXPENSIVE LITIGATION: ONE QC TO ANOTHER!

RACHEL, YOU'RE THE BEST AT THESE COMPLEX CASES – FAR BETTER THAN I AM.
COULD YOU HELP OUT?
AS ONE OF OUR MOST ABLE AND VALUED ASSOCIATES, WE KNOW YOU'LL DO AN EXCELLENT JOB.
THANKS RACHEL. I'LL SEE YOU ON MONDAY!
SIGH!
ONE OF US IS THE BRAINS OF THIS OUTFIT – AND IT'S NOT ME.

CRIME:
the BARRISTER'S PROGRESS
① the STUDENT
I WANT TO BE A CRIMINAL LAWYER SO I CAN DEFEND THE WEAK AGAINST THE STRONG.
LAW
THE JUNIOR BARRISTER
MY CLIENTS AREN'T REALLY GUILTY, THEY'RE JUST UNDER-PRIVILEGED.
THE EMINENT SILK.
WHAT I NEED IS SOME RICHER CRIMINAL CLIENTS.
...WHO CAN AFFORD MY FEES.
THE JUDGE
QUITE FRANKLY, THEY'RE OBVIOUSLY ALL GUILTY.

AMAZING... A WHOLE DAY WITHOUT INTERRUPTIONS! I'VE ACTUALLY GOT SOME WORK DONE!
TAP TAP
NO CLIENTS CALLING, NO PARTNERS BUGGING ME, HARDLY ANY EMAIL...
TAP TAP
A WHOLE DAY OF PROPER WORK!
SHAME IT ONLY HAPPENS ON A SUNDAY.

DID YOU KNOW THAT YOU CAN BE CHARGED UNDER NO LESS THAN FIVE PIECES OF ANTI-HATE SPEECH LEGISLATION?
THERE'S THE PUBLIC ORDER ACT 1986 AND 1994, THE RACIAL AND RELIGIOUS HATRED ACT 2006...
ALL OF WHICH PROVIDE FOR LARGE FINES AND/OR PRISON SENTENCES.
I DON'T CARE. I STILL HATE YOU AND I'M NOT EATING MY PEAS.
RIGHT. I'M CALLING THE POLICE.
PLIK

WHICH JUDGE ARE WE IN FRONT OF TODAY?
MR JUSTICE CARBUNCLE.
CARBUNCLE? NO! HE'S HALF ASLEEP!
YES... QUITE USELESS...
WRONG ON THE LAW... UNRELIABLE ON THE FACTS...
M'LUD, YOUR LORDSHIP AS EVER MAKES AN EXCELLENT POINT.
MOST APPOSITE...
I DEFER TO YOUR LORDSHIP'S LEARNING...

SO, RICHARD, WHAT'S OUR NEXT MOVE?
WHAT WE NEED IS A REQUEST FOR FURTHER INFORMATION.
AN RFI?!?
BUT THEIR PLEADING IS 300 PAGES LONG! THERE ARE 200 BOXES OF FILES TO GO THROUGH!
WE'RE SWAMPED AS IT IS! I MEAN, WHAT WE REALLY NEED...
... IS A REQUEST FOR LESS INFORMATION!

THIS CASE IS GOING INSANE... I NEED ALL HANDS ON DECK! WHERE IS RACHEL?
SHE'S NOT IN.
WHY NOT? EVERYONE NEEDS TO WORK THROUGH THE NIGHT!
ER... SHE'S GOT THE WEEKEND OFF.
WHAT?! WHY?!?
SHE'S HAVING A BABY.
OH, WELL THEN...
... I WANT HER IN FIRST THING ON MONDAY MORNING!

AS I LOOK BACK ON MY LIFE, I AM GLAD I CHOSE TO BECOME A JUDGE, RATHER THAN STAY AT THE BAR.
AS A BARRISTER, WHEN YOU BECOME TOO OLD AND TIRED AND SICK TO GO ON, YOU HAVE TO GO.
WHEREAS, AS A JUDGE...
... YOU GET TO GO TO THE COURT OF APPEAL

BREAKING AWAY AND BECOMING INDEPENDENT COMES WITH BIG RISKS!
BREXIT FEARS
IT'S A LEAP IN THE DARK! AND THE FINANCIAL BENEFITS MAY BE ILLUSORY.
BREXIT
I DO HOPE YOU'LL VOTE TO STAY, RACHEL
NOW ISN'T THE TIME TO LEAVE AND START YOUR OWN FIRM!
BUT... IF NOT NOW... WHEN?
FINGERS CROSSED
STAY WITH US... YOU'LL MAKE PARTNER SOON!

I CAN'T BELIEVE A BARRISTER WOULD LIE ABOUT HIS DAILY COMMUTE
BARRISTER IN RAIL FRAUD
WELL, HE ISN'T THE ONLY ONE!
REALLY? YOU DON'T MEAN...
...NOT IN THESE CHAMBERS!
I'M AFRAID SO!
YES DEAR... HOME NOW... ANOTHER 5km POWER WALK ACROSS THE PARK...
TAXI
£20
?

HOW CAN ANYONE SELF-IDENTIFY AS SOMETHING THEY ARE NOT?
OH... HALF THE MEMBERS OF CHAMBERS DO JUST THAT!
WOMAN SELF-IDENTIFIES AS BLACK
... CRAWLEY SELF-IDENTIFIES AS A COMPETENT BARRISTER...
ER...
QUAKE TREMBLE
... BERNARD SELF-IDENTIFIES AS A PERSECUTED MINORITY...
TAX LAWYER
...AND SIR GEOFFREY SELF-IDENTIFIES AS SOBER AFTER LUNCH.
ZZZ

NOW THAT FIONA WOOLF HAS RESIGNED FROM THE ABUSE ENQUIRY, SIR GEOFFREY THINKS HE'S IN WITH A CHANCE!
CHAIR NEEDED
REALLY?
BUT SURELY HE'S AN ESTABLISHMENT FIGURE TOO? HE MUST HAVE HAD DINNER WITH ALL THE GREAT AND THE GOOD!
WELL, ACTUALLY I DON'T THINK HE GETS ASKED TO MANY DINNER PARTIES.
WHY NOT?
MY LATEST CASE TURNS ON A FASCINATING POINT OF LAW... LET ME EXPLAIN IT IN DETAIL...
ZZZ
ZZZZ

THESE CUTS TO JUDICIAL PENSIONS MEANS OLDER BARRISTERS DON'T WANT TO BE JUDGES ANYMORE. IT'S CAUSING A CRISIS!
... TO THE ADMINISTRATION OF JUSTICE?
WHAT?
NO!
... TO THE BACKLOG OF COURT CASES?
NO.
... TO MY CAREER! THEY'RE ALL HANGING AROUND CHAMBERS ALL DAY, PINCHING MY BRIEFS!
ANYTHING FOR ME TODAY, DEREK?
CLERKS ROOM
DON'T FORGET ME!

RIGHT, I'M OFF TO CATCH MY FLIGHT TO EDINBURGH TO CAST MY VOTE IN THE REFERENDUM.
REALLY?
VOTING FOR UNION, I TRUST?
OF COURSE NOT!
I'LL BE VOTING "YES" FOR INDEPENDENCE.
BUT WHY?
SIMPLE!
...307 YEARS OF LEGAL CONTRACTS TO RE-WRITE...

HOW'S YOUR NEW LAW TEXTBOOK SELLING?
NOT GOOD I'M AFRAID.
HEY – LOOKS LIKE YOU'VE GOT A GOOD REVIEW AT AMAZON!
"...BRILLIANTLY CLEAR ... THE ONLY TEXTBOOK YOU'LL EVER NEED."
THAT'S GREAT!
THAT WAS BY ME.
OH

FOOTBALL AND LAW HAVE A LOT IN COMMON.
BOTH ARE A GAME OF TWO HALVES.
BEFORE
MR SPROCKET, I'M VERY CONFIDENT IN YOUR CASE.
AFTER
WELL, I ALWAYS SAID YOUR CASE WAS A TRICKY ONE...
I'M RUINED!

ECONOMISTS THINK A.I. AND ROBOTS WILL REPLACE HALF THE NATION'S JOBS WITHIN TWENTY YEARS.
A.I. NEWS
I DON'T THINK THE BAR WILL BE IMMUNE.
A.I. NEWS
SOME THINGS WILL STAY THE SAME, THOUGH.
A.I. NEWS
HAVE YOU MET MY GOD-SON? HE'S LOOKING FOR A PUPILLAGE...

THANKS FOR COMING IN. IT'S ABOUT YOUR RESPONSE TO THE CLAIMANT'S LETTER BEFORE ACTION.
NOW, I KNOW THAT THE COUNTRY IS GRIPPED WITH FOOTBALL FEVER...
...AND PASSIONS ARE RUNNING HIGH...
BUT REALLY, IS "DEAR SIRS, COME AND HAVE A GO IF YOU'RE HARD ENOUGH" REALLY AN APPROPRIATE REPLY?

RACHEL, I'M ON HOLIDAY NEXT WEEK AND I NEED THAT BRIEF TO COUNSEL DRAFTED.
...AND THE SCHEDULE OF COSTS... MONTHLY BILLINGS...
EVERYTHING NEEDS TO BE WRAPPED UP AND BROUGHT UP TO DATE!
PREPARING FOR RICHARD'S SUMMER HOLIDAY IS HARDER THAN ORGANISING MY OWN.

IT'S OUTRAGEOUS THAT THE SCOTS NOW WANT A SECOND REFER-ENDUM!
STURGEON SEEKS 2ND VOTE
...AND TONY BLAIR WANTS A SECOND VOTE ON BREXIT!
YOU CAN'T JUST KEEP ASKING PEOPLE THE SAME QUESTION UNTIL YOU GET THE "RIGHT" ANSWER!
M'LUD, THE JURY MAY ALREADY HAVE CON-VICTED MY CLIENT, BUT WE NOW SEEK A RE-TRIAL...

VERY WORRYING, ALL THESE INCRIMINATING PHOTOS BEING USED FOR POLITICAL GAIN
TRUMP IN HOOKER SCANDAL
OH... I DON'T KNOW... A COMPROMISING PHOTO OR TWO CAN BE QUITE USEFUL.
REALLY?
... LIKE PHOTOS OF DONALD TRUMP?
NO, NOT TRUMP!
...LIKE THESE PHOTOS OF A CERTAIN JUSTICE IN THE BALLIOL JCR IN 1974...
I'M SURE THIS WILL SWING THE JUDGEMENT IN MY FAVOUR...

IT'S VERY HARD LEARNING A NEW LANGUAGE
I TRIED TAKING LESSONS, BUT IT DIDN'T WORK.
I GOT BOOKS... GOOGLE TRANSLATE, BUT STILL I CAN'T UNDERSTAND...
... A SINGLE WORD MY LAWYER SAYS TO ME!
RES IPSA LOQUITUR...
EL VINO
...EX POST FACTO...

COME ON SWEETIE, EAT YOUR PEAS.
NO!
LET'S CHANGE YOUR NAPPY.
NOOOOOOO!!
LET'S GO TO THE PARK
NO! NO! NO!!
HOW'S FAMILY LIFE?
IT'S TEACHING ME A LOT ABOUT SUCCESSFUL NEGOTIATING STRATEGIES.

BEING ORDERED ABOUT BY A SADISTIC OLDER MAN...
GREY
... DOMINATED AND ABUSED...
GREY
WHY DOES THAT SEEM FAMILIAR?
... SOUNDS JUST LIKE MY LAW FIRM...
*!?!

I NEVER REALISED THAT BEING A PUPIL BARRISTER COULD BE SO PHYSICALLY ONEROUS!
PUFF!
WE GET TREATED LIKE PACK ANIMALS HAVING TO FETCH AND CARRY FOR SENIOR BARRISTERS!
... BUT WORST OF ALL ...
... IS SIR GEOFFREY'S ANNUAL SHOOTING AND FISHING TRIP TO SCOTLAND...
EUSTON
AHA! THE CALEDONIAN SLEEPER ...
HURRY UP CRAWLEY...

THE BEST THING ABOUT BEING ON HOLIDAY IS THAT NO-ONE CAN REACH ME.
NO PHONES, NO INTERNET, NO CLIENTS OR BOSSY PARTNERS
...SOLITUDE AT LAST...
AH RACHEL, THERE YOU ARE... YOU STILL HAVEN'T SUBMITTED YOUR TIME SHEETS ...

HELLO, I'M YOUR CONSERVATIVE CANDIDATE. I TRUST I CAN RELY ON YOUR SUPPORT?
ER...
AS YOUR MP, I WILL FIGHT FOR YOU ON ALL THE VITAL ISSUES THAT FACE THE COUNTRY!
LIKE BREXIT?
...NOT BREXIT!
WHAT THEN?
...PAY RISES FOR LEGAL AID LAWYERS, BETTER PENSIONS FOR JUDGES, AND PROPER BRIEFS FOR SENIOR MEMBERS OF THE BAR...

YOU WANNABE MPs, WITH YOUR SECOND JOBS - IT'S NOT RIGHT!
VOTE
DON'T WORRY, I ASSURE YOU THAT IF I AM ELECTED AS YOUR MP...
... I INTEND TO DELEGATE ALL MY CONSTITUENCY WORK TO MY AGENT!
...IT WON'T INTERFERE WITH MY LUCRATIVE CAREER AT THE BAR AT ALL!

SO, SIR GEOFFREY, YOU'D LIKE TO BE OUR CONSERVATIVE CANDIDATE FOR THE GENERAL ELECTION?
YES
CV
CV
WHAT ARE YOUR VIEWS ON TAX POLICY?
VERY SIMPLE.
CV
CV
I'M FOR MUCH MORE COMPLEXITY AND LOOPHOLES.
ER...
CV
CV
...SURELY YOU MEAN "GREATER SIMPLICITY"?
NO. COMPLEXITY IS WHAT KEEPS US BARRISTERS IN BUSINESS!
CV
CV

SORRY TO HEAR YOU LOST TO THE OTHER CHAP IN THE ELECTION
I'M GUTTED!
ELECTION FIASCO
... BECAUSE YOU LOST TO LABOUR?
NO... NOT THAT!
... BECAUSE HE'S A COMMITTED LEFT-WINGER?
NO
WHAT THEN?
HE'S A...A...SOLICITOR!
OH DEAR
THE SHAME!

BACK FROM YOUR HOLIDAY? HOW WAS RYAN AIR?
AWFUL!
... CRAMPED CONDITIONS, NO STORAGE SPACE, BAD COFFEE, AND CONSTANT INTERRUPTIONS...
SIR, BAGS UNDER YOUR SEAT!
SOUNDS TERRIBLE!
WELL ACTUALLY...
...IT'S NOT UNLIKE BEING A PUPIL IN CHAMBERS...
CRAWLEY, MAKE ME A COFFEE, AND PHOTOCOPY THESE PAPERS...

HOW WERE YOUR HOLIDAYS?
EVENTFUL. ON THE PLANE ON THE WAY HOME, THE PILOT ASKED US...
... "IS THERE A DOCTOR ON THE PLANE?"
WOW! WHAT HAPPENED?
I PUT MY HAND UP!
BUT... YOU'RE NOT A DOCTOR!
I SAID: "I'M A LAWYER. I'LL HELP YOU SUE THE DOCTOR"!

I HEAR THE POLICE WERE CALLED TO SIR GEOFFREY'S HOUSE BY HIS NEIGHBOURS.
YES
THERE WAS LOTS OF SHOUTING AND SWEARING, AND THE SOUND OF PLATES BEING SMASHED.
WHAT COULD IT HAVE BEEN ABOUT?
...HIS NEW CLEANING LADY RAN HIS WIG THROUGH THE WASHING MACHINE BY MISTAKE.

I WENT TO A PARTY LAST NIGHT; ALL THE PEOPLE ON MY TABLE WERE LAWYERS.
MY DAD'S A LAWYER, I MARRIED A LAWYER, AND BOTH MY KIDS ARE IN LAW SCHOOL.
ALMOST ALL MY FRIENDS ARE LAWYERS.
SOMETIMES I THINK IT WOULD BE EXCITING TO MEET AN ACCOUNTANT.

QUENTIN, I SEE HARRY AND MEGHAN HAVE KEPT ARCHIE'S GODPARENTS A SECRET.
YES.
ROYAL BAPTISM
I WISH MY PARENTS HAD DONE THE SAME FOR ME.
WHY?
ROYAL BAPTISM
ER... WELL...
ROYAL
THAT YOUNG PUPIL QUENTIN...
NOT VERY BRIGHT, IS HE?
...ONLY GOT INTO CHAMBERS AS SIR GEOFFREY IS HIS GODFATHER...
SHAME
ROYAL BAPTISM

HAWKEYE HAS TAKEN SOME OF THE FUN OUT OF WIMBLEDON.
I USED TO ENJOY THE DISPUTES BETWEEN THE PLAYERS AND THE UMPIRE
McENROE 1981
IT REMINDED ME OF MY YOUNG DAYS AT THE BAR...
YOU CANNOT BE SERIOUS, M'LUD!

IT'S EXHAUSTING PACKING FOR THE HOLIDAYS.
BAGS, BEACH TOYS SURFBOARDS ... ENDLESS STUFF TO LOAD INTO THE CAR
BUT WHAT A RELIEF WHEN IT'S DONE AND THE CAR IS STARTED ...
SLAM!
... TAKING THE WIFE AND KIDS TO FRANCE SO I CAN GET BACK TO THE OFFICE ...

I LOVE THE OFFICE IN AUGUST, EVERYONE LEAVES AND ALL GOES QUIET...
KNOCK! KNOCK!
RACHEL - TAKE CARE OF THIS WOULD YOU? I'M OFF TO UMBRIA FOR THREE WEEKS.
SORRY RACHEL, I'M AWAY ALL MONTH AND NO-ONE ELSE CAN DO THIS BUT YOU
THANKS RACHEL, I'LL BE BACK IN SEPTEMBER TO SEE HOW THE CASE TURNED OUT.

I DREAD GOING INTO CHAMBERS THESE DAYS.
REALLY? WHY?
THERE'S NO-ONE AROUND! DIGITAL CASE MANAGEMENT MEANS EVERYONE WORKS FROM HOME.
THE ONLY PEOPLE LEFT TO TALK TO...
... ARE THE ONES WHO DON'T HAVE ANY WORK TO DO...
AH, EDWARD, LET ME SHOW YOU ALL MY HOLIDAY SNAPS FROM UMBRIA...
PLIK

AH, MR SPROCKET, YES... I'M LOOKING AT YOUR FILE RIGHT NOW...
AH, MS WALTON, YES... I'VE GOT YOUR FILE IN FRONT OF ME RIGHT NOW...
AH, MR PHIPPS, YES... I'M LOOKING THROUGH YOUR CASE RIGHT NOW...
SO HOW WERE YOUR HOLIDAYS IN BARBADOS?
OH, WORK, WORK, WORK...

Milton Keynes UK
Ingram Content Group UK Ltd.
UKHW052140021123
431838UK00002B/3

9 781912 687565

Kings of the Land
Book 1

JRC Cox

Published by Farland Valley Ltd

Follow us on Facebook at 'Kings of the Land'

'To fight for the king, may be the greatest honour.
To fight for the land is the greatest deed.'

Merlin 496 AD

PROLOGUE – TWELVE YEARS AGO

The thud of the firing catapult boomed out and Uther saw the tar-flamed rocks tear towards his castle. A roar rose from the enemy lines, and thousands of soldiers and mounted knights charged at his gates. He'd been fighting the Lady for two years, battling her onslaught for power, but all his resistance had counted for nothing. Now she was attacking his last remaining stronghold, and he knew he couldn't win.

He turned to the young maid beside him and pulled her with him, away from the edge of the stone walls. 'Get the children away,' he said, as the firing of more catapults echoed from behind them.

'Yes, sire,' she replied nervously. She glanced back as more blazing rocks rose from the enemy's lines and sped through the air. She edged further towards the steps leading down to the courtyard, now eager to get going.

'All the children, both noble and common,' Uther stressed. 'Dress everyone plainly so the enemy can't tell the difference. Maybe that way my infant boy will survive. You must save him from the Lady's wrath.' For an instant Uther's face softened just a little. 'Please.'

The maid nodded, then she flinched as the first impact shook the wall they stood on. 'What about you, sire? You look so tired. Can't you negotiate with them?'

Grim determination returned to Uther's face. He reached down deep inside and called up the blazing courage in his heart one last time. 'No, there must be no surrender to the Lady.' His expression hardened further as he got ready for the battle. 'I'll fight with my army until my last breath. We will buy you time to save the children.'

Uther stopped briefly before the steps. His hand tightened on his sword, and magical flames erupted along its blade. Now his face showed no sign of fatigue or weariness at all. 'The Lady may destroy us today, but it will not be clean or bloodless. I will give her death and destruction the likes of which she has never seen before.'

The maid shied back from the force of his words. Then she looked down at his hand. 'And the sword? What will happen to Excalibur?'

'Before my end, I will drive the sword into the ground and the land will take it back.' Uther walked down towards the packed courtyard, scanning for his private squad amongst the hundreds of troops.

'Are you sure it's wise to let go of our most powerful weapon?' she asked quietly, leaning in towards him once more.

'The Lady's dark heart must never use Excalibur.' He increased his grip on the sword as the flames along its blade flickered. 'I might have failed to protect our land, but my boy must not! The sword will wait, it will find him somehow.'

Uther paused at the bottom of the steps. 'No more talking. Go.' He gestured her away as his royal guard massed around him. 'Do as I command. Get the children to safety.'

The young maid ran reluctantly to the keep, leaving King Uther and his sword to their fate. Before she entered the doorway, she turned and watched him signal the archers to get ready. They raised their tar-flamed arrows as the main gate shattered and blew inwards. Hundreds of rampaging soldiers burst through the entrance and the archers cut them down with flaming arrows. But as quickly as the invaders fell, more of the Lady's troops streamed through the ruined gatehouse, and she knew Uther would not hold the castle for long.

With her eyes glowing red in the gathering flames, the last

thing the maid saw was the flash of Uther's sword as he entered the fight and dealt out death around him, one final defiant act of a desperate man. Then she turned and ran for the nursery, to see to the children.

The young girl paddled in the shallow water of the pond while the castle burned around her. Soldiers were everywhere, some fighting the invaders, others scrambling back to defensive positions. Desperation showed on their faces and weariness in their movements. Then one man noticed her and stopped.

'What the hell are you doing out here playing in the pond?' he said between ragged breaths. 'Get inside for heaven's sake.' As he reached out with a hand to help her, his foot sank into the water up to his calf. He looked at the girl in surprise as she splashed about on the surface of the pond, but before he could utter another word, an arrow tore through his chest, and he went down hard. The girl stopped her game and watched sadly as the life left his eyes. She stepped towards him as another arrow came flying. Her little face creased in concentration, and she sank briefly into the water, the arrow passing over her head by a few inches. When she reached fallen man, she bent down and gently closed his eyes.

'Where do they go?' she asked.

The pond rippled at her feet, tickling her toes.

'I wish we did know,' she replied. 'It makes me sad when they leave us.'

The pond lapped at her ankles a little more forcefully, breaking her away from the morbid distraction and urging her to get going.

'Ok, ok,' she said. 'I am four years old you know. You don't have to tell me everything.'

She reached down to the pond, and just before her fingers hit the surface, the ripples leapt up and splashed into her hand.

She smiled at the comforting weight of the water in her

palm. 'Right,' she said to the pond, 'let's go find him.'

The girl stood in the nursery doorway and glanced around at the cowering children. Some of them were with their nursemaids, while others cried on their own. A look of worry crossed her normally determined face.

'There's so many of them. How am I supposed to know who he is?' She opened her hand just a little, but the tiny pool of water remained motionless. 'Well, you could be more helpful,' she said somewhat petulantly. 'Do I really have to go ask them all?'

She went to move, and the water in her hand shook with force beyond its size. 'Oh, silly me,' she said and looked down at her feet to the infant crawling towards her. Slowly, his tiny hand reached out and grabbed at her big toe.

The girl giggled. 'That tickles.'

The water in her hand shook again.

'Already? Do we really have to go now?' she asked. 'Can't we play a little?'

Before the pond could reply, the nursery shook, and a blast of magical fire boiled up the corridor towards them. The girl bent down and grabbed the young child. With both arms wrapped around his small body, she ran towards the washbasins in the corner. As nursemaids and children panicked all around her, she tipped one onto the floor.

'Can't we bring them with us too?' she pleaded. The water in her hand rippled ever so gently, and a tear trickled down the girl's cheek.

'I'm sorry,' she said quietly to everyone and no one. Then, holding the infant tight, she stepped into the water just as the red flames tore through the room and blew the nursery apart.

PART 1 – THE BATTLE OF GLENN

CHAPTER 1

The blade swung viciously over the boy's head as he ducked under its swipe. He watched the weapon continue its journey and embed itself in the knight standing right behind him. The young squire stared for an instant. Then the victor pulled his sword from the dead man as he fell, and the boy felt a large hand grip his shoulder.

'What are you waiting for?' came the rough voice of his knight. 'Go get my second sword before we're both killed. This battle is going badly enough without you standing about.'

The boy turned and ran through the gathering mist. The clash of weapons came from all around him, along with shouts and screams. Then a rush of fighting men broke through the mist, and the boy ran around them. He saw their soldiers defending desperately, trying to repel the invaders. But swords found gaps in armour, and the overwhelming numbers cut down his comrades.

The boy wished he could help, but even though he was strong for his age, he knew he would never survive the fight. Years ago, the squires were left alone to serve their knights, but not anymore. A dead squire led to a dead knight, so they became the first targets.

The mist closed in behind him as the boy dodged away from the last enemy. Just as the hill felt like it was getting steeper than ever and his legs too tired, he broke through the mist at the top. He was relieved to see the colours of his own side. A few soldiers were posted here to guard their backup supplies. It looked like they still held the top of the hill, at least for now.

The boy scanned around quickly and found his knight's pack leaning against the others of their battalion. He took out the small sword, so short it was almost dagger like, and rapidly checked it was still sharp. Then he turned and started back down the hill. The young squire was not sure why his knight wanted his second sword. Few knights were skilled enough to use two blades at once, and unfortunately, he didn't think his master was among those.

Still, he found it hard to judge his knight's true worth. His master showed wisdom and pigheadedness, harsh words and kindness in equal measure, and often with little apparent thought for either choice. Still, unlike so many others they had known, neither of them were dead yet. So maybe his knight was doing something right after all.

Back down the hill, another group of fighting knights came crashing out of the mist. This time, the boy ran straight through them as fast as he could, ducking under the flashing blades. He knew he was being reckless, but he didn't want to get turned around in the mist and lose his way back to his own knight. Regardless of his master's erratic behaviour, the boy was loyal and really didn't want to fail him.

He started to breathe hard again, but he pushed himself to keep going. The surrounding mist thickened, and it cut his vision to less than twenty paces. Then, right on the edge of the mist, he glimpsed his knight fighting a much larger opponent. His master was defending well against the massive blows from his huge foe. But with each strike, he fell back a little, conceding ground as he went.

The boy sprinted faster, but before he could close the gap to his knight, he noticed an archer lining up to fire at the duelling knights. 'Look out,' he shouted, not knowing if the archer was friend or foe, but not wanting to take the chance.

The archer stopped at the sound, then turned his aim

towards the boy and fired. The arrow skimmed past the boy's head as he lurched to one side, but the archer persisted and took aim again. Before the boy could even wonder what to do next, the mist swirled thickly, and he lost sight of the enemy completely. He crouched down a little more, wondering how the mist could move like that with no wind about. Then, from out of nowhere, a voice beside him made him jump.

'I suggest you move away from the aim of that archer. Before he fires again.'

The boy spun around at the sound, raising his short sword. He saw an old man sitting on a rock. 'How can you see where he's aiming, sir?' he whispered.

The old man calmly ignored the question as he concentrated on his hands. He held them together, and a fine blue dust fell to the ground from between his parted fingers. Without looking up, the old man spoke again. 'I would still advise you to move. A few more feet to the left should suffice.'

The boy took a crab-like step, and an arrow whistled past the back of his head, nicking at his short hair. He crouched down even lower and peered into the thick mist, trying to see where the archer might be, or maybe even catch a glimpse of his knight. He thought he heard the creak of a bow and then finally nothing. Impossibly, all sounds of the battle had ceased.

The boy looked back to the old man, noticing for the first time that the swirling mist seemed to emanate from the strange blue dust when it hit the ground. The boy patted at the back of his head where the arrow had passed. 'Thank you, sir?' he offered.

The old man glanced up. Once more, he ignored the boy's questioning. Instead, he asked a question of his own. 'And why might you be here? Are you not a little young to be in a battle of this size?'

The boy weighed up his options and decided to answer. 'I'm helping my knight, sir. He needs this second sword I'm bringing him.'

A slight smile crossed the old man's weathered face, and amusement flickered in his eyes. 'I notice you did not mention for which side you fight. A good strategy when you do not know what you are facing. After all, battlefields are dangerous places.'

'Yes, sir,' said the boy, shifting his stance, unsure whether the remark was a friendly warning or an outright threat.

'Worry not,' the man replied, as if looking inside the boy's head, 'you have nothing to fear from me.'

The boy stared at the unnatural mist, all sight of the ferocious battle still gone. He needed to get back to his knight, but he also wanted to know what was going on.

'How are you doing this, sir?' he asked, gesturing to the quiet around them and the shifting mist. 'Are you wielding magic to stop the battle and protect us? Can you help my knight too?'

The old man opened his hands, and the boy saw a small glowing ball gradually fading away into the blue dust. 'From a certain point of view, the answer to both those questions is yes.'

Not really reassured by the answer, the boy watched anxiously as the dust continued to blow away, and then he noticed the ball of magic was getting smaller and smaller. 'What happens after when your magic runs out? Will the fighting return?' The boy shifted uncomfortably, and though he tried to hide it, the old man saw the fear and uncertainty edging onto his young face. 'My knight said we're losing this battle. He won't admit it in front of me, but I don't think we'll survive today.'

A strange smile fell across the old man's face again, but his eyes held a hint of sadness. 'Well, young Arthur, I can see that you are nobody's fool. I believe there are interesting times ahead for you.'

At hearing his name, Arthur raised his sword again, but held his ground. The old man watched him closely, and he saw something else in Arthur's expression. 'Excellent. I see you have some bravery mixed in with your curiosity. An admirable combination, and something you will need to survive this day. As you have correctly judged, the odds are not in your favour.' The old man held Arthur's gaze. 'However, I may be able to help.'

Help who? thought Arthur, but instead he just asked. 'How do you know my name, sir?'

The slight amusement returned to the old man's face. 'Well, as you can see, I have my ways and means. But unfortunately for you, I am not here to answer your questions. Right now, I have some questions for you.' The old man glanced around them. 'Who do you think I am? Why I might be here?'

'I've heard the stories,' remarked Arthur, sinking down into the damp grass. 'Tales of Merlin the magician, Merlin waiting for the king's return. Are you really a powerful sorcerer? Is the king going to return now?' A little hope crept into Arthur's voice. 'Can he help us win this battle?'

Merlin raised an eyebrow again, and a tiny blue spark flashed in his eye. 'Once again, the answer to your questions is yes. But likely not in the way you expect.'

Arthur looked up at Merlin as the fine blue dust finished falling and the small ball of magic was gone. The sounds of battle returned beyond the edge of the mist, and the air grew heavy again with the stench of fighting. Merlin glanced around. 'The device I just used took me years to construct, yet I have spent it in mere minutes. I am afraid that everything will return to normal rather quickly, so you best get ready boy.'

'Ready for what, sir?' shouted Arthur against the growing noise, his voice almost drowned out by the deluge of crashes and screams. Arthur stood up, raising his short sword again and scanning the mist for his knight.

'No need to call me sir all the time. You may call me Merlin.'

He glanced at the sword in Arthur's hand. 'And I am afraid that small sword will not help your knight as much as he requires.'

'Why not?' persisted Arthur with his questioning, wanting a straight answer at least once.

Merlin raised an eyebrow and looked to his right. Arthur followed his gaze to the outline of the archer, now emerging from the mist. 'Well, for a start,' said Merlin, as the enemy raised his bow. 'If you do not avoid that next arrow, the sword will not actually make it as far as your knight.'

Arthur desperately threw himself aside from the speeding arrow. He looked around in vain for cover before his foe could fire again, but there was only the grassy slope of the hill. Arthur stared helplessly at the archer, then seemingly from nowhere, the man was struck down himself, an arrow embedded deep in his neck. Arthur looked for his saviour, but the friendly archer was nowhere in sight. All he saw was more chaos of the battle. Mostly there were knights locked in combat, swords arcing viciously towards weak spots in armour, but scattered about were a few squires, helping where they could.

With no sign of his knight, Arthur spotted Lancelot, one of the older squires. He was fighting alongside his own knight, trying to help him gain an advantage. Lancelot came from a high-born family, but his father had insisted he start at the bottom and learn everything he could about war. And Lancelot was good at learning.

Despite seeing him, Arthur didn't shout out. He knew there should be no distractions, unless to warn about a killing blow. Lancelot had taught him that. The older squire was generous with his advice, even to boys like himself. Without a drop of noble blood in his veins, Arthur knew he was bottom of the pile. But Lancelot paid no attention to bloodlines, he dished out praise and scorn on merit alone.

Wondering how on earth he could help, Arthur saw

Lancelot parry a strike, giving his knight the advantage he was looking for. Together, they began to drive their enemy back. As they disappeared into the mist, Arthur saw his own knight, Aurelius, emerge. He was still fighting the same large knight, and the strain was showing. The enemy knight was incredibly strong, and despite all his armour, he was fast. Even though his knight was battle hardened, Arthur didn't like what he saw. Arthur could hear Aurelius grunt with the effort as he caught another blow from his opponent's sword, breathing ever harder as he repelled the powerful onslaught.

Arthur started towards him. 'I've got to go help my knight,' he shouted back to Merlin.

'Be careful, boy,' the old man called after him, adjusting his position on the rock. 'Your knight will need you alive. As do I.'

Ignoring the caution, Arthur ran as fast as he could. Fighting soldiers were all around him, and he had to weave even more to stay out of the way, but he kept his eyes on Aurelius, knowing he had to help somehow.

He saw his master stagger back again under renewed blows from his opponent, the big knight swinging his huge sword ever harder. Much more, and even the best defence in the land might not stop those blows, thought Arthur. Then Aurelius dropped to one knee under another vicious strike. As he turned to counter the next blow, he saw Arthur running towards him.

'Right shoulder,' shouted Aurelius, before lunging back at his opponent.

Arthur didn't hesitate or wonder, he just raised the short sword to his right as a swipe came in from the fight next to him. Not even aimed at Arthur, the blow smashed into his sword, and the blade snapped in two. Surprised by the sudden stop of his swing, the attacking knight hesitated a fraction and his opponent took advantage, driving his own sword under the knight's helmet. The victor looked down at Arthur, and with a small nod turned away. Friend or foe, Arthur couldn't tell, but the knight had shown his gratitude anyway.

Another loud clash of swords brought Arthur back to Aurelius. His huge opponent seemed to grow ever larger, and the blows raining down forced Aurelius lower still. Arthur speed desperately towards his knight, his sword extended to try anything. Aurelius sagged down further, and his opponent raised his sword high for one last swing. Then Aurelius' left hand shot out and Arthur threw the short sword the last few feet. Aurelius caught it and in one smooth movement buried the broken blade into a narrow gap between his opponent's armour plates, the one revealed by his over extension. The huge knight crumpled, and another fight was over.

'Glad you could join me, young Arthur,' remarked Aurelius, breathing hard.

Expecting the usual cross words for his efforts, Arthur was a little surprised.

'Bloody well get a move on next time. That big oaf was hard work and nearly finished me off.'

Ah, thought Arthur, that's more like it.

'So, what kept you?' asked Aurelius, scanning the surrounding battle.

'I was talking to Merlin, sir. He saved my life with magic.'

Aurelius stared at him, somewhat caught off guard. 'Not that old fairy tale again,' he finally sighed. 'If those words came from any other squire, I'd take the flat of my sword to him. But from you, I suspect there's no lie. Least not intentionally. Where is this supposed magician then?'

'Over here, sir,' replied Arthur in earnest, as he turned and started back.

'Old man with a beard I presume? Told you he was Merlin no doubt? Showed you a jester's trick? You're too trusting,' remarked Aurelius, but he followed Arthur nevertheless. Whether this was to duck around the fighting or in genuine curiosity, Arthur couldn't tell. But when they got there, the rock where Merlin had sat was empty.

'He was here, honest,' said Arthur desperately.

A kinder look crossed Aurelius' face just briefly, then another large group of knights in desperate combat broke through the mist and Aurelius was drawn back into the battle. This was not a fight for squires, and he shouted to Arthur. 'Get back over the hill to the castle. They're pushing us back more and more. We won't hold this ground much longer.' Then he turned to deal a surprisingly powerful blow on an enemy knight.

Arthur remembered his weapon and ran to the large knight's body. He pulled the broken sword from the dead knight and started back up the hill, keeping low and out of sight as best he could. By the old oak tree, he stopped and looked down the hill. Through the mist, he could see patches of fighting, and amongst it all, he could see them losing. Bit by bit he saw their knights fall, only to be replaced by soldiers in the dark red colours of their enemy.

Arthur looked over the other side of the hill, across to the castle. Torn between returning to help his knight and obeying his command, Arthur paused, not knowing what to do.

'A hard choice, is it not?'

Arthur jumped again at the sound of Merlin's voice and turned to look at the sorcerer standing next to him.

'How do you do that?' asked Arthur, after his heart had stopped hammering in his chest.

'A little gentle magic,' replied Merlin. 'It can be surprisingly easy to persuade people to not see something, when it is something they do not expect to find.' Merlin raised an eyebrow. 'After all, how often do you see an old man in the middle of a battlefield?'

Arthur conceded the point. Then he looked down at his sword. 'You were wrong about this sword. It did help my knight in the end.'

'Yes, it did indeed,' said Merlin. 'But I regret to say, that was not the fight I was referring to.'

'What fight do you mean, sir?'

Merlin remained silent, just watching the fighting down the hill. Arthur tried to see what Merlin was looking for, but all he could see was the ground they were conceding. 'We're losing this battle. Can't you use another magical device to help us, sir?'

'Sadly not. I have only one magical device remaining, and despite your dire need right now, I must save that one for later.' Merlin's eyes continued to search the battle. 'And, to add to your woes, I fear that control of this hill is not the only aim of our enemy today.'

Arthur sighed, not really understanding what Merlin was getting at. He looked down again at his broken sword. 'Maybe I should just do what Aurelius says and get back to the castle.' He gestured past the old oak tree. 'I noticed some rocks down the other side of the hill. They might provide some cover so we can make it back to the castle without a fight. Now that my sword's broken, I don't think I'm going to be much help anyway.'

'Do not underestimate the help you could give,' Merlin said with another slight smile. 'However, I believe you are correct, cover would be wise.'

Arthur looked around and saw some of the rocks on the edge of their vision, disappearing into the mist. 'Over there,' Arthur pointed.

They walked through the gloom, and into the beginnings of the scattered rocks, as the battle raged on behind them. With the mist closing in again, it was all about the noise. The clash of weapons seemed to be endless, without let up for a single second. Arthur worried the sounds were getting closer, and he encouraged Merlin to move faster so they could reach the relative safety of cover as soon as possible.

'Can you work more magic without a device?' Arthur asked

as they walked. 'Could you hide us both like you hid yourself?'

'Unfortunately not. Hiding another person is far more difficult than just hiding myself. And triggering that device took a lot of effort. I must rest for a while before working any large amounts of magic. For now, we are left with merely our own intelligence and guile.' Then Merlin smiled at Arthur. 'And the might of your sword of course.'

Before Arthur could question Merlin any further, they rounded a large rock formation and arrived in a small grassy clearing surrounded by towering stone. Arthur walked over to the edge where some of the larger rocks overhung. In the enclosed space, the noise of battle was dulled. 'This cover looks good,' he said. 'We can't be seen from outside this clearing.'

'A very sensible choice with excellent cover.' Merlin found a seat seemingly from nowhere and settled down. 'There is however, just one small problem. Can you tell me what it is?'

Arthur concentrated as he looked around. 'Where's the problem? I can't see anyone, and no one can sneak in without us seeing them.'

'Aye, well observed young squire,' announced an unknown voice, and the sound of weapons being drawn came through the mist. 'And so, you cannot leave without being caught.'

Five men stepped out of the mist. The first knight was small and wiry, but his four companions were not, they were huge. None of them had any clear colours, which usually meant mercenaries. Not a good sign, thought Arthur. Mercenaries generally took what they wanted and didn't have a need to keep their prisoners alive.

'I see you've met our old friend,' said the smaller man, with a slight accent from the North. 'No doubt he's told you a tall tale or two. Well, let me tell you something a bit more practical.' He shifted his sword as he spoke. 'If you leave now, I'll only send one of my men to chase you off. To be honest, they're a bit lazy when it comes to killing squires, so you might even get away.'

Arthur stole a quick glance at Merlin and raised his broken sword. 'And what about the old man?'

The mercenary watched Arthur plant his feet. 'Good Heavens, not another brave and stupid squire,' he said to his men. 'Does this country produce them by the bucket load?'

He began to advance on Arthur, his men fanning out around him. 'You're just a wee boy with half a sword, defending an old man you don't even know. Why risk your life in such a meaningless way?'

'I...' started Arthur.

Suddenly, one of the large mercenaries broke forward, and without a word, took a huge swing at Arthur with his sword. The powerful blow was directed at his neck, and Arthur ducked under it just in time. A rock behind him took the strike and large chunks shattered from it. The leader of the mercenaries looked annoyed, but remained still, just glancing briefly at the rest of his men.

The large mercenary regained some balance after the failed blow and moved a little more cautiously. 'You're trickier than you look, but you should've taken up Morgan's warning. Now I'm going to carve you up so your own mother wouldn't know you.'

The look of annoyance increased on the mercenary leader's face. Why's that, thought Arthur briefly, wondering if he'd live long enough to find out?

He raised his sword, more for defence than attack, as the large mercenary continued forward. The big man grinned, making fainted swings from time to time. 'You really think that broken sword will do much good?' He swung another powerful blow at Arthur's side.

Arthur dodged right and angled the blow along his own sword, trying to deflect it away from his body. The blade missed his flesh but caught on the broken edge of his sword and whipped it away. The mercenary lunged in again, but Arthur jumped inside the blow, giving the large man a kick to his knee. A small grunt of pain escaped from the man before he shouted at Arthur. 'Enough playing, now you're dead.'

The mercenary limped towards him, a little slower than before, and Arthur thought he heard a small chuckle from Morgan. He scanned desperately for his sword, then to his left he saw the handle sticking out from the rocks. He moved towards the hilt as the large mercenary advanced. Another swing caused Arthur to leap left, and he continued into a desperate dive for the sword's handle.

Arthur seized the hilt, and it felt stone cold. Then he tightened his grip and it strangely warmed in his hand. With no time to wonder why, Arthur pulled at the sword, and it slid from between the rocks with a grinding screech. This is not my sword, thought Arthur, its undamaged blade emerging from the rocks. But with no time for anything, he just raised it in hope as the large mercenary swung down hard. The swords crashed together and the noise from the blades boomed out. Somehow, Arthur's sword held its ground and the mercenary's blow didn't hit his head as intended.

His opponent's sword didn't fare so well, and it snapped clean in two. The large man cried out in pain and gripped his wrist, the rest of his sword dropping to the ground. With agony and fury etched on his face, he lumbered towards Arthur. Then the big mercenary stopped, and his face relaxed. He stood still for a second before collapsing slowly forward. Behind him, Morgan pulled his dagger from the large man's back and looked Arthur in the eyes.

'I don't have time for needless violence and even less for careless talk. I really should choose my reinforcements more carefully.' Morgan took a step closer, returning his dagger to his belt and drawing his sword once more. 'Now young laddie, you need to step aside, or I will deal some very necessary violence.'

Merlin shifted on his seat. 'Maybe you should do as the mercenary asks, young Arthur,' he said. 'Despite his recent actions, I believe this man will fight unsparingly to get his way.'

Morgan didn't take his eyes off Arthur for a second. 'Aye squire, what's it to be?'

Arthur just raised his sword. 'I'm sorry, sir, but the answer's still no.' The sword, warm in his hand, felt comforting. Its presence didn't boost his courage, but did somehow confirm his decision was right.

The mercenaries closed in and Morgan stepped forward quickly, his sword whipping up to Arthur's head in the fastest movement he'd ever seen. Arthur tried to duck again, but this time he was too slow. Morgan's blow struck him hard on the side of his head, and Arthur fell to the ground. He waited for the blackness that should follow, but instead he felt pain and his vision turned red. Morgan stepped back and tapped the flat of his sword, just as a knight would do when sparring hard with his squire to teach him about pain.

'Last warning,' growled Morgan more forcefully. 'I won't turn aside my blade the next time and it will kill you. So, step away.'

Arthur slowly got to his feet. Surprisingly, his sword was still in his hand, and he raised it again. 'No,' he said quietly. The sword's warmth increased, and his vision began to clear.

'You cannot win you know,' said Merlin. 'Just let it go.'

'I know he bloody well can't win,' cursed Morgan. 'But the stupid boy doesn't seem to care.'

'I wasn't talking to Arthur,' remarked Merlin, looking directly at Morgan.

With that, Morgan stepped in again and aimed an even faster blow at Arthur's head. But this time Arthur didn't try to avoid the blow, and with a slight movement, raised his sword higher to counter the vicious strike. The clash of the swords seemed to deafen them all, and Morgan's blade just shattered. The mercenary fell back from the explosion of his sword, small shards of metal embedded in his armour and flesh. He looked up with pain on his face as his men advanced on Arthur.

'Hold,' Morgan said. 'The old man is right, we can't win.'

Morgan's men stopped. Confusion showed on their faces, but loyalty held them still.

'So, you told the truth,' said Morgan as he turned to face Merlin, 'and the Lady told lies. I think you were just a means to an end. I reckon this sword was her real target.'

Morgan shifted painfully and started to pull the small pieces of sword from his face. 'Nae wonder she was willing to pay so highly.' He moved on to pulling shards from his hands. 'I really don't like disappointing an employer. But in this case, I think I'll have to pass on the task.'

Morgan glanced back at his men. 'Most don't believe in the tales of Merlin, even less the legend of the sword, and you could include me in that number. However, I'm nothing if not adaptable, and after what I've just seen, I'm changing my mind. You can continue, but I recommend you do not.'

The largest of Morgan's remaining knights studied Arthur briefly. Then he held out a hand to help up his boss. 'I think we will follow your lead,' he said simply.

Morgan nodded, then looked at Arthur. 'Now what?'

Arthur stood still for a second, totally stunned. He turned to Merlin. 'Why's he asking me what to do? Who is this lady? What lies did she tell, sir?'

'You really should just call me Merlin you know,' he said, adjusting his position to get comfortable again on the rocks. 'However, those questions are not important for now. There is only time for one. So please choose your next question carefully.'

Arthur looked at the sword, then at Morgan and his men, then finally back to Merlin. 'What on earth do we do next? How do we get back to the castle alive?'

Merlin considered this briefly, then replied with a small smile. 'Not quite one question, but a good choice nevertheless. I think we will be just fine.'

'But Merlin, that doesn't answer anything...' Arthur started, then the noise of the battle washed over them, and horses came thundering around the edge of the rocks. The leading knight and squire, followed by their soldiers, were dressed in the same blue colours as Arthur, and they headed straight for his small group.

The rest of the chasing knights were in the dark red colours of their enemy, and they stopped at the edge of the clearing, blocking everyone in. Dismounting and drawing their swords, over fifty armoured knights started to advance towards them.

CHAPTER 2

Arthur recognised Lancelot as he rode nearer, but he didn't know the old knight with him. They drew their swords as they dismounted. The knight looked around quickly, then spoke to Morgan. 'Mercenary, on what side do you stand?'

'I stand with the young laddie here, as will my men,' replied Morgan. 'He will pay us later.'

'Not sure I follow your meaning, but I'll hold you to your word,' said the knight. 'If we live long enough that is.'

He pointed to Arthur and asked Lancelot. 'Will this young squire fight?'

'Yes, father, he'll fight hard despite his age and won't be a hindrance. Maybe some of us can hold out until our reinforcements get here.'

'Enough!' shouted the largest of the advancing foe. 'Lay down the sword, Lord Bane, and surrender. If you do not, we will have all your heads, from the old man to the young boy. Then we'll save the last few blows for you and your son.'

Bane's expression hardened, and he raised his sword. 'Group round me,' he said to the others. 'Even numbers on either side.'

Morgan and his mercenaries split quickly beside Bane, and the soldiers did the same. Arthur and Lancelot closed in to be on his right. Only Merlin stayed at the back, still seated and uninvolved.

As the enemy advanced, Arthur set his position and whispered to Lancelot. 'Where's your knight? Are you really our commander's son? Who's that big knight?'

'Always so many questions, even in battle,' whispered

Lancelot with a tight smile. 'My knight is slain. Brave, but reckless. A bit like you really. And yes, Lord Bane is my father, though we try to keep that quiet. Mainly to prevent situations like this. The big knight is Lord Falcon, commander of the enemy forces, and under the orders of the Lady we think. He's been leading the drive to take this hill.'

As Arthur started to ask something else, Lancelot scowled. 'No more questions, time to fight.'

Falcon advanced with his knights in front of him and addressed Lord Bane as they raised their swords. 'Actually, I've changed my mind. I think we'll start with you and the mercenaries. Once you're dead, we can despatch the others at our leisure.' He looked at his knights and shouted. 'You four take Bane, and you lot kill the others. That should be easy enough, there's not many of them. The rest of you stay with me.'

Bane's group adjusted their spacing, placing the rocks to their backs and choosing secure footing on the ground. 'Lancelot, Arthur, hang back,' said Bane quietly. 'Watch their swings, then stab out at anyone who leaves themselves open. If you get a chance, break for a horse while we distract them, and try to get away. Understood?'

'Yes, sir,' they both whispered.

Bane's soldiers and the mercenaries waited for the leading enemy knights to make their move. With the rocks covering one side, their foe couldn't attack all at once without getting in each other's way, so ten of them led the charge. The first one swung his sword hard at Bane's neck. Bane blocked the blow and dealt back a powerful counter strike. The red knight fell, as did two more with strikes from Morgan and the others, but one of their soldiers limped back injured, a slow trickle of blood coming from the wound.

The red knights kept up their attack, with more stepping in to replace their fallen comrades. The mercenaries fought back hard, matching their enemy blow for blow. But Bane's soldiers were outclassed as well as outnumbered. One by one, they were cut down and dropped to the ground.

Lancelot deflected a blow from one knight fighting his father, but before they could take advantage, another stepped in with a strike to Bane's arm. There was a crunch of bone as Bane's arm broke despite the armour. Instantly he dropped his supporting dagger, all movement in that arm gone, and was reduced to fighting one handed.

'We won't last,' said Arthur. 'There's too many of them.'

'Be quiet and fight,' came the harsh reply from Lancelot. He managed a swipe at the unguarded knee of the knight who'd hit his father. The red knight came down, and when his armour moved in the fall, Bane finished him with a stab to his exposed neck. But another knight immediately dealt a blow to Bane's extended arm. His armour blocked the hit better this time, but his sword still fell from his weakened grip.

Bane threw himself forward, desperate to push back the tide of red knights, but Arthur knew this wouldn't stop them for long. He also saw the mercenaries suffering. Two were down and Morgan was bleeding from his shoulder.

'Get the boys away,' called out Bane to Morgan, as he managed to briefly push back their foe. At the same time, Falcon shouted at his knights. 'Get Bane's sword.'

'Keep them occupied,' Morgan called to his men. Then he side-stepped a red knight's swinging blade and moved over to cover Lancelot and Arthur. 'Get behind me and we'll try for the horses.'

We don't have long, thought Arthur. He looked at Morgan's shoulder bleeding as they backtracked, and saw Lord Bane wrestled to the ground. Then he finally watched Falcon being handed Bane's sword.

'We won't all make it,' said Arthur, louder this time.

'Aye, but you might,' grunted Morgan, the pain showing through on his face.

23

'We need to go now,' said Lancelot, tugging at Arthur. 'I can't let my father sacrifice himself for nothing.'

'No.' Arthur stopped retreating with them. 'We're not leaving anyone.'

He turned and held his sword up high. He shouted as loud as he could. 'Falcon, is this what you are looking for?' Then he plunged the sword back into the rocks. It slid in down to the hilt with an ear-splitting grind of metal on stone.

The knights on both sides stopped and stared at Arthur and the sword. Lord Falcon raised his hand, shouting at his men. 'Stay your weapons.'

Falcon glanced at his knights and their vastly superior numbers, then he smiled. 'Yes boy, you might well be right.' He signalled to his men. 'Hold those mercenaries and bring Bane over here.'

The two knights standing over Bane pulled him up roughly and a grunt of pain escaped, despite him clamping his jaw shut. The red knights dumped Bane behind Falcon as he stepped up close to Morgan and the boys. 'If you stand aside now, mercenary, we may be able to use you later. Oppose me and I will cut you down.'

'No, I've changed sides for the last time today. I'll not move. I stand by the boy.' Morgan brought his sword up with his good arm.

'Have it your way,' said Falcon, and he sent a tremendous blow crashing towards Morgan's injured shoulder. Unable to swing his sword fully to block, Morgan twisted and took the blow across the back of his armour. The armour split and more blood showered down his back. Morgan fell to his knees, but didn't go down completely. Slowly, he pushed himself up again, his sword wavering slightly in his hand, but his face set hard.

'You'll have to do better than that,' grunted Morgan, grinning despite the pain. 'Being born in the South has bred you soft Lord Birdy.'

'You won't live long enough to regret those words,' said Falcon, lashing out with an armoured boot to bring Morgan down to his knees once more. 'Line up this mercenary with Bane,' Falcon commanded. 'We'll get the sword then kill them all.'

Despite the advancing enemy, Lancelot turned on Arthur and shoved him. 'Now we'll all die. I hope you and your stupid bravery are happy.'

'We're not dead yet,' said Arthur as he steadied himself by the sword.

Falcon strode over to them. 'Boys, boys, boys. You can argue in the next life.' He stood by the sword embedded in the rocks and pushed Arthur aside.

Falcon glanced at Lancelot who was inching closer. 'Raise that blade one inch higher, and your father dies painfully.'

'Now,' continued Falcon. 'I shall take the sword, and with it I will conquer this land.' He grasped the sword by its cold handle and pulled hard.

The sword did not shift. Falcon adjusted his grip, put his foot on the rock, and pulled harder still. His huge muscles bunched with power, but even then, there was no movement. 'What have you done, boy?' Falcon shouted at Arthur. 'What trickery is this?'

Falcon picked up his own sword and stared at Arthur. Then he thought better of it, and with lightning speed, slapped Lancelot across the head with the flat of his blade. 'Get me that sword little boy, or the next blow takes your friend's head off.'

Lancelot held the side of his face and swayed, but he managed to remain standing. 'Don't give him anything,' he croaked.

Falcon slapped him with his sword again. This time, Lancelot went down and didn't move. Falcon raised his sword for one last blow.

'Wait,' shouted Arthur, and placed his hand around the handle of the sword. The hilt went from as cold as stone to the warmth of a person's touch. A feeling of familiarity filled Arthur, and he pulled the sword from the rock with another ear-splitting screech. Some of the knights held their ears to block out the noise. 'You want the sword?' Arthur pointed it at Lord Falcon. 'Then come and get it.'

'No, I don't think so,' said Falcon, holding his ground. 'Someone pulls the legendary Excalibur from a stone; I think I'll keep my distance.' He leaned down and grabbed Lancelot by the throat, making his intention perfectly clear. 'Now for the last time, give me that sword or I will kill your friend.'

'Why should I? You're going to kill us all anyway,' said Arthur, inching a little closer to Falcon.

'You know what? You're right. Knights, kill them all. Then we'll rush the boy together. No way he can fight us all at once.' With that, Falcon adjusted his grip on Lancelot and raised his sword for the fatal blow.

Without thinking, Arthur swung Excalibur as hard as he could and let go. He saw Lancelot starting to wake and raise his head to watch the downward blow from Falcon's sword. Just as Falcon's blade reached Lancelot's neck, Arthur's sword flew right through it and severed it in two. The tip of Falcon's sword spun away, slicing Lancelot's cheek as it went, then fell uselessly to the ground. Excalibur carried on its flight and embedded itself in the knight standing over Bane. The knight looked down at Arthur's sword in surprise, then fell over silently.

The other red knights looked on stunned and the mercenaries took their chance, lashing out at ankles and knees to unbalance their foe. Lancelot kicked out at Falcon and began to run unsteadily. Arthur sprinted towards his sword, overtaking the staggering Lancelot. He retrieved Excalibur from the dead knight, then tried to help Bane to his feet. Lancelot and the mercenaries joined them. The largest mercenary took over from Arthur and effortlessly lifted Bane up.

This time Arthur was standing at the front. He was a bit breathless, but he looked steadily at Lord Falcon.

The enemy knights regrouped as Falcon rose and strode to his horse to fetch another sword. Still outnumbering them by four to one, Falcon looked back with confidence. 'Enough of this childish brawling,' he said to his knights. 'We kill them all right now.'

Just as his hand closed on the hilt of his sword, an arrow sped through the air and took down a red knight. Then another arrow followed, felling a second knight and killing him instantly. Without a word or any hesitation, Falcon's hand moved from his sword to the saddle, and he mounted his horse in one swift movement. With a kick and no backward glance for his knights, he fled the small clearing as fast as he had arrived.

The red knights continued to fall, and Arthur moved towards their remaining number. He raised his sword, shouting. 'Hold fire, hold fire.' One more arrow flew in, then the barrage stopped.

'What the devil are you doing, boy?' came a familiar shout from the top of the rocks.

Instead of looking up, Arthur turned to the red knights. 'You can't win now. Will you lower your swords and surrender?'

All bar one, they dropped their weapons. Arthur walked up to the remaining knight still holding his sword. Slightly shorter than the rest but stocky in build, he held his sword steady. Arthur stopped just out of range. 'You know you're surrounded and beaten, but you don't give up. Why's that?'

'I could have asked you the same question a few moments ago,' replied the short knight, who looked much younger than Arthur had first thought.

'Drop your sword and we can talk. What's your name?'

Arthur lowered his sword a little to show he meant well. Around him, he could hear soldiers descending from the rocks, commands being shouted.

'Marcus,' the knight replied, still holding his sword at the ready. 'How do I know I can trust you? I certainly can't trust the lot I'm currently with.' He glanced after his departed commander.

'I'll show you,' said Arthur and he stepped in, swinging his blade around fast. Marcus was quicker and brought his sword up in a perfect block, but as the swords clashed, Marcus's blade was severed clean in two. Arthur's sword continued unhindered, and he stopped it right at Marcus's neck, where Excalibur drew a small bead of blood. They both watched, dead still, as the drop ran slowly down the sword and boiled away with a faint flash of blue.

'What was that?' said Marcus, still without fear in his eyes.

'To be honest, I don't know,' replied Arthur, completely lowering his sword. 'But it feels like a good sign. Pleased to meet you, Marcus. I'm Arthur.' He extended his arm in welcome and Marcus took hold in return.

Knights gathered all around them, picking up weapons from their foe and organising the prisoners. Once more Arthur heard the same familiar voice shouting. 'I'll ask again, what the hell are you doing, Arthur?' Aurelius came striding towards them. 'Are you trying to get yourself killed all over again?'

'Sorry, sir,' said Arthur, 'but I think we're going to need all the friends we can get today.'

'Well, you're right about that, but stop taking such bloody great risks to get them. You're just lucky that knight's sword broke when you hit it.'

Aurelius turned to Bane. 'What are your orders, sire?'

'From what I have just witnessed, that will be up to the king,' he replied. Aurelius looked at him curiously, but before he could say a word, Bane continued. 'Secure the area for now and get me an update on the battle. Let me know how long before we're completely overrun. Right now, I want to talk to Arthur.'

More of their soldiers arrived, and Aurelius directed them while Lord Bane led Arthur across the clearing. The prisoners were undressed from their armour and searched; Marcus included. As the soldiers worked, whispers spread through them, and some looked over towards Arthur.

'You pulled the sword from the stone.' Bane looked down at the weapon in Arthur's hand. 'By legend, only the line of the king can free Excalibur. How do you explain this?'

Arthur shook his head. 'I don't know, sire.'

Bane looked from Arthur over to Aurelius, then he called him back. 'Where exactly did this young lad came from?'

Aurelius saw the look on Arthur's face and knew what was coming. He held up a hand to stop Arthur before he opened his mouth with a hundred questions.

'Arthur was brought to us as an infant, the only living thing pulled from Uther's castle when it was destroyed by dark forces. No idea how he survived that, bloody miracle we thought.' Aurelius looked around as others started to listen in as well. 'Wrapped in cheap cloth, my wife presumed he was a servant's child, but she insisted we care for him anyway. I know what my brother, King Uther, was like. He would have wanted me to look after anyone under the care of his sovereignty.'

Aurelius paused briefly and lowered his gaze just a little. 'I couldn't find it in myself to look after the kingdom. I never wanted the responsibility of being a king. My brother would have been disappointed in that, so the least I could do was take care of the boy.' He turned from Bane to Arthur and looked closer at the sword in his squire's hand. 'From what I'm seeing and hearing, maybe not a servant's child after all. Maybe I have a new nephew and a new king!'

'Yes,' confirmed Bane. 'I believe we all have a new king.'

Astounded, Arthur looked at Lord Bane, at his newly discovered uncle, and then finally settled on Merlin, who had quietly appeared beside them. 'But I can't be king. I'm just a squire. I'm not strong enough or wise enough. The legend must be wrong Merlin, I can't be a king.'

Aurelius looked at the old man. 'Well, this day just gets better and better. So you're Merlin, huh?'

'Yes,' replied Merlin firmly, holding Aurelius' gaze with a determined look of his own. 'You have just witnessed a small part of what Excalibur is capable of. Is it so difficult to believe that I exist too?'

Aurelius remained quiet but continued to study the sorcerer closely. In return, Merlin's expression softened. 'I understand your scepticism, Aurelius. However, I am here to help young Arthur. Let me speak with him alone for a moment. After that, you may judge me all you wish.' Without waiting for an answer, he gently led Arthur away from the group.

When they were seated on their own, Arthur looked imploringly at Merlin. 'You did say you'd help me today. What should I do?'

'It is not for me to tell you what to do. However, I will assist you with some good advice.' Merlin studied the boy standing before him. 'As you have so correctly stated, you are not strong enough or wise enough.'

Arthur's mouth dropped open. 'With respect sir, that doesn't help me very much.'

'Boy, the point you are missing, is that you are not those things yet. So while you wait to become wise enough and strong enough, what do you think you should do now? What are you going to say to them?' Merlin indicated to the gathered knights and Lord Bane.

Arthur's face creased in concentration for a while, then he broke his silence. 'I think I should probably find people who are already wise and strong, then I should ask them to do what they do best.' Merlin looked at him like a teacher pleased with his pupil.

Arthur walked back to Lord Bane. 'Sire, is your arm ok? Can you continue to command the battle?'

'I think I should be calling you sire,' replied Bane. 'However, to answer your questions, young sire. Yes, my arm can be bound, and yes I can rally our forces. Falcon may be a little spooked by these events, and even if he's not, his soldiers should be. So we might be able to press some advantage and hold this hill for a while longer. At least long enough to better prepare the castle for a siege. Would you agree Aurelius?'

'Agreed. A hard drive at the enemy will give us some losses, but if Falcon fails to rally them quickly, then they could fall back far enough to give us time to retreat the rest of our troops.' Aurelius rubbed at his tired face. 'However, we all suspect who's the genuine power behind this. We need to find out more about the Lady and her plans. Even after all these years, we still don't know who she is, but we're seeing her dark influence return more and more. I want to talk to Morgan and Merlin about this, they could know more than us. Maybe I can escort them back to the castle, before I return to the fight.'

'If King Arthur agrees, then certainly,' replied Bane. 'While you do that, I will take our forces here and try to push the enemy down the hill before you return. You can escort the others back to the castle, then bring back another battalion to reinforce us for the retreat.'

Lord Bane looked to Arthur. 'Do you agree, sire?'

Still stunned, Arthur slowly nodded. Bane turned to Lancelot and the gathered troops and shouted. 'Let's mount up and get ready to battle. We have a king to fight for and a strategy to survive this day.'

CHAPTER 3

When Bane's group had departed, Aurelius instructed his knights to get the prisoners ready for the hike back to the castle. Once he was happy the prisoners were being secured, Aurelius turned to Morgan. 'What do you know of the Lady and her plans?'

'Instructions were delivered through her messenger, so we never met. She paid us to find the old man. I mean Merlin.' Morgan corrected himself as he glanced at the sorcerer. 'She wasn't sure if he was really here, but we found him yesterday before he slipped away from us. However, seeing Falcon's actions just now, I reckon the actual target was the sword. We were probably just one small part of her overall goal.'

Aurelius looked to Merlin and waited.

'I believe Morgan is correct in our enemy's desire for the sword,' stated the sorcerer. 'Quite possibly the taking of this hill and the castle were merely strategic targets on the way towards gaining the sword. But now that Arthur has Excalibur, I think the Lady's plans will have to change.'

Aurelius sighed. 'We need to know more.' He regarded Arthur for a moment, then called Marcus over, ordering his knights to let him be. He looked steadily at Marcus as he approached. 'You better not betray the trust my nephew has placed in you so quickly. What do you know about our enemy's plans?'

'We were ordered to capture the hill and then the castle, with no prisoners to be taken alive.' Marcus grimaced. 'This wasn't popular. Most of us have been on the losing side at some point, and we like to live to fight another day. Falcon wanted Lord Bane's sword and yours too, but he didn't want any witnesses to how he got them. We presumed he and the Lady were looking for King Uther's sword to claim some kind of right to the throne. Everyone knows you're his brother, and we presumed you and Bane were still arguing over who should become king. Maybe you were even going to fight him for the throne.'

Aurelius snorted a laugh. 'No chance of that. I've no intention of fighting the best commander I know, for a throne I don't want. Mind you, not that he wants it either. Truth be told, even after all this time, we still didn't know what we were going to do. We just knew that the Lady and her alliance shouldn't get hold of the throne. However, young Arthur here has changed everything today.'

Arthur looked at his newfound uncle and thought about everything he'd just heard. He glanced at them all in turn and finally settled on Aurelius.

'Go on, young, sire, ask your questions,' said Aurelius. 'You may be the new king, but you're also that same inquisitive squire my wife and I raised all these years.'

'What if there's a way for everyone to survive the battle for this hill? Could we let the enemy take the hill faster than they planned by ordering a full retreat right now under the cover of the mist? Maybe we can make enough noise to start with so they think we're attacking, not retreating, and fool them into letting us get back to the castle without a fight.' Arthur's face creased in concentration as he spoke. 'After that, how about we show them Excalibur as we prepare to defend the castle? Show everyone that we already have the sword. Falcon knows I've already got it, but do all the others? If all the lords in Falcon's alliance see us hold the sword, will that weaken Falcon's grip on them and force him to back down? Maybe that will end this battle and save the loss of life on both sides. What do you think, sir?' To Arthur's side, another smile appeared unnoticed on Merlin's face.

Aurelius rubbed at his stubble. 'Well, you're certainly right about holding this hill, it has been very costly and our odds don't look good. But if the enemy is spooked enough by you wielding the sword, then what you say might work. But we'll have to act quickly.' He looked over at the prisoners. 'What about them, sire? We don't have time to take them in.'

Arthur turned to Marcus. 'Who will fight with us?'

'My unit of soldiers will fight with me, and I'll stand with you.'

'We should bring them with us and find Lord Bane. The rest just let them go unarmed,' Arthur said to Aurelius. 'Then we can start right now. Would that work, sir?'

'Bloody hell, king for five minutes and you don't stop with the bold plans,' said Aurelius. 'But yes, that could work. And you should probably stop calling me sir. If we're going to show the sword to the enemy, then we'll have to show you as well. You'll need to start behaving like the king people expect.'

'Morgan, get your shoulder stitched up by one of your men,' said Aurelius as he turned to get started. 'Marcus, come with me and let's get these prisoners sorted out. We need to get moving right now.'

While the others got busy, Arthur sagged and sat down next to Merlin, who seemed to have found another comfortable rock.

'I suspect you are feeling the weight of the land on your young shoulders already. Would you care to share your thoughts with me?' prompted Merlin gently.

'There's so many things I know nothing about, and yet they all believe I'm the new king and should lead them.' Arthur looked at the sword still gently warming his hand. 'I know I have good ideas sometimes. But I'm nothing compared to a squire like Lancelot, let alone Lord Bane or Aurelius.'

Merlin saw the concentration again on Arthur's face and

waited for him to continue. 'And now there's you as well, Merlin. The legend no one quite believes. What's your place in all this?'

'I have given the matter much consideration before I sought you out, but to be honest, I am not fully sure myself,' replied Merlin. 'Why, do you have something in mind?'

Arthur paused and then became a little more intense. 'I don't want to be rude, Merlin, but if you really want to help us, why can't you just win this battle with magic after you've rested?'

'I take it you are somewhat of a believer in me then?' Arthur slowly nodded. 'That is a good question, boy, but I am sorry to say, rather complicated. The easy reply is mostly more questions. Even when I am fully rested and able to wield more magic, what if the other side counters with their own? Has the Lady grown more powerful over the years? Should I battle with blazing magic, only for those around me to be turned to dust?'

'I choose not to kill with magic unless there is no choice, but the Lady would not be so considerate. Should she become involved, I fear the cost would be far beyond your worst nightmares.' Merlin looked at Arthur once more. 'For much of the time after the destruction of Uther's castle all those years ago, she has been very quiet, and I do not know why. Maybe the victory cost her more than she bargained for, or maybe she is simply saving herself for something else. Until I discover more, I would prefer to observe quietly and not risk provoking the Lady's direct involvement.'

Arthur nodded in understanding, then something else occurred to him. 'This is all so unbelievable. Magic. A legendary sword. Me.' Arthur shifted uncomfortably. 'Am I really the king's son?'

'Well, boy, what do you think?' said Merlin.

'I don't feel like it. I didn't know King Uther of course, but Aurelius doesn't feel like my uncle. He has a good side and can even be quite nice when he thinks no one is watching. His wife is the kindest lady I've ever met and has given me a roof over my head in a good household. But despite all that, they don't feel like my family. This is all so strange.'

'Yes, I would agree it is indeed strange. This is probably the one aspect I have thought about the most,' said Merlin. 'You know, when I was young, someone told me a lie to protect me. For a long time, I believed it was a kindness, but I grew to find it was a grave mistake. So, I will always tell you the truth as I know it, good or bad. I suspect that Uther's poor son perished with all the other children in the destruction of his castle. Therefore, I think you are correct, I believe you are not King Uther's son.'

'What!' Arthur almost fell off the rock. 'But they all think I'm the king now, and you're saying I'm just an imposter.'

'Ah, my boy, I did not say you were not the king. I just said that you are very likely not Uther's son.' Merlin laid a steady hand on Arthur's shoulder. 'Uther was a good soul, certainly compared to many kings and queens, but he was quite different from you. The sword allowed him to use it, and he used it well, for the most part. But the sword never truly became his. For you, I think it is different. The sword belongs in your hands more than I have ever seen. I think you can feel that too. This is because of who you are in your heart, and not because of the blood in your veins. That is the reason why you should be king.'

Arthur stared at the ground. 'But they're all about to follow my plan as if I'm their true king.'

'Yes boy, and that should clear all doubt from your head.' Merlin rose to stand. 'Your plan may save many hundreds of lives on both sides. And what king could be more worthy than that? It is your actions, not your bloodline, that will make you the king we all need.'

Aurelius came striding back with the others. 'We need to leave now to reach Lord Bane before he attacks too heavily. Are you ready, sire?'

Arthur looked back to Merlin, who gave him a barely perceptible wink with a flash of blue in his eye. Arthur breathed in and straightened himself up. 'Yes, I am. Lead the way.'

'Let's mount up,' Aurelius instructed the others. 'Morgan on the left, Marcus on the right, my knights with me and King Arthur in the centre. Let's avoid any fighting unless we have to. I want to reach Bane as fast as possible. When we get there, we'll let the commanding knights know the plan, but tell them to wait for Bane's signal.'

'I've given you a quiet horse,' Aurelius said to Arthur as he mounted. 'I know squires don't get much riding practice at your age.'

Arthur took up the reigns. 'Don't worry, Lancelot has been giving some of us extra lessons. It's one thing he said I'm actually quite good at.'

'Why am I not surprised? Let's move fast then.' Aurelius spurred his horse and they took off.

Arthur stuck to the centre of the group, and they met no trouble. When they approached the back of their lines, the knights and foot soldiers parted for them quickly when they recognised Aurelius. The sounds of battle had returned and they saw fighting in the distance.

Arthur noticed the mist was beginning to slowly clear. He glanced at Merlin who was riding quietly beside him, seemingly unnoticed by all. 'Are you clearing the mist now?'

'Just a little helping hand. After all, everyone must be able to see you holding Excalibur later, if your plan is to work.'

When they arrived at Bane's group, he was issuing orders to prepare for the counterattack. Squires of the lords loyal to Bane were coming and going as they received orders and took them away to their masters. Lord Bane spotted Arthur with Aurelius and looked over questioningly.

Aurelius dismounted and wasted no time in greeting. 'Change of plan. From our new king no less.' He described the outline of Arthur's idea.

'Risky, but I agree it could work,' said Bane. 'If this mist continues to clear and the archers come into play while we counterattack, then the losses on both sides will increase significantly.'

Arthur looked up at Bane and asked. 'Sir, if I was not your new king, would you follow this plan of your own free will?'

'Yes, I might,' replied Bane. 'However, I do have one addition. A rather dangerous suggestion.' He held Arthur's stare and his face became more grave. 'Because this is the largest castle we hold in this county, we cannot afford to lose it. Therefore, we must drive home the existence of you and your sword to every single one of the enemy's force, beyond a shadow of doubt. If that's done in the most public way, then it will demonstrate your right to be king.'

'Don't know if I like the sound of that,' interrupted Aurelius. 'What are you getting at?'

'Right of Challenge,' replied Bane. 'It's rarely used, as it's viewed as very unpredictable. But by the old laws, a group of knights can challenge the enemy, and they must send an equal number of knights to meet that challenge in combat. The outcome decides who wins the entire battle without further bloodshed.'

'Falcon's well on his way to winning this battle. Why on earth would he even accept that challenge?' questioned Aurelius. 'And even if he did accept, he could just ignore the outcome if we win and overrun us as if nothing had changed.'

'Two good questions. Both solved with one simple but regrettable answer,' replied Lord Bane, glancing back to Arthur.

'Hold on. You're not seriously suggesting Arthur leads the Right of Challenge personally?' asked Aurelius. 'Even though he has Excalibur, he's still just a boy.'

'I know, I don't much like my own suggestion, but Right of Challenge would be the least bloody way to resolve this conflict and probably the only realistic chance of us actually winning. If Arthur leads the challenge, there's no way Falcon could refuse, and he would have to take part himself or be seen to be weaker than a boy. And most importantly, if Arthur beats Falcon personally, then he'd have to accept the result.'

Aurelius grunted. 'Ha, considering a Right of Challenge is generally a fight to the death, if Arthur beats Falcon, he won't be around to argue the point.' He sighed and looked at Arthur. 'I guess we could send you out with a company of knights to protect you. But the problem there, is that the other side can send a company too. This plan might save many lives on both sides, but it will not be easy.'

Lancelot moved over from the edge of the group and spoke up. 'Sir, what about squires?'

A look of suspicion, followed by a dawning of understanding, crossed Bane's face and he jumped in before Aurelius could speak. 'What exactly are you getting at, son?'

'Well, I remember from my history lessons that the rules applied to squires too, so they can go with their knights into the challenge. Seeing as the Right of Challenge must be an equal match, why not go small? Maybe just send three knights, but also their squires too. Arthur would be the first squire of course. I could be another one. Marcus here looks like he could pass for a squire, so he could be the third. I can fight as well as many knights and better than any squire. Maybe that will tip the balance in our favour. Fewer fighters, more skill. It also means Excalibur would make a bigger difference comparatively.'

'Bloody hell. I'm being told what to do by a bunch of children, and the worst part is you could well be right. It would be like sending out five knights, and that would give anyone a run for their money. Then adding the power Arthur can wield with his sword, that could ensure a victory.' Lord Bane looked to Arthur. 'I regret to put your life in danger so quickly, but I think we're out of options. Not that I want to risk my son's life either, but together we might just have conjured up the best chance of success. Shall we proceed, young sire?'

Arthur mustered all the confidence he could and tried to look like he knew what he was doing. 'Yes. Please order the immediate retreat to the castle and tell everyone we're issuing a Right of Challenge.' Arthur thought for a moment longer, and something else occurred to him. 'The whispers should spread through the enemy, and that can only help us. From what Marcus has said, they're not as keen on this battle as their commander.'

Bane started giving orders, and Arthur rode back to the castle with the others. The mist was clearing further, and he saw the walls appear before him. The castle was built on the top of the next hill to the west. That hill was smaller than the one they were fighting for, but closer to the bend of the river, and more importantly, giving access to an underground stream.

Constructed over many years, the castle was enormous. As far as Arthur knew, it was one of the largest in the county after the destruction of King Uther's. The local Lord of the castle was determined not to bow to Falcon's alliance, so he had sent word to Bane for help. His determination meant it would be a long and bloody siege if they had to defend the castle, and with the massed army of the Lady and her allies, probably not one they could win. The losses on both sides would be terrible. Arthur really hoped they could avoid that.

As they approached the gatehouse, the sentries recognised Aurelius and stood aside. The gates were still open as the battle was confined to the other hill, but a full battalion of one hundred knights and archers had been placed around the gates to cover any returning comrades or defend against a sneak attack. Aurelius spoke to the commanding knight and told him the plan. 'Cover the retreat,' he said, 'and let everyone know we're issuing a Right of Challenge.'

Arthur continued to the main square and dismounted with the rest of them. He tugged at his uncle's arm. 'Can someone explain the Right of Challenge to me a bit more?'

'Yes. Let's talk and eat, sire. You lot too,' said Aurelius, indicating to Morgan, Marcus and Lancelot. 'Especially you, Lancelot. I'd also like to hear more of what you've learnt from your history lessons.'

Arthur walked towards the main hall, and they all entered together. Aurelius spoke to a servant, who then hurried off to the kitchens.

Lancelot sat down and looked to Aurelius. 'What would you like to know, sir?'

'What's the general role of squires in a challenge?'

'We were taught two versions of that,' started Lancelot. 'At first, when the laws were created, squires were there to purely serve their knights. If a squire's knight was killed, then they retreated and were left alone. Unfortunately, as times have changed, so the second version came into common practice. Just like the battle today, a squire is often the first and easiest target. We also heard that some knights may even sacrifice their squire to gain an advantage.' Lancelot ran his hand through his hair. 'Nowadays Right of Challenge is not a popular method for deciding a battle. Partly because no one wants to risk the result of an entire campaign on the skill of a few fighters, but mostly on account of all the cheating.'

'On the upside,' commented Morgan, in between mouthfuls of bread. 'If you fight them at the bottom of the two hills, then both armies will see Arthur with Excalibur as Bane said, and help drive home his right to be king.'

'Ha, even if we win, they could crush us with their sheer weight of numbers before we retreat back to the castle,' commented Aurelius. 'We'll need to work something out for that for a start.'

'Don't forget the ditches my father had dug near the bottom

of the hill,' pointed out Lancelot. 'They don't have pikes in them yet, but they should still delay their advance for long enough. Give us a little more time to get back to the castle.'

'Maybe some old-style Roman shield walls would offer more cover as well?' suggested Morgan. 'They won't have time to set up their catapults, so you only need to guard against archers and mounted knights.'

'Yes, that could do it,' conceded Aurelius, though he still regarded Morgan with suspicion. 'But why would you care?'

'Och, I expect to be in that group of knights fighting the Right of Challenge, so I want my arse well covered when it all goes wrong.'

'Hold on, that's for Lord Bane to decide, not you.'

'Actually, I rather think it is for King Arthur to decide,' said Merlin, breaking his quiet observation for the first time. More food arrived, and he regarded Arthur. 'Like it or not, young sire, you are now responsible for the lives within your kingdom, both friend and foe alike. You must decide how best to save them or use them.'

Arthur thought about the situation, his mind full of many possibilities. 'Aurelius, you're still my knight even though I'm now your king. We know each other really well, we've trained together and fought together, so I should take you. I think Lancelot is right about the squires, so I would take him along as he suggested, and probably Marcus too.'

Arthur looked at Marcus. 'You were fast today, but how well can you fight in a duel?'

'I'll wager I can best any young knight you have,' he replied. 'I'm not sure I could beat Falcon, but I reckon I'd give him a run for his money.' He shifted a little in his seat. 'Trust me, I don't particularly want to do this. I'd prefer the stakes to be a little less high. But you could easily have killed us all in that clearing and you didn't. I owe you my life and I will fight for you.'

'Thank you,' said Arthur. 'Morgan, I'd like you to be Marcus' knight. I think the enemy will underestimate you both, and that's got to help us.'

Morgan slapped Marcus on the back and grinned. 'Lucky you laddie, you're with the handsome man from the North.'

Arthur turned to Lancelot. 'So, who should fight with you? Lord Bane is the best commander I've ever seen, but maybe a bit old for single combat?'

'Yes. My father doesn't like it, but he knows this and would agree. Not that it's even an option. His broken arm isn't going to heal itself anytime soon.'

'Oh yes, of course,' said Arthur, a little sheepishly at forgetting. Then his face lifted as he thought of something else, and he looked back at Morgan. 'To reach us, you made it through the heart of your enemy during the battle. That couldn't have been just luck. Who's your best knight?'

'Geoffrey,' replied Morgan immediately. 'He's the largest of my knights, the one who spoke when we met. He looks slow and witless, but he's far from either. I haven't seen anyone as big as him move so fast nor with so much purpose during battle. He would work well with young Lancelot here.'

'Good, please ask him if he'll join us. Then you, Marcus, Geoffrey and Lancelot, should go practice. I need some rest. I might be the king, but I'm still only twelve.'

As the others departed from the main hall, Aurelius remained to speak quietly with Arthur. 'Before you rest, young sire, please go see my wife. I know she cares deeply for you and she will want to hear your story.' Then he left without another word.

Arthur sighed tiredly and looked at Merlin, the last remaining person at the table. 'The legends speak of Merlin the sorcerer and his place by the king's side. And yes, I know you said you didn't want to burn our enemies to the ground, but surely you can help us more? More than just telling me to decide who lives and dies? Like I said to them, I'm still just a boy.' As he spoke, his hand moved to the hilt of the sword, and it warmed to his touch once more.

Seeing this unconscious movement, Merlin smiled. 'You can feel the warmth, can you not?'

Arthur nodded in reply.

'How much of the sword's legend do you know?'

'King Uther and his sword, Excalibur, were invincible.' Then Arthur's face dropped a little. 'I guess that was true, right up until he got killed.'

'You quickly get to the heart of the issue there, my boy,' said Merlin. 'I believe Uther could feel the warmth of the sword, just as you do. Whenever he felt that warmth, he was greatly assisted by Excalibur and was undefeated. And, as you so aptly put it, so that remained true right up until he was slain.'

Merlin sighed. 'When he lost to the Lady all those years ago, I was away as I often was, searching the land for more sources of magic. In hindsight, maybe I should have stayed more often instead, and guided Uther a little more closely.' A look of regret crossed Merlin's features. 'When I did finally return, the battle had been lost and Uther was dead. Possibly for some reason, the sword did not warm to his final actions, and therefore failed to aid him in his greatest hour of need. Or maybe the odds were so large against Uther, that the sword became unwilling to deal out that much death. Unfortunately, I have no way to know.'

'I feel a similar circumstance would befall Aurelius if he took up the sword. He has good qualities like his brother, but also some failings. He probably knows this in his heart, even if his head does not fully understand why. That is possibly the real reason why he does not take up the crown. And that is one more reason why you must.'

Some warmth returned to Merlin's face, and he smiled at

Arthur. 'But, returning to your first question, yes I will help you in my way. First, please go see Aurelius' wife as he asked. I find her to be a significant source of knowledge and sound advice.'

'You know...' started Arthur.

Merlin held up a hand. 'Listen to my advice please. There will be time for your questions later.' Merlin composed himself once more. 'Second, do get some rest. I believe you will need to be fully refreshed for the challenge ahead. Third, I will assist as much as I can without risking the Lady's direct involvement. Though I suspect she will try to influence events as well, so do bear that in mind. And fourth, trust the sword as it trusts you. Whilst it is warm in your hand, I believe it will aid you with all its might. But remember this. Though the sword may be incredibly powerful, it does not make you invincible.'

Merlin placed a hand gently on Arthur's shoulder. 'And finally, while the sword can cut through almost anything and anyone, ultimately it stands for life and not death. Please use its power wisely.'

With that, Merlin rose and left Arthur alone.

'Thank you,' whispered Arthur to the sorcerer's retreating back.

Without a pause in his stride, from halfway across the hall, Merlin replied. 'You are most welcome, young sire.'

CHAPTER 4

Arthur walked over to the cluster of houses built inside the large castle. Here, the Lord of the castle had welcomed his allies and their families. He found Aurelius' wife, Lady Anne, in her temporary chambers. She was making one of her unique bowstrings, working with slender dagger-like needles as she often did.

Forgetting his troubles for a moment, Arthur couldn't stop himself from asking. 'I still don't understand how you make those bowstrings so strong, what's your secret?'

Lady Anne smiled at him with genuine warmth as he approached. 'I will tell, but only once you have told me all your many secrets, young sire.'

Arthur stopped in surprise. 'You already know?' he exclaimed. Lady Anne just smiled and waited for him to continue. 'Do you know about the Right of Challenge as well?'

'Yes, an acquaintance from the stables did mention it in passing, and a few details about all the new friends you have made.' She stopped what she was doing and held her needles still. 'Morgan, I am aware of, and though he is a mercenary, I hear he has a code of honour of sorts. I believe you can trust him. The man called Marcus I do not know, so please be careful.'

Arthur paused before he responded, looking pensive. 'How do you feel about the whole nephew thing?'

Anne smiled again and reached for his hand. 'I have seen you grow from an infant into a young man, and I care for you dearly, Arthur. Aurelius does too, though he would scarcely admit it, and certainly not out loud. However, I know you are not Uther's son and you are not Aurelius' blood. In my own time I will tell him, we have no secrets from each other, but for now we should let them all believe, my husband included. It will help everyone accept you as their king.'

Arthur stood in stunned silence, many questions forming in his head. This kind lady was so much more than he had ever supposed.

Anne saw the distant look in his gaze. 'I know you all too well, Arthur. Therefore, I will try to answer some questions, so you can rest a little easier.' She put down his hand and held up the wicked-looking needles. She moved them expertly with her fingers, and Arthur thought they looked more like weapons than ever. However, when she held them still, they glowed faintly with a blue light. 'I have made many friends over the years and one of them happens to be a sorcerer of legend. Like you, I have a gift for making friends, and I have tried to use that gift wisely. Though Merlin has lived in the shadows for many years, I have known him for a long time. From time to time he's been kind enough to share some magical wisdom, with those of us who have the right nature and talent.'

With that, she pulled a fine strand of her long hair and expertly blended it into the growing bowstring with her needles. As she did this, the string briefly glowed with that same strange blue light.

'When you were brought to us, I believed you to be one of the servant's children.' A hint of sadness crossed Lady Anne's face. 'Aurelius and I could not have children of our own, but as I had not been seen to be pregnant, we couldn't pass you off as our own. So, you became Aurelius' squire. When Merlin later told me some of your story, I almost wished you were of Aurelius' blood, but such good fortune is often not the way of the land.'

Then she smiled again, and the warmth returned to her face. 'As time passed, I became content to help care for you and

Aurelius did the same in his own way. As Merlin has no doubt told you by now, and something I hold dear myself, the intentions in your heart are more important than the blood in your veins. You are the best squire Aurelius has known. I suspect he keeps count of the times you have saved each other's lives. I hope you can do that again today, and from what I hear, you may well save many more lives in the process.'

She took his hand once more and held it a little closer. 'I know you are still very young, but today in the battle ahead, you must start to become a man and a king. All I ask is that you become the king that you want to be.'

She laid down his hand and took up her needles. 'Now, if you would kindly excuse me, sire, you need some rest, and I feel the need to finish this bowstring. It will be a gift for someone I would like to become one of my friends.' With that, she lightly kissed him on the forehead and turned him around to face the door.

Still dazed, Arthur walked slowly back to the squires' rooms. He stumbled through the door without really noticing the extra guards standing watch. With so much to consider, he thought back to his training sessions as he got ready to rest. 'Keep it simple, Arthur,' Aurelius had repeatedly taught him. 'One thing at a time. Eat, sleep, think, fight.'

Aurelius is so much smarter than he looks, realised Arthur, as he slipped into a deep sleep with the sword glowing softly by his side.

'Wake up, sire,' said Lancelot as he shook Arthur. 'My father has sent a runner to issue the challenge and they should be back soon. He also told them the rightful king will be present. He's still hoping to tempt Falcon into the battle. Some stories of your actions today are already spreading, and there's talk that you've found the king's sword and will pass it to Aurelius as both your knight and Uther's brother. Most believe your uncle will lead the challenge and will claim the throne if he wins.'

'Maybe that would be better.' Arthur rose and picked up his boots. 'But I don't think Aurelius would ever accept. How did your session practice go?'

'Bloody hell, Morgan was right. Geoffrey is fast,' said Lancelot with admiration. 'I like to assess my enemy before a fight and I know I'm good at it, but I still underestimated him. He beat me to the ground with one move. Even then, I'm sure he was holding back a lot. After that we worked on simple signals for strategy during the fight.'

'Morgan and Marcus are almost as quick too, and certainly more devious.' Lancelot paused for a second, studying Arthur. 'It's like you've conspired to bring together the perfect fighters for what we need. But how could you even know?'

Arthur turned a little red. 'I'm just making it up as I go along, really.'

'Hmm, I think you should give yourself a little more credit than that. Still, however you're doing it, keep it going.' Lancelot sat himself down while he waited for Arthur to get finish getting ready. 'Though you might want to keep quiet about making it as you go along. Not really very kingly that.'

'Thanks for the advice,' said Arthur genuinely. 'Anything else you can think of to improve our chances of winning?'

'Well, if I hadn't seen your sword in action today, I would have said you and Aurelius were the weakest link by far and should be replaced. And if Falcon takes Excalibur from you somehow, then you're done for. But I don't think there's much we can do about that. You have to be there.'

'Thanks,' said Arthur dryly.

'Just being honest,' replied Lancelot a little sharply, with some of his youth still showing through. 'You should know that from the training I've held for you and the other squires.'

'I'm just kidding,' said Arthur, breaking into a grin and patting Lancelot on the back of his shoulder. 'And thank you for the training. Between you and my uncle, you've saved my life a lot.'

Lancelot shook his head in exasperation. 'How can you make jokes right now?'

Arthur looked at Excalibur. 'Merlin just told me this sword stands for life, and I guess he's trying to tell me something. Even though we've got this powerful weapon, everything's not just about fighting and killing and dying.'

Arthur looked up from the sword and smiled at Lancelot. 'To be honest though, I like my version better.'

'What's that?'

'Have fun when you can.'

'Bloody hell, now I'm being given advice by a child.' A slight smile appeared on Lancelot's face, showing the man he was becoming. 'No offence, sire,' he added.

Arthur lowered his voice. 'None taken, young squire,' he said with a passable impression of Lord Bane. They both laughed as they left the room.

The others were gathered in the main hall with Lord Bane and the allied lords. Bane turned to Arthur as they approached. 'The runner has returned, and the challenge has been accepted, sire. I've outlined the situation to everyone. They accept it as the truth and will abide by your decisions. But to be honest, there is some unrest. Many of the troops believe Aurelius should be given the sword and the crown. We will support you Arthur, but what do you want to do about this?'

Arthur scanned the expectant faces and settled on Merlin and Aurelius. 'I think my uncle would make a fine, if reluctant, king. But the sword is now my responsibility, and I have to live up to that. My actions will speak louder than any words I can think of, so I have to lead this challenge. If we win, that will show I have the strength needed and remove people's doubts.'

Arthur turned back to Bane. 'Please organise some basic chain mail for us squires to go under our clothes, but keep it simple. We need to stick to the rules, three armoured knights and their squires. We need to show some honour as well as our strength.'

'Aye, you do need to show honour,' said Morgan, who was flexing a short bow at the edge of the group, 'but you also need to win.'

'I've been thinking about that and I have another idea to tip the challenge in our favour some more.' Arthur noticed the bow in Morgan's hands. 'Looks like you do too.'

'The laws say no horses in the challenge. Nae mention of bows though,' grinned Morgan. 'But enough of that, what's your idea, sire?'

'It's simple really. Everyone focuses on protecting me from any attack, while I try to cut their weapons in two,' said Arthur, feeling a little embarrassed again, but trying his best to project confidence to them all. 'That will prove the power of the sword and my right to have it. It might even end the challenge without anyone dying.'

'Simple is good, sire,' confirmed Aurelius with a nod. 'Let's get ready.'

Arthur walked to one of the armoury rooms with Lancelot and Marcus. He started dressing in chain mail as Merlin approached their group of real and bogus squires.

'It's a little heavy,' commented Arthur, 'but it should give us some protection.'

'I think I can assist with that,' said Merlin, and he asked Lancelot and Marcus to come closer as well. He gently touched their chain mail one by one, and a blue shimmer transferred from his hand to each mail. All three glowed briefly, then returned to their usual grey colour. 'Now cover them up with your shirts.'

As Arthur dressed, he felt the mail lighten.

'I'm impressed,' said Marcus, flexing his arms. 'Just the cunning edge I approve of. Feels like it's only an extra shirt now, no weight at all. Will the effect last long?'

'Long enough,' commented Merlin.

They finished dressing, and Merlin led Arthur to one side. 'Take this, my boy. It may aid you in your moment of greatest need.'

Arthur took the small sphere from Merlin's hand. As it settled in his grip, it glowed with a faint blue light. 'What is it?'

'My last remaining device. Pure magic in a container of my own making.'

'You're giving me some of your magic?' Arthur stared down at the glowing ball in awe and apprehension. 'What on earth do I do with it? I've never even seen magic before today, let alone had some.'

Merlin patted Arthur on the shoulder. 'Worry not, young sire, just follow your heart and do what you feel is best.' Merlin turned at the sound of approaching boots. 'Just remember, it is only a small amount,' he said quietly over his shoulder. 'So, whatever you do use it for, please remember, it will not last long.'

As the others arrived, Arthur saw that Aurelius, Morgan and Geoffrey had dressed in armour built for hand-to-hand combat. Their heavier pieces reserved for mounted battle had been replaced by lighter sections.

'Are you ready, sire?'

'Yes, I think so.' After glancing up at Merlin one last time, Arthur took a deep breath and looked them all over. They dipped their heads in return, one by one, and Arthur started for the door. 'Ok, let's get going.'

Arthur led them through the castle gates and out past the battalion of sentries. Despite being armed with large shields and spears, nervous rustles could be heard from the soldiers. However, as Arthur passed, not a word was uttered. Loyalty to their lords holds them steady, he thought, but I'm going to need to do something really special to earn it myself.

He stopped at the base of the hill and looked up. The enemy's army was spread out across the opposite ridge. Easily twenty battalions or more, with catapults already being constructed at the very top of the hill.

'We better win this challenge,' whispered Arthur to Aurelius, 'or there really will be a lot of bloodshed.' Looking up the hill, he saw the enemy's challengers emerge, walking towards them.

'Ha, their squires are huge,' said Morgan quietly from behind Arthur as six fully grown men approached. 'I know we've pushed it, but they're not even close to the rules. So much for Falcon's honour.'

Their foes crossed the temporary bridge constructed over the ditches dug by Bane's engineers and stopped before them. The first knight raised his helmet and Arthur saw that Lord Falcon was indeed leading them.

'Your Right of Challenge has been answered, Aurelius,' he called out for all to hear. 'Uther was too weak to unite the lords of this land, and as his brother, you are no better. But I will take on that task. I will prove my strength with your defeat today.'

Arthur stepped forward with his sword raised, and a distant murmur rose from the enemy lines. A cold smile appeared on Falcon's face. 'So it really isn't Aurelius. This will be easier than I thought,' he hissed. Then, without waiting for any reply, he swung a fast and vicious blow at Arthur's head.

Arthur side stepped and raised Excalibur to deflect the attack. The swords clashed heavily, and Arthur could feel Excalibur warm as it absorbed the blow and spared him from the full force of Falcon's swing. However, the sword could do nothing to stop the kick Falcon launched to the centre of his chest and Arthur flew back, landing awkwardly on the ground.

Winded, Arthur slowly got to his feet. Lord Falcon advanced, the other knights still holding back.

'Wait!' called Arthur, raising his sword again. 'If you yield now, we can discuss terms and save the bloodshed. No one else has to die today.'

'Yield to a boy, I think not,' laughed Falcon. 'The only blood spilled will be yours. Your supporters are too cowardly to take the crown, and you are no match for me and my men. Time for you to die.'

Falcon swung his sword again, and Arthur caught the blade full on with Excalibur, the clash ringing out across the hills. Excalibur became hotter in his hand as it held its ground, and this time Arthur moved faster. He pivoted aside to avoid the follow-on attack, then swung back hard at Falcon.

But as Excalibur hit Falcon's sword, instead of cutting right through it, there was a sound like tearing metal, and dark red sparks exploded from where the swords collided. Stunned, Arthur pulled back and Falcon laughed again. 'You're not the only one with a bit of magic,' he whispered fiercely.

So that's why the other knights are holding back, thought Arthur. Then, when Falcon stepped away and raised his left hand slightly, Arthur heard the sounds of arrows being fired by the enemy bowmen, and he realised that was not the only reason.

Arthur shouted out a warning. 'Archers.' He tried to dive to the ground, but felt a massive blow to his shoulder that spun him around. The pain was enormous, and he grabbed at the top of his arm expecting to find blood.

The others had fared little better. Geoffrey had an arrow through his right arm and Aurelius through his calf. Marcus and Lancelot were pinned to the ground, and Arthur couldn't see how badly they were hurt. Only Morgan had escaped unharmed, and he raised his short bow.

'You'll not reach my archers with that child's toy,' sneered Falcon.

Without reply, Morgan loosed off two arrows, bending the

bow back further than Arthur thought possible. The arrows flew to the back of the enemy's lines and two longbow men dropped. 'Obey the challenge laws, or face the consequences,' shouted Morgan across the field, lowering the bow only slightly. Arthur could see the faint blue glow recede from the bowstring, and he caught the brief look of surprise on Morgan's face.

'Very cunning, but that won't help you,' said Falcon. 'You're now one against six.'

'Two,' said Arthur, standing up and flexing his arm. It hurt, but there was no blood, the chain mail having somehow stopped the path of the arrow.

'Three,' said Geoffrey, swapping his sword to the other hand and quickly driving in at the two closest knights. He put them both down in an instant, and dead or dying, they didn't move. 'Against four,' he finished.

The three opposing knights backed away a little, and Arthur saw the first glimmer of fear in Falcon's face.

'Maybe we should discuss this more,' said Falcon as he came closer. Then, without warning, he swung again for Arthur.

Arthur caught the blow full on with Excalibur, but instead of red sparks, this time Falcon's sword just shattered, and he staggered back in surprise. Arthur stepped in closer and looked Falcon in the eye. 'No more talking,' Arthur said. 'You can never be trusted.' He swung Excalibur hard across Falcon's armoured torso. The sword burned hot in Arthur's hand and sliced through the armour as if it wasn't there. Blood burst from the man's chest and he went down hard.

Arthur gripped Excalibur tightly, despite the heat, as he approached Falcon's form. The man was still alive, and he weakly raised a hand. In it was a glowing red sphere. 'Don't think you've won. I'll take you all with me.'

Arthur watched as Falcon crushed the ball in his hand. Through Falcon's fingers, Arthur saw dark red magic shine out.

He stood there, somehow unable to tear his eyes away from the sight.

Morgan grabbed Arthur by the shoulders as Falcon's hand fell to the ground and the dark magic pulsed stronger. 'I think we should get out of here right now, laddie.'

Tendrils of red magic whipped out from Falcon's limp hand, flames erupting along their length, and Arthur shook his head clear. He looked around at the flat ground. 'Where?'

'The defensive ditch, it's the only cover close enough.'

'But that's heading right towards the enemy,' said Aurelius as he limped over. 'Are you mad?'

'He's right,' stated Geoffrey, 'it's our only hope.' Despite the arrow through his arm, he took hold of Lancelot and Marcus, and in one powerful tug tore them free of the arrows that pinned them to the ground.

Without another word, they all ran for the ditch, Morgan helping Aurelius over the ground as fast as he could. As they leapt in, there was a great pull in the air, then red fire exploded all around them.

The dark red flames blazed over the ditch, and the rushing heat was intense. Arthur just held his hands over his head and tried to keep as low as possible. When the explosion was finally spent, Arthur cautiously poked his head over the top of the ditch to look around.

'Let me guess,' said Aurelius as he removed the arrow from his calf and tore a strip of cloth from his under tunic to wrap around the wound. 'Two thousand heavily armed soldiers are now baring down upon us?'

Morgan sneaked a glance over to top as well. 'No, just one battalion.'

'Great, only a hundred to fight then. Any more bright ideas?'

'Sorry, I'm all out.'

Arthur stood up and looked at the advancing troops, ten rows of knights and soldiers. Then he remembered the sphere of blue magic Merlin had given him. He grabbed it from his pocket for the others to see. 'I have this.'

He climbed back up to the top of the ditch on their side. He could now hear the sounds of the advancing troops. The others joined him, watching the enemy get closer by the second.

'At least we can take a few of them with us,' said Lancelot, looking at the magic in Arthur's hand as he got ready to meet the rushing battalion.

'Actually, I want to do something else. I hope.' Arthur threw the sphere of magic into the ditch and it shattered at the bottom. Trapped by the edges, it blasted out along the ditch, blue fire erupting twenty feet in either direction.

The advancing frontline stopped in its tracks as the first soldiers reached the fire. All of them afraid to venture too close to the flames. However, those at the back were not so concerned, and they continued to push forward. The soldiers at the front began to panic as they were shoved helplessly towards the intense heat.

'We should get out of here while we can,' gestured Morgan from beside him.

A pained look crossed Arthur's face. 'No, I didn't mean to burn them to death. I just wanted to stop them. I don't care what side they're on, they don't deserve to die like that.' The blue fire flickered towards Arthur's sword with its flames, and he looked down at Excalibur in his hand.

'Maybe the sword can do something with Merlin's magic,' said Arthur. Without really knowing what he was doing, he raised Excalibur high over the fire for all to see, then he lowered the sword into it. The blue flames leapt up the sword's length and it burned hot in his hand. Arthur cried out, but he kept hold and practically willed the sword to devour all the fire. The flames raced towards the sword, and as the first enemy soldiers fell into the ditch, the last flicker of fire rushed into Excalibur.

Before Arthur could think too much about what he'd just done, sheer exhaustion hit him hard, and he started to sag. Geoffrey moved to his side and casually put his hand on Arthur's shoulder, inconspicuously holding him up.

Arthur looked down at Excalibur, somehow still gripped in his hand. Blue flames gently lapped along its blade. Morgan leaned in. 'Time for you to say something, laddie.' Then he gave a bow of his head for all to see.

Arthur looked down at the relieved soldiers in the ditch, not a single one of them burned, then up to those behind them on the hill. 'The fighting here is finished for today,' he called out as loud as he could. He searched the ditch and found a frightened young soldier staring up at him. 'What is your name?'

'Edward,' stammered the young man.

'Find your knight and give him my message, then tell him to find his commander and do the same,' commanded Arthur. 'Work your way up to your lords.'

The squire and surrounding soldiers watched Arthur expectantly.

Morgan leaned in again and whispered. 'And your exact message would be what, young sire?'

Arthur looked up at the enemy forces and back at their castle. 'Care for your wounded and get ready for a new age,' he called out. 'At dawn tomorrow we will meet with all lords from both sides. I will unite this land and together we will have peace.'

With that, Arthur held Excalibur up high one last time, the blue flames along its blade burning brightly. Then he lowered the sword and turned around. 'Don't let go,' he whispered to Geoffrey, and the huge knight smiled as he helped Arthur down to the base of the hill. 'How is everyone?' asked Arthur as they walked.

'I'll live. There's not too much blood,' replied Aurelius. 'The others too.'

Lancelot and Marcus were poking their fingers through the holes in their clothes. 'Holes in our shirts, but none in us, sire,' added Lancelot. 'Merlin's magic deflected the arrows and saved us.'

Arthur nodded with relief and turned to Marcus. 'Don't look back,' he said, 'but do you think the lords in Falcon's alliance will meet us tomorrow as I asked?'

'After what you've just done, I reckon they'll at least talk, especially without Falcon to drive them on. This fight has been costly and even the most ambitious lord needs someone left alive to rule over. However, it's the reaction of the Lady I'd be more worried about. She was the real power behind Falcon.'

'Let's get back. I want to talk to Merlin about that.' Excalibur warmed in his hand, and Arthur felt some energy return. He stood up straight and with one last look at the enemy, he walked unhurriedly back to the castle gates.

'Well done, my boy,' said Merlin, when they were finally left alone. 'You had a brave plan, and you improvised well when everything went spectacularly wrong. As you are no doubt finding out, even the best of strategies can turn to dust in battle.'

Merlin paused briefly, then smiled, as if something slightly amusing had just occurred to him. 'I have one question for you for a change. How did the sword feel in your hand?'

'Warm most of the time, like it was full of power and giving me extra strength at the same time.' Arthur sat down and examined the sword a little more closely. 'But it got really hot when I cut down Falcon.'

'I think Excalibur was supporting your decisions for the most part. However, you should be careful. I believe the heat of the sword has twin reason,' Merlin said. 'King Uther found the sword would become hotter as it became more powerful. This seemed to be in response to both his desire and need becoming more intense. But be warned. For Uther, if he asked the sword to do the wrong thing, then it would become too hot and eventually lose all power completely.'

'From what I saw today, I believe your heart guided you well. However, if the sword became very hot, then you may have been on the edge of right and wrong. I know you will always try to do what is right, but be careful you do not follow Uther's path too closely.'

'Not more things to think about,' said Arthur tiredly. He slumped a little in the chair. The exhaustion seemed to weigh on every bone in his body. 'I need to sleep, but what about the Lady? If she's the real power, what do we do about her?'

'It appears we have some good fortune there. Lady Anne has shared the reports from her network of friends. It seems that the Lady has left for now. Though I must reluctantly admit, we do not know why and we can only speculate on her reasoning. Maybe without Falcon's ear, her position was not as strong as she thought. Or possibly she has some other plan to move on to.' Merlin paused briefly in thought, then his face relaxed a little. 'However, I think we can rest easy for today. From what I observed, the Lady is not quite as powerful as I feared. Did you notice her magic in Falcon's sword?'

'Yes, it only worked once,' replied Arthur, as his eyes began to close.

'Indeed. It takes less power to create magic for one-off use. Either she is still finding her way to more power, or she is holding back for now,' said Merlin.

Arthur slouched further into his seat. 'With everything you've done today, you must be much more powerful than her then,' he mumbled before finally falling asleep.

'Ah, my boy, the land would already be saved if that were true,' lamented Merlin to himself as Arthur started snoring. 'Let us just be thankful that the enemy let loose only one volley of arrows upon you.'

With a gentle pat on Arthur's head, Merlin watched the new king sleep. 'Rest well, my boy,' he whispered quietly. 'For the years ahead, I believe you are truly going to need it.'

PART 2 – THE TOURNAMENT

CHAPTER 5

Arthur side-stepped and the blade just missed his ear. He gave a push to the swinging arm to exaggerate its movement, and his attacker overbalanced and fell. Arthur lunged in for the killer blow, swinging his sword down hard and fast, but the blade didn't connect as his attacker kicked up with an armoured foot and blocked the blow.

Arthur knelt on his attacker's thigh and pushed the blocking foot away. He steadied his sword with both hands and drove it down hard. 'I have the better of you now, vile knight,' shouted Arthur as he sank his sword in to the hilt. He rose exhaustedly and leaned on his knees; glad the fight was over.

'Aye, very funny, Arthur,' came the dry reply, 'but you've not won yet. Look down at your side.'

Arthur did and saw a small line of blood where his armour joined at the waist. 'Damn, I thought I'd finally beaten you this time.' He held out a hand to help Morgan rise and noticed the smear of blood on his dagger.

'Four years of training and you've pretty much taken my blood every day. Are you sure you're not trying to kill me?'

'Nae point to having safe training only to be killed in your first proper battle,' replied Morgan, pulling Arthur's training sword from the ground next to where his head had been. 'You've grown a lot, and you're much faster and stronger. But you still take too many risks. You're always aiming for the killer blow, and when that doesn't succeed you end up in trouble.

Aye, you may have killed me, but my dagger had found your weak point. You were dead too; you just didn't know it.'

'Yes, but with Excalibur I could have sliced your foot from your leg and ended the fight much earlier.' Arthur picked up the magical sword from where it lay next to their training area.

'Nae doubt,' agreed Morgan as they walked out of the courtyard and back to the armoury, 'but then maybe my dagger would have found your armpit. I'd died from my wounds, but you could have been badly injured too. Anyway, one day someone will catch you without Excalibur. Then you'll thank me for all this training.'

Morgan stopped walking and looked steadily at Arthur. 'Do you remember what I've always told you, sire?'

'Yes yes. I may have to slay many enemies, but they only need to kill me once. It's amazing that any king lasts longer than a week,' said Arthur, slapping Morgan on the shoulder. 'Luckily, I have some good friends to help me. When they're not trying to drain my blood that is.'

Arthur entered the armoury with Morgan and began to take off his armour. Each discarded piece was collected by one of the squires and taken for cleaning.

'Thank you,' said Arthur to a particularly young squire struggling with the large breast plate.

'Yes, sire,' came the barely whispered reply from the boy as he redoubled his efforts and hurried off.

Morgan grinned at Arthur once they were alone again. 'You know those young laddies are terrified every time you talk to them?'

'Yes, I know, but sometimes it feels like only yesterday that I was one of them. I'm nearly sixteen and finally about to be ceremonially crowned on my birthday next week. But often I feel that I'm still just a common boy.'

'Nothing wrong with being common, sire. In my experience,

common folk usually make the best ones.'

'Talking about people,' said Arthur. 'How's your castle?'

Arthur heard Morgan groan as usual and couldn't help but laugh.

'You know I didn't want Falcon's castle or his land, but you gave them to me anyway,' replied Morgan.

'Yes, but I also knew you'd take good care of it and its people. How's the harvest going?'

'Not bad at all,' replied Morgan, a little pride creeping into his voice. 'In fact, we might gather more than last year. Even the livestock tend to stay put nowadays. Took a couple of seasons to sort out the local gang of thieves, but they're useful now.'

'I liked your solution to that problem,' said Arthur. 'Giving them jobs in the castle garrison worked out well. They get paid not to steal stuff and do a proper day's work as well. Though I hear you cracked a few heads to start with.'

'Aye, not everyone was so happy, but the majority came around to seeing the advantages of lawful employment. Speaking of which, we haven't settled on my fee for my services to you.'

Arthur looked at Morgan, a little surprised. 'Oh, sorry. I remember our first meeting and your promise to stand by me for future payment. I guess I thought the castle and its lands would be enough.'

'Aye, most would agree with you on that, and justifiably so. But I see them both as part of my service to you. The land is beautiful, but I don't want its ownership. I look after the land and people on your request alone.'

'So, what payment do you want?' said Arthur. 'Next week I'll no longer be the boy king in waiting. I will officially be crowned king of all our lands. I could grant you almost anything, if I thought it was right.'

Morgan turned and picked up his dagger, hiding it in his belt now he was redressed in his court clothes. The collection of the dagger almost instinctive while he pondered. 'Well, sire, that is a good question. You see, every other contract I've accepted has had the requirements and payment set out up front. This is the first service I've performed without knowing the task or the pay. I don't even know how long my service will be. To be honest, I have no idea what my fee should be.'

'So why did you stand by me four years ago?' asked Arthur, the curiosity clear on his face.

'Sometimes you just have to do the right thing,' replied Morgan. 'Then you're left with working out the rest later.'

'Okay, when you do figure out your payment, be sure to let me know,' said Arthur as they walked to the main hall. 'I always keep my promises.'

They stopped at the doors as they waited for the others, Morgan awkwardly straightening his tunic. 'Aye well,' he said, 'if you spared me from attending court functions, I might find that payment enough.'

The centre of the large hall was full. Lords, ladies and knights stood around in conversation, with tables set at the edge for the evening's feast. A few children played quietly around the tables, carefully shepherded by nursemaids and squires so as not to disturb any lords quick to anger. The noise of a hundred conversations filled the hall. However, it lowered to whispers as Arthur strode into the room, accompanied by Morgan, Marcus, Geoffrey and Lancelot.

Arthur looked around and saw Merlin, Aurelius and Lord Bane together, with Lady Anne by her husband's side. Arthur nodded to them, and they joined him in front of the head table. Behind it, a temporary display had been mounted for the crown, surrounded by several guards. 'Time for a speech,' said Arthur, and he turned to face the crowd in the hall.

'Lords, ladies, knights and all,' he called out across the

crowded room in a loud, confident voice, 'I welcome you and your families to Dunstan Castle. And thank you, of course, to Lord Gallow for hosting the royal tournament before my confirmation to the throne next week.'

Arthur paused briefly whilst he looked across to Gallow, who acknowledged this with a smile lacking any warmth or humour. Arthur turned back to his audience in the hall. 'Tomorrow we shall start the tournament and compete in battle games for one week. When we are finished, I will invite the seven most worthy lords and eight most noble knights to join me at Camelot. Together we will meet at a round table, and we will work with equal voice to unite the entire land in peace.'

Whispers rose across the hall at the unexpected news, and Arthur waited patiently for the quiet to return. 'I will make a further announcement tomorrow morning at the opening of the tournament, but for now please enjoy the feast our most gracious host has prepared.' With that, Arthur walked around the head table and sat next to its central seat.

Slowly, the crowd took their seats. Some finding places easily with friends and allies, others being guided by Lord Gallow's knights to positions carefully chosen to benefit his politics. A few people however, were charmed by Lady Anne as she led them to tables and subtly broke up some of the groups. Arthur made himself comfortable and Gallow joined him, sitting in the central seat at the head table.

'Shouldn't the future king sit at the head of the table?' said Gallow to Arthur, with the same wintry smile on his face.

Arthur studied Gallow and he could see the resemblance to his dead half-brother Falcon, though Gallow, if anything, was even larger. Why do all my enemies have to be so bloody big, thought Arthur to himself.

He gave a slight nod to Gallow. 'I feel it's polite for the host to sit at the head of the table in his own castle. The king's chair will be wherever I sit, its position doesn't really matter.'

Gallow's smile didn't waver, but his eyes hardened further. 'As you say, sire. The king's chair will be wherever the king is sitting.' Then his smile widened with fake warmth. 'Please excuse me, I see my servants are bringing out the first dishes. Like any good host, I wish to ensure my guests are well taken care of.'

'Of course, please continue,' said Arthur, and Gallow turned away as the food started to arrive.

From his other side, Lancelot leaned over and whispered in Arthur's ear. 'Are you really sure we can eat here?'

'We should be fine. Lady Anne has mixed us in with Gallow's allies, so just eat what they eat. Remember what your father said, it's the tournament games we really need to worry about.' Then Arthur chuckled. 'Oh, and no midnight walks around the castle walls on your own.'

They returned to their lodgings after the dinner, and the others joined Arthur bit by bit. However, when Lady Anne arrived, she began to usher them all away except for Merlin.

'Please gather your thoughts tonight and talk to King Arthur tomorrow morning about the deadly duelling,' she said to the men. 'For now, I need to talk to him and Merlin about politics.'

Aurelius took his wife's hand and kissed it. 'We shall certainly leave you to that, my dear,' and he led the others away, leaving two guards on Arthur's door.

Once they'd left, Arthur closed the door and found a seat. 'That feast was every bit as hard work as you predicted,' he said to Lady Anne. 'I think I'd rather fight them all in battle.'

'Oh, but I heard you handled yourself rather well, my dear Arthur,' she remarked. 'The king's seat is where I sit, was a particularly nice touch I thought. Your easy-going confidence has them confused, it makes you seem stronger and wiser than your years.'

'However, we should beware. Your enemies will have many

plans for this tournament. As your good friend Morgan is so keen to point out. They only need one victory to ensure your demise, whilst we on the other hand, must foil every plot of theirs. Luckily, I have a good friend here in this castle, and that will certainly help, but he's just one person and your foes here are many.'

Lady Anne turned to Merlin, her face betraying her concern. 'Why did you advise us to hold the tournament here, within these lion's jaws? I trust your judgement Merlin, but I didn't truly believe your stated reasons.'

'You are as observant as ever, Lady Anne,' replied Merlin with a slight bow of his head. 'Many of my reasons are simple and familiar to you. However, there is something that even you and your network of friends do not know.'

'As you all heard, I wished to confront Gallow in his own lands. If we defeat him here in this staged tournament, then we should prevent the need for a long and very real conflict. But as you suspect, that is not my only reason. As you mentioned, you have a friend in this castle. That person can be very valuable to our current cause, but they can only be useful here. We will ask a favour of your friend soon I expect.'

Anne looked at Merlin and gave a small sigh. 'He'll do as I ask if he can, but he will probably get only one chance. After that he will be revealed and in need of our protection.'

'I can offer sanctuary,' said Arthur, 'and no, don't tell me what you're up to. I'm not great at lying, so it's probably best if I don't know. Though don't cross any lines I might regret?'

'It is certainly less than Gallow himself would try,' replied Merlin.

Arthur held a grim smile on his face. 'Well, that doesn't count out much then.'

He stood up and walked over to the small window. Outside, there were torches alight in both the castle and the fields. People were still working on the last structures for the tournament opening, and he could hear the mallets even from this distance. 'Was there another reason?'

'Yes,' stated Merlin. 'It is the simplest reason of all and the most dangerous. If the Lady is here too, then our alliance may be in deep trouble unless we do something about it.'

'How so?' asked Arthur.

'There is a large build-up of natural magic in this area, and just like a field of corn, we may be able to harvest it soon. If I can gather this magic, then we can use it for the good of the land. But if the Lady were to gain it, she would have power the likes of which you have never seen before. Even with Excalibur and all your allies, you might not stop her. That is why we must be here now.'

'Great,' said Arthur. 'I'm about to be crowned king but I'm not actually the king's son, my combat tutors draw my blood almost every day, my host is trying to kill me, and a woman I've never met before wants to turn me to dust and take the throne,' he paused for breath and looked at Merlin. 'Oh, and there's powerful magic that you may or may not be able to get hold of. Did I forget anything?'

'Just one part,' said Merlin, raising his eyebrow. 'What is your plan, Arthur?'

That made Arthur smile, but this time with more enthusiasm. 'To the point as always.' He considered the situation for a moment. 'I don't have much of a plan yet, just one question. Is anyone going to kill me tonight?'

'No,' replied Merlin. 'We can prevent that.'

'Excellent.' Arthur guided them to the door. 'Eat, sleep, think, fight. A man wiser than he looks taught me that. So now I'm going to rest. Goodnight.'

With that, Arthur ushered them out and closed the door.

CHAPTER 6

Arthur entered the armoury with his guards just after dawn and found Aurelius already waiting.

'Sire. I hope you slept well?'

Arthur grabbed his forearm in greeting. 'I did, and now I've had some time to think.'

'Glad you remember at least some of what I've taught you,' Aurelius replied in his gruff way, just like he would all those years ago. He started to dress in the heavy armour necessary for mounted battle. Then his tone grew more respectful, as if only just remembering how much things had changed. 'The squires have been keeping an eye on our armour and weapons as you requested. Some of the knights volunteered too, just to be sure. No tampering was found. What do you need from us next?'

'For starters, stop dressing in that heavy battle armour and put on something lighter for now. I'm going to make some changes to the traditional tournament order. Although I do want to hear your opinion before I announce them.'

Aurelius nodded, and Arthur continued. 'Normally it's jousting for the knights, archery for the lords, and then finally one-on-one duels for the strongest. I think we can skip the jousting, it's mostly just for show and almost always fixed. Instead, I want to finish with something new. I'd like to stage a field battle, one hundred knights and soldiers on each side. Lord Gallow's best against mine. A tournament defeat like that will lessen the support for Gallow and may prevent the larger conflict.'

'Great idea, very audacious. Just two trifling points,' said

Aurelius. 'How the hell are you to stage that without a bloodbath? And what makes you so sure you can win? Sire.'

'Tournament rules state, when battling in a duel, blunted weapons only and horses without armour,' replied Arthur. 'I think we can expand on those rules with a larger field battle. That should prevent fatalities and keep the damage to a minimum. As for winning the battle itself, I'll leave that to Lancelot and Morgan to figure out.'

'You're going to do what?' exclaimed Lancelot, not wanting to believe what he'd just heard.

'I told you not to hit him so hard on the head during training,' commented Morgan.

'You know you can't use Excalibur during the tournament, and especially not during a sporting field battle. Even your own rules forbid it!' Lancelot paced around the room. 'How on earth can you guarantee winning? I know there's a lot at stake, probably more than I'm aware of. But that's even more reason why this is all too risky.'

'You're right, I can't guarantee winning the field battle,' said Arthur. 'That's why I need you and Morgan to figure out how to improve my odds.'

'Unbelievable!' Lancelot threw his hands in the air and looked over at Morgan.

'Aye, leave it to the common folk to do the actual work,' said Morgan with a sly grin on his face. He put his arm round Lancelot. 'Come on laddie, let's go put our heads together.'

'Go find Merlin as well,' called out Arthur to their retreating backs. 'He's got something that might help.'

'My son does have a point, sire,' said Bane after Lancelot had left, 'and I suspect Aurelius has commented on this too. There's certainly a lot of risk in this plan of yours. However, I will not labour the point. I imagine you and Merlin have debated this long and hard.'

Not as such, thought Arthur, but he held his nerve and waited for Bane to continue.

'Have you thought about the tournament structure?'

'Just the beginning and the end,' answered Arthur. 'There's sixteen lords to start with, and I'd like to work down to two lords leading their allies in the final battle. One side being mine of course, and ideally Gallow being the other. I was rather hoping you could fill the gaps in between.'

Bane considered the problem for a minute. 'You'll need to carefully control the tournament matching to ensure you and Lord Gallow meet in that last battle. However, that should be possible. I'll get my knights to work on it. But once Gallow sees what you're up to, no doubt he'll try to get his Master of Ceremonies to influence things in his favour.'

'Yes, that's certainly what I'd do,' added Marcus, listening in while he oiled his sword.

'I know, but we'll just have to do the best we can,' said Arthur. He turned to Bane again. 'One more thing. I want you to lead my side. I'll just be a knight in the battle. You have a lot more experience at tournaments than me.'

Arthur looked back to Marcus. 'As someone who used to fight for the other side, what do you think?'

'To some, they may think it shows weakness,' Marcus paused in his labours. 'But to those who matter, it shows cunning. Play to your strengths is good in my book.'

'Good. Let's hope they think that,' said Arthur. 'Either way, I guess we'll see soon enough.'

The spectator enclosures were full and the surrounding fields crowded. Thousands of people had come to see the tournament and their new monarch-to-be. Arthur stood at the front of the royal box and waited for a hushed silence to settle.

'Welcome all to our royal tournament,' he called out across the crowd, trying to project the supreme confidence he did not quite feel. 'Over the next few days, our lords and knights will compete in games of skill and strength to find the most worthy amongst them. At the end, I shall choose seven lords and eight knights to sit at a round table in Camelot. Together we shall unite this land of ours in peace.'

After waiting for the whispers to quieten, Arthur raised his voice again. 'There will also be some changes to the tournament. There will be no jousting this year. As fun as it is, we all know it's just for show and results are fixed for political favour. Instead, we shall have a skill-based tournament with the losers being knocked out as we progress.'

This time, the whispers rose higher and there were some shouts above them.

'You can't take out jousting!'

'What will you give us instead!'

Arthur waited for the crowd to quieten down.

'At the end of the tournament there will be a full field battle, with knights, horses and soldiers. Sporting rules will apply, with the battle being fought by one hundred combatants on each side. It will be won by the last ten fighters left standing with their lord.'

'During the tournament, Lord Bane will lead my forces, and I shall fight as one of his knights. Lady Anne will take my seat in the royal box and will act as final judge in any dispute.'

More murmurs arose in the crowd. No woman had judged a tournament in living memory. Arthur looked out and held his gaze until the quiet returned. 'Lords and archers prepare for the first event. Let the games begin!'

A cheer went up, and Arthur made his way out of the royal box to get ready. Passing Lady Anne, she put a hand up to his shoulder and whispered in his ear. 'Very bold, young sire. You are showing confidence and determination beyond your years. But be careful not to make changes too quickly. You may find that some people do not want to keep up.'

Then she leaned across to kiss his cheek. 'And look after my husband will you, I am rather fond of him. I'd really hate having to put an arrow through someone just to save his grumpy old derrière.'

Arthur dressed in light armour, whilst Bane and Morgan got ready for the archery. 'I see you're up last. Who are you pitted against?' asked Arthur.

'Lord Cador, one of Gallows allies,' replied Bane. 'Though it must be said, probably one of Lord Gallow's more reluctant friends. He has no love for the man, but his lands are directly north of here, so he would be unwise to stand openly against Gallow. Lady Anne has suggested I talk with Cador at some point during the tournament. This should be an excellent opportunity to do just that.'

'Is Cador any good with a bow?' asked Morgan.

'Very,' answered Bane. 'Better than me on most days.'

'Not better than me, I bet,' stated Morgan.

'He doesn't have to be,' said Bane. 'Lords compete with lords, and their seconds only compete if there's a tie.'

'Then I guess this will have to be one of those days when you win,' remarked Morgan before leaving for the archery field.

'Are you sure we shouldn't use some of Lady Anne's bowstrings?' Bane asked Arthur.

'No, I want us to show this tournament is fair.'

'Even if your foe does not compete fairly?' questioned Bane.

'Especially if they don't. Remember what I said in my opening speech. I told everyone that the most worthy will join me at my round table. I didn't say anything about the winners.' Arthur grinned.

'Anyway. I have faith in our people and faith in my friends. We can be honourable, and we can win.' Arthur gripped Bane's shoulder. 'My goal here is to show I deserve the throne, that I have the strength and wisdom to rule the whole country. Defeating Gallow fairly in his own lands will certainly demonstrate that.'

Towards the end of the day, Arthur stood waiting in the archers' shelter with Morgan and Bane. 'Give me your quivers and I'll act as your squire,' he said to them both.

Bane passed over his quiver of arrows, but Morgan held on to his. 'I'll hold my own arrows, sire, if that's all the same to you. Nothing personal, just habit.'

'No problem. I only need one excuse to be here.'

'Actually, sire, why are you here?' questioned Morgan.

'To observe and learn,' said Arthur, without further explanation.

Cador arrived at the firing range and offered his arm in greeting. 'Good afternoon Bane.'

'Good day Cador,' replied Bane, gripping Cador's arm back in friendly greeting. 'This is my second, Morgan.'

Cador nodded at Morgan. 'And this is my second,' he stated, indicating to the tall wiry man beside him. Cador then bowed slightly to Arthur. 'Good afternoon to you, sire. I look forward to competing with you in this tournament. May the best and most worthy win.'

That's odd, thought Arthur as he acknowledged Cador, no mention of his second's name, I'll keep an eye on that one.

Bane stepped forward to the front of the shelter where the archers' places were marked. 'Shall we start?'

Cador nodded in return, and they signalled their readiness to the royal enclosure.

'Lords, ladies and gentlefolk,' called out Gallow's Master of Ceremonies. 'After a fine day of archery, with seven clear winners so far, we now have the final round. Lord Cador versus Lord Bane. Lord Bane, please begin.'

'That's strange,' whispered Arthur to Morgan. 'Why would Gallow's Master of Ceremonies allow Bane to go first and have the advantage? Surely he can't want us to win?'

Morgan shrugged. 'No idea. We'll have to wait and see I suppose.'

With the best of three rounds, the first round was an even match with four bullseyes each. The second round was also evenly matched with three, Lord Bane dropping the second and fourth shot and Cador the fourth and fifth. With the scores tied on two draws each, the lords took a break.

'Good shooting,' said Morgan to Bane. 'Not to insult your archery, but I think Cador should be beating you.'

'No apologies needed, you're right. I noticed he slightly drops his aim to miss after I do. I think he just hit the third bullseye so as not to make it too obvious.'

'Why would he want you to draw?' interjected Arthur. 'He must know that Morgan is unbeaten with a bow for the last four years. What's the point in Cador drawing just for Morgan to then win?'

'I wish I knew, but you can bet he has a reason, or more likely Gallow does,' replied Bane. 'Cador does not seem very comfortable, and he's making that clear to me as we shoot. I haven't had a chance to talk to him yet, but I'll try harder at the end of this final round.'

Bane stepped up, and the last round commenced. Both lords took their shots well and they eventually tied at four each. Sweating hard with extreme concentration, Bane took his final shot. The arrow flew straight into the golden bullseye and he scored his first perfect five. Cador stepped up and with barely a pause hit the bullseye as well. The crowd erupted with cheers and the Master of Ceremonies announced the first perfect round of the day.

Exhausted but happy with his performance, Bane turned to his opponent and offered his arm in congratulations. As Cador took his arm, Lord Bane started to speak, but Cador shook his head and mouthed just one word. With that, both of them departed the firing area and made it back to their companions.

'What did Cador say?' Arthur asked him.

'Just one word,' replied Bane. 'Sorry.'

'What for?'

'I don't know,' stated Bane. 'But whatever's going on, it's clear he doesn't want any part of it.'

The Master of Ceremonies announced the tie-breaker match, naming Cador's second only as Jon. Both men stepped forward to their firing positions, with Jon clearly towering over Morgan.

'After you, little man,' he said.

'Aye, you will be,' replied Morgan, and he shot a perfect bullseye.

The match continued and they tied on ten bullseyes, each shot demonstrating their expert skill. They retired for a short break before the final round, the exertion showing on both men.

'I hate to say this, but I'm not sure I can beat him,' said Morgan. 'I can hit another five bullseyes I reckon, but I suspect he'll just do the same. Likely the best I can give you is a draw, sire.'

'Miss one,' said Arthur.

'Why?' replied Morgan. 'Surely you don't want me to lose?'

'No, and I don't think you will.'

'I believe Arthur is correct,' said Merlin, who had quietly arrived to observe the last round. 'It seems Jon is Gallow's man. It appears both he and Cador have been instructed to draw with you.'

'Blimey, that's quite a task to expect over two matches,' said Bane. 'And anyway, even if we draw on bullseyes, they'll measure the distance of the final two arrows to the centre. No way those distances could be the same for both archers. How could anyone possibly guarantee a draw?'

'Very difficult indeed,' agreed Merlin. 'Yet here we are on the verge of a draw. Cador is probably the most skilled lord in the land with a bow, so he could match you most days. As for Jon, watch his bowstring carefully.'

Morgan returned to the front, and the final round began. He hit four perfect bullseyes, as did Jon, then with his last arrow Morgan hit just outside the bullseye.

Jon looked across curiously, then he turned to take his final shot. This time he did not fire quickly. He pulled back the bowstring with a shrewd look on his face.

Arthur watched closely as Jon let loose his arrow, and he saw the faint dark red shimmer on the bowstring. The arrow flew and landed just outside the bullseye too.

The crowd went silent as the Master of Ceremonies ordered both arrow placements measured. After several moments of cross checking, two surprised stewards looked up and announced that both arrows exactly equal in distance from the centre. The Master of Ceremonies declared a draw, and the crowd remained eerily quiet as they waited to hear how the draw would be resolved.

'You saw the red shimmer?' whispered Merlin to Arthur. 'That means the Lady is certainly here. I imagine she is helping Lord Gallow whilst searching for the magic I mentioned.'

'That can't be good.' Arthur looked back to the royal enclosure and saw Gallow step forward. 'And I'm probably not going to like this much either.'

Lord Gallow confidently took in the audience, then he called out across the fields. 'As the host of this tournament, I shall choose how to resolve this archery draw. Tomorrow there will be a joust, and I invite our future king to compete in this most noble of sports.'

The spell was broken, and the crowd erupted with a

tremendous cheer.

'No, not good at all,' whispered Merlin to himself.

CHAPTER 7

'This is a very bold move by Lord Gallow and quite ruthless,' Lady Anne proclaimed to everyone gathered in Arthur's quarters. 'If you do not compete in the joust, then Gallow can call you a coward in closed circles. If you compete and win with Merlin's magic, then he can openly call you dishonourable. And if you compete and lose, then everyone will see you as weak and unworthy of the crown.'

'Oh, there are two more options,' added Merlin. 'First, you could compete and get killed.'

'I hope the second option is an improvement,' commented Arthur.

Merlin looked to Lady Anne.

'You could compete and win without Merlin's magic or Excalibur,' she said. 'Merlin needs to leave soon to continue his search for the gathering magic. He could leave tonight to dispel any suggestion of involvement. Then tomorrow we just need you to win.'

Aurelius scratched at his stubble. 'Hold on, I know Arthur's quite handy with a sword and bow, and I've seen him joust a little with Lancelot to learn the ropes. But winning a tournament event is a big step up. I'm not sure this is a good idea.'

'But I have to compete,' said Arthur. 'I don't think I have much choice.'

Lady Anne laid a hand on his shoulder. 'You're right, you don't. That is why I shall lend you a helping hand instead of Merlin. Come with me Arthur my dear, there's someone I would like you to meet.'

Arthur walked through the main stable door with Lady Anne. 'What are we doing here? Is your friend going to hobble my opponent's horse? I'd rather not.'

'Certainly not,' she replied sternly. 'I hope you don't think I would orchestrate something like that.'

'No, not really.' Arthur shook his head and ran his hands through his short hair in frustration. 'I just don't know how I can win. Jousting's all about power and weight, technique comes second most of the time. Lancelot taught me that the hard way.'

'Look at this horse for instance,' he said, walking over to the nearest stable. 'He's beautiful in his own way, strong and experienced from the look of him. But a bit on the small side for a tournament stallion and peppered with ageing grey hair and battle scars. Just like me, this horse is not really built for jousting.'

Arthur absentmindedly reached out and patted the horse on its shoulder. Then he stopped for a second and patted the horse again, feeling the rock-hard muscle under his hand. All the while, the horse held still and patiently watched him.

'Ok,' said Arthur, 'maybe a little more powerful than I thought.'

'Would you care to revisit some of your other assumptions,' suggested Lady Anne, with a little smile on her face. 'Take a closer look. I hear this horse won't bite, as long as you show the proper respect that is.'

Arthur opened the door to the stable and led the horse out. With a gentle hand on the horse's neck, he inspected its eyes. 'Not so old after all,' remarked Arthur. 'His eyes are clear and youthful.'

The horse returned his stare and gave him a nudge backwards.

'Either he doesn't like me or I'm missing something,' said Arthur, and the horse nudged him again a little harder.

Arthur stepped back further, then smacked his head with his hand. 'Oh, that's very arrogant of me. Not his, her. Her eyes are clear and youthful. I'm very sorry young lady.'

The horse took a step forward, and this time playfully pushed him with her nose.

'Hold on, is this some kind of magical horse that understands what I say?'

'Not quite,' answered Lady Anne, 'but she is the smartest animal I have ever encountered. And you see those battle scars? Many look like they came from the tip of a lance, so plenty of experience there. Intelligent and experienced, what more could you ask for in a jousting horse?'

'But what about all the hits she's taken, surely that can't be good?'

'It wasn't so much the number of scars that caught my attention,' remarked Lady Anne. 'It's the fact that she's still alive that rather intrigued me.'

'Do you remember what I taught you last year?' said Lancelot, as he helped Arthur into his battle armour at the first light of day.

'Kind of,' Arthur winked at Lancelot. 'Don't get hit seemed to cover it mostly.'

'It's not funny.' Lancelot slammed down a clip and slapped Arthur's breast plate to emphasise his point. 'They'll be out to hurt you badly at the very least. Gallow is bound to put one of his own men into the joust, and from the look of things, Lord Cador doesn't have much choice. Gallow only needs the joust to look fair, that doesn't mean it actually will be.'

'And if you happen to get killed falling off your horse, then Gallow has his chance to openly challenge for the throne.'

'I'm just kidding,' grinned Arthur. 'I remember all the

techniques and tricks you taught me. How could I possibly forget, those lessons hurt far too much.'

His friend smiled a little at the memories. 'Ok, maybe it's a little funny. I think you must have fallen off over a dozen times one lesson.'

'That's the spirit.' Arthur clapped Lancelot on the back. 'A little merriment is good for us all. Anyway, I have a new horse and the support of my friends, what more could any king need?'

'A brain,' said Lancelot, as he placed Arthur's helmet on his head and gave it a rap with his knuckles. He turned as the door opened. 'Maybe Lady Anne can encourage a little caution in that head of yours. I'll leave you to it.'

Lady Anne took in Arthur's armour while she waited for Lancelot to leave the room. 'A good choice of words, Arthur my dear, trying to raise your friend's spirits with a little humour and confidence at a dangerous time. How much did you mean them?'

'Not a lot really, but I didn't want to tell him how terrified I am. That wouldn't help anyone. I'm learning that a king must often stand alone and bear the weight of our troubles.'

'Oh, a king is not always so alone. As you say, he has his friends to help him,' smiled Lady Anne. 'I hear from the stable hands that Gallow's man is an excellent jouster, but he heavily favours his right. If you can hit his right shoulder and force him to swap his lance to the left, then your skills will be far more evenly matched.'

'Thank you, Anne. As always, I owe you more than I can ever repay,' said Arthur.

'I know,' she said smiling and giving him a kiss on the cheek. 'Not bad for a pretend aunt.'

'Only pretend by blood,' replied Arthur before he left the room. 'Not in my heart.'

Arthur and Gallow's man rode out into the hastily constructed jousting arena to tremendous cheers from the crowd, and the Master of Ceremonies called out his announcement.

'On my left and representing Lord Bane, is our king in waiting, Arthur. And on my right, in a magnanimous gesture of fair-mindedness, Lord Cador will be represented by a humble squire, a noble knight in waiting, Lord Gallow's first-born son Kay.'

Hardly generous, thought Arthur, Kay is five years older than me and almost as big as his father.

The riders met in the middle of the arena, Kay's stallion standing a good two hands higher than Arthur's horse.

'Nothing personal, Arthur,' said Kay while they waited for the traditional speeches to finish, 'but you're too young and inexperienced for the throne. Even your choice of horse shows weakness. Could you not even tame a real stallion as your war horse? I can't see how a mare would strike terror into your foes. Bessy the farm horse doesn't really impress me.'

'Actually, no one seems to know her name,' said Arthur, brushing aside the goading. 'So, she's just called Horse for now.'

'Huh, a fifteen-year-old boy on an unknown horse. This is almost too easy.' Kay studied Arthur for a second. 'Whatever weaknesses you have, I don't believe stupidity is amongst them. Maybe I should keep a closer eye on you than I first thought.'

'I guess we shall see,' said Arthur, wishing he had said nothing at all. Live and learn, he thought to himself, well hopefully anyway.

With the speeches finished, Arthur clicked and gave Horse a nudge with his feet. He cantered to the other side and turned Horse around carefully, whilst Kay galloped to the edge of the arena and expertly spun in a spray of mud. Positioned at each end, both riders lowered their lances and waited.

Lady Anne held up her white scarf, then let it fall to indicate the start of the joust. Kay kicked his horse into a gallop and came charging towards Arthur. Without instruction, Horse started to canter, then picked up speed more steadily as she broke into a slow gallop. Arthur held his lance steady and aimed as best he could, gladly noticing he was not bouncing about as much as usual.

The distance between them closed quickly. Arthur concentrated through the narrow slit in his helmet and tried to aim for Kay's right shoulder as they got close. Then instantly there was blinding pain, and he felt himself fly through the air. The pain in his left side was so great, he hardly even noticed when he hit the ground. It all went quiet, and Arthur stared up at the sky, his face guard thrown up over his head.

A shadow fell across him, and he heard Kay speak. 'Stay down. If you stay there, you may live to see the end of today. There's no shame in losing to an opponent of greater skill.'

'Ugg,' replied Arthur, barely even understanding Kay's words. A second shadow fell across him, and he felt a large hairy nose nudge his cheek.

'Yup, still alive thank you,' he managed to croak as he reached out to stroke Horse's mane. When his hand touched her hair, he felt a jolt through his left side.

Horse lifted her head and Arthur's arm flopped back down. She lowered her head again, and this time prodded him more forcefully. Arthur took hold of her mane again and felt heat burning through his arm and body. But when the sensation finished, the immense pain in his left side had become just a dull throb. Horse lifted her head and Arthur held on to rise with her.

'Erm. Thank you?' he whispered in astonishment as he gingerly climbed back into the saddle. Slowly, he rode back out to the edge of the arena once more.

'Well, lords, ladies and gentlemen, it seems we are not finished after all,' called out the Master of Ceremonies as the crowd cheered excitedly, baying for more. 'We have a second round. Jousters begin.'

Arthur pulled down his face guard, and everything became narrow again. He geed Horse forward and she broke into a canter. He concentrated on Kay's right shoulder and Horse increased to a gallop. Far quicker than before, they sped towards Kay. Arthur held his lance high, the effort burning his muscles, and Horse increased her speed yet again. Arthur saw Kay's lance rush towards him. I'm going to die, he thought. Then Horse stumbled to the side at the last instant and Kay's lance missed by a fraction. But Arthur's did not.

Kay took the full force of the lance on his right shoulder and went spinning from his horse. He landed hard on the ground and lay still. The crowd went silent.

Horse stopped and turned around, as if waiting for Arthur to decide. 'Come on then,' he said. 'Let's go see if he's ok.'

Horse cantered over and Arthur jumped down from her back. Bending down to investigate, he saw only shallow breathing coming from his opponent.

He looked back to Horse. 'Can you help him like you helped me?' he asked, feeling a bit stupid talking to her, but not really knowing what else to do.

She lowered her head and nuzzled Kay's neck, then he groaned and opened his eyes. 'Bloody hell, that hurts,' he croaked.

'I think you'll live,' said Arthur and he held out his arm.

'If I allow you to help me up, then I forfeit the joust,' said Kay.

'It's not an offer of defeat, it's an offer of friendship,' said Arthur. 'We can ride again if you want.'

Kay grabbed Arthur's arm and rose unsteadily to his feet. He leaned in towards Arthur to talk quietly. 'Thanks, but I'll pass on another joust, if it's all the same to you. Nearly being killed once a day is enough for me. I've never seen a lance move so accurately before.'

Kay stole a quick glance at Arthur's horse. 'You're certainly not all that you seem, young Arthur. Who knows, maybe I will take you up on your offer of friendship one day.'

The Master of Ceremonies remained quiet, and Lady Anne stood up. 'Would you care to announce the winner young man, or shall I?'

In the castle hall, the lunch was loud and boisterous. Several lords and knights came over to Arthur and clapped him on the back. Many congratulated him enthusiastically for his jousting victory, though others did so more reluctantly. When Kay limped over to offer his formal congratulations, Arthur led him to the edge of the hall.

'I'm guessing your father wasn't happy,' said Arthur.

'That would be an understatement. Even his favourite goblet was dented when he threw it across the room. He's adamant you're too weak to rule and that our land will descend into further conflict over the throne,' said Kay. 'He's an experienced leader and often a fine judge. But in this matter, I think he might be wrong. I suspect you are not too weak, and possibly you will unite the land one day. Though I do agree you're still a bit too young for all this.'

'Time will tell,' replied Arthur. 'In the meantime, I will continue to lead as best I can. One thing I have decided, you'll be the first knight invited to my round table. You fought fairly in our joust and accepted the loss with good grace, despite your father's wishes. You also reassessed the situation when needed and didn't let emotion cloud your judgement.'

'I must admit, I am interested in your round table. I'm beginning to suspect it's better to work with you to change what I don't like, rather than work against you. But what about my father?' asked Kay. 'He's really not going to like this, even if you invite him to. He thinks he's far more suitable to rule than you, and he certainly doesn't want to be your subject.'

'The invite does not extend to your father,' said Arthur more firmly than he expected. 'I don't like his political games or some of the people he chooses as friends.'

'Well, that's one thing we can agree on,' sighed Kay. 'He has one particular friend who always stokes the fires of his ambition when she visits. She was also an old friend of my half uncle, though her influence on his unsavoury character was far more extreme. But then you and Lady Anne already know this I suspect.'

'Tell you what, Arthur, I'll make you a deal. You help me remove this Lady from my father's circle of friends. You stop her leading him into the deep waters of conflict, and I'll sit at your round table. But be warned, I won't be a spy for you. If that's your game, then I'm not interested.'

'Nothing so clever or political,' said Arthur. 'I'm expected to lead our land, but I also want to unite it. To do that, I need help. It started when I fought with your uncle and I sought to avoid the larger conflict. There I had help from a mercenary I'd just met that day. Now I intend to make more friends from my so-called enemies. As you so rightly pointed out, people are not always what they seem. I think we may be closer to friendship and peace than you think.'

'Ha, not clever my arse,' said Kay with a laugh and clapped Arthur on the shoulder. 'You might just be our king in the making after all.'

Arthur parried the blow and lashed out with his boot, forcing his opponent to grunt heavily as he fell to the floor. Unfortunately, this was a short-lived victory, as his second opponent weighed in with a fast punch to his head and Arthur went down.

He rolled with the punch to lessen the impact and continued the momentum back onto his feet. No sooner had he regained his footing, than Arthur waded in with two hard punches to his attacker's ribs and one to the solar plexus. That should put an ox down, thought Arthur, as he retreated to assess the situation.

'You'll have to do much better than that little man,' laughed his huge foe. Then he winded Arthur completely with a lightning-fast shove to the chest. Hardly able to breathe or stand, Arthur staggered back, desperately trying to get out of range. Then his first attacker stuck out a leg and tripped him to the ground. Arthur just put out his hands in desperation to break his fall, no graceful rolling this time.

'And now you're finished,' said the larger of the two as he advanced towards Arthur. 'This is the end of your tournament.'

A clapping came from the edge of the room, and Morgan tossed Excalibur to Arthur while Geoffrey brushed himself off and Lancelot got to his feet. 'And that is why you'll not be fighting without your sword at your side in this tournament. Sire.'

'But surely having Excalibur is cheating and breaking my own rules,' said Arthur. 'Even if I don't use its full power and kill anyone, Excalibur still gives me an enormous advantage. At the very least it will make my opponents wary of me.'

'What, and you don't think Geoffrey's massive size and speed give him an advantage? What about Gallow's army full of seasoned knights, or even the size of his son Kay compared to you?' said Morgan. 'There's no cheating in warfare, only winners and dead people. And there's nothing noble about being dead.'

Arthur thought for a moment. 'So, if I'm always going to have Excalibur with me, why do you still persist in training me without it?' he asked.

'Aye, that is a good point,' conceded Morgan, as he and Geoffrey packed up to leave the room. 'Two reasons, my young king. First, no matter how close you keep Excalibur to you, one day someone will likely separate you from it. And second, I just like to win when we fight.' Then he grinned and left.

'He makes a good point,' said Lancelot as he rubbed his ribs where Arthur had kicked him, but he broke into a rare smile despite the pain. 'It is fun to see you bested from time to time, even though that's not so often anymore. Speaking of which, how was your chat with Kay? Is he going to back down, now you beat him? Will he defy his father's ambitions for the throne?'

'I think he will. But only if we can remove the Lady's influence from his father,' replied Arthur. 'Oh, and I invited Kay to my round table.'

'What! Are you mad? How on earth can you trust the son of your most powerful enemy?'

Arthur rubbed his sore hands as a drop of his blood fell onto Excalibur and fizzled away with a gentle blue glow. 'If I fill this round table with only my allies, then the land will never be united. I need to make friends of my foes as well. I know it won't work for all of them, but I believe it will for some.'

'Hmm, not sure you're right about that,' said Lancelot somewhat distracted, watching the last glimmer of blue on Arthur's sword. 'Why don't you just test their blood on the sword? It glowed blue for Marcus and was red for Falcon's blood all those years ago.'

'I'm not sure that's what it's for,' replied Arthur. 'I've asked Merlin about it, but he's a bit guarded and won't say why. Possibly he doesn't actually know but doesn't want to admit it.'

'Ok, do you trust me?' said Lancelot.

'Of course, with my life.'

'Ok, then let's test my blood.' Lancelot took his dagger and made a small cut on his thumb. He squeezed and a drop of blood fell onto Excalibur. It boiled away with a bright blue glow at its heart, but also some fiery red at its edge.

'What on earth does that mean?' said Arthur.

'I don't like that at all,' replied Lancelot. 'That looks like dark magic to me. Maybe I'm the one who shouldn't be at your round table.'

'Nonsense.' Arthur put a hand on Lancelot's shoulder. 'There's no one I trust more than you to do the right thing, under any circumstance. You've proven yourself many times, and I expect you'll do that again before this tournament is finished.'

As the two friends left the training room, Lancelot did not look entirely convinced.

CHAPTER 8

Arthur looked on as the first round of duels progressed. The weakest champions were pitted against the strongest. Eight lords had made it through to this round, and Arthur had seen the first three duels go as expected. The largest and strongest had won each time, and the losers were bloodied and bruised but still alive. Even Gallow's champion had fought fair and deserved the win.

Now Geoffrey was competing on behalf of Lord Bane and Arthur. The fight was going well, with Geoffrey gaining the advantage. Arthur could see that he was holding back, doing just enough to ensure a win. They wanted to keep people from seeing his full capability until the final field battle. 'Better to keep them guessing,' Morgan had commented that morning.

Geoffrey swung a heavy-handed blow with his sword, which his opponent easily ducked. But instead of over balancing, Geoffrey rolled to the ground and swung up his leg. The kick knocked his opponent to the ground. Geoffrey rose to his feet and placed the tip of his sword on his opponent's neck. The man immediately held up an arm to concede the duel.

With the first round complete, the lords retired to the castle with their champions and courtiers. However, Arthur and the others remained on the field to discuss the next round.

'Who's matched with me next?' asked Geoffrey.

'It's Kane, Lord Galahad's champion. Probably the best fighter in this tournament that we've seen,' replied Morgan. 'Except you of course.'

'Yes, I watched him in the first round. He is very good, but you're right, I am better,' said Geoffrey as a matter of fact and with no trace of arrogance. He turned to Arthur. 'How do you want me to fight, sire? Just enough to win again?'

'No,' replied Arthur. 'I want you to beat him as hard and fast as you can. Though try to avoid any serious injury. He fought fair and doesn't deserve that.'

Geoffrey nodded, but Lancelot stepped forward. 'Are you sure that's wise? You'll show everyone how good Geoffrey is. No more surprise element.'

'All part of the plan,' said Arthur as he winked at his friend.

The first duel continued as expected, Gallow's man winning with ease. Lastly, the Master of Ceremonies called out the duel of Kane and Geoffrey.

The two knights approached one another in the centre of the field, swords drawn but at rest. Lady Anne dropped her white scarf to signal the start of the duel.

Kane raised his sword, but instead of rushing in as he had done in his previous bout, he circled Geoffrey slowly.

'I'm not fooled by your fight last time you know,' said Kane. 'It was a performance; I could tell you were holding back. But you seem like a good man. You could have hurt your opponent badly or humiliated him, but you didn't.'

Geoffrey circled in response to Kane's movement. 'Maybe, maybe not. But why are you telling me this?'

'Because I have to kill you or die trying,' stated Kane. 'And I'll have to start soon, or they'll become suspicious. Gallow's man gave me those instructions and this sword to use. My own Lord doesn't know. If I fail, then my family will die. So, bring your best or face the consequences.'

Kane feinted left, then swung in a fast and powerful blow from the right. Geoffrey parried with his sword in one hand and countered with an even faster punch to Kane's side. Kane staggered back a little but regained his defence.

'Knew I was right,' he said. 'Enough testing, time to fight,' and he launched at Geoffrey with a series of attacks, both strong and skilled. Geoffrey countered the blows, but noticed his sword taking damage with each attack. Small red sparks coming from Kane's sword as it struck his own.

Kane finished his attack and the two fighters stepped back, both breathing hard.

'Seems you've had a little extra help with that sword,' said Geoffrey.

'So, it does,' replied Kane. 'That will be why Gallow's man insisted I use it. No matter, I'll take any advantage I can when I'm fighting for my family.'

Kane dove in again, this time faster still. The attacks were relentless, and even the crowd were gasping in surprise at the viciousness. Geoffrey kept blocking and countering with blows of his own, but his sword was taking yet more damage. Kane himself was breathing harder and harder, his lungs not able to keep up with what he was pushing his muscles to do.

Looking on, Arthur could see both fighters were in trouble in different ways. He moved to draw Excalibur, but Morgan laid a hand to stop him. 'Let it play out, sire. Remember what Merlin said. You could try to solve everything with magic, but that doesn't mean you should. Anyway, Geoffrey wouldn't want you to interfere, no matter the outcome.'

Kane came in for a close blow, and Geoffrey's sword finally snapped. The two men looked at each other for an instant, one fighter to another.

'Sorry,' said Kane quietly.

'Me too,' replied Geoffrey, then he dropped his sword and grabbed hold of Kane's blade. Blood poured down Geoffrey's hand as Kane tried to pull his sword free, but Geoffrey just pushed it higher. Then lightning fast, he took his dagger from his belt and drove it into Kane's side under his armour.

Kane grunted with pain, but instead of pushing and twisting

the dagger to finish him off, Geoffrey leaned in. 'This is going to hurt, a lot.'

Through a haze of pain, Kane looked surprised for an instant, then Geoffrey gave him a sharp punch to the side and pushed him in the chest to topple him to the ground. Kane grunted once more as he hit the ground. After which he became silent and still.

Some of the crowd were whooping at the sheer violence, but others were deathly quiet. Lord Gallow rose and left the royal enclosure without a word, and his Master of Ceremonies looked lost.

Arthur stood to quieten the crowd. 'We have a winner, but not without loss. We will remember the bravery and fight of the man who fell. Rest assured his family and those he leaves behind will be cared for. Now we shall break for today, to prepare for the final event tomorrow.'

The crowds dispersed as Arthur made his way over to Geoffrey. He looked at him and then at the body of Kane lying on the floor.

'Was that entirely necessary?' asked Morgan as he joined them. There was no hint of accusation in his voice, just a plain question.

Arthur bent down to examine Geoffrey's broken sword. Touching the end, he could still feel the heat where the blade had been severed. 'I thought I saw flashes of red. Morgan, I think the Lady has been at work here. So unfortunately, I suspect it was entirely necessary.'

'When you've all finished judging me,' interrupted Geoffrey, as he wrapped his injured hand. 'I think we need to see to Kane.'

'What on earth for?' asked Morgan.

'Well, for a start,' replied Geoffrey simply, 'he's not actually dead.'

Geoffrey carried the unconscious Kane off the field, and Lady Anne tended to his injury. She carefully removed the dagger and used a heated knife to seal the wound, both inside and out.

'I did wonder why you hadn't pulled your dagger out to reclaim it,' she commented to Geoffrey, whilst Aurelius used surprisingly delicate skill to stitch the wound closed. Arthur left them to it and sat with Lancelot and Morgan in the next room.

'Bloody hell, the conspiracies and deceptions never end do they,' he said. 'Apart from the war it would cause, part of me would like to take Excalibur and separate Lord Gallow's head from his shoulders.'

'Really?' asked Lancelot.

Arthur breathed out and rubbed his face. 'Ok, not really,' he admitted. 'Anyway, at least we have some time to plan for the main event tomorrow. Now that your father and Gallow are the last two lords in the tournament, we can organise the one hundred knights and soldiers we need for the final fight. I'd very much like to see what alliances we can form. I know Lady Anne has been working on some potential allies.'

Before Lancelot could reply, his father strode into the room. 'Sorry, not much time for anything, young sire,' Bane said. 'Cador came to see me after the duel. His scouts have spotted some of Gallows' soldiers with a hooded woman. They're on his land by his western farms. They might be there to help the Lady gather this magic. It might even be the Lady herself. But whoever it is, I think we need to find Merlin and try to stop them.'

'Ok,' said Arthur, 'Go get Aurelius and some soldiers. I'll meet you in the stables shortly. Morgan, you work with Lady Anne on the battle strategies for tomorrow. Oh, and go get Marcus as well, he usually has an idea or two.'

'Told you he'd leave the actual work to us common folk,' Morgan joked to Lancelot as Arthur made for the door and left the room.

'Mind you,' Morgan added. 'There's a great king in the making there.'

Arthur walked down the corridor, not knowing quite what to do, but agreeing with Bane that they should find Merlin. He reached the stables and started to saddle up Horse.

'We really should find you a proper name,' he said while he worked. Horse just looked back at him with a quiet stare and Arthur noticed her watching.

'Or are you happy with Horse?' he asked, still feeling a little daft talking to an animal, despite all he had seen.

She turned her head some more and gently placed it on his shoulder. Arthur nodded and rubbed her ears. 'Horse it is then,' he said decisively.

As he put his foot in the stirrup and climbed up, Lord Bane arrived with Aurelius, Lancelot, and twenty soldiers in tow. Then Lord Cador entered the stables with another ten.

'I'd like to lend a hand,' he said to Arthur. 'I'd rather not openly stand against Gallow, but helping you and Merlin feels like something I must do. Anything to resist Gallow's onslaught for more power.'

Before Arthur could respond, another voice called out from the back. 'It's not an onslaught,' said Kay. 'My father may be arrogant, but he does believe what he's doing is right. His choice of friends has led him to these extreme actions, but his intentions are for the best.'

'After all your father has done to control my policies and actions, I'm not sure I can agree with that,' said Cador.

Arthur held up a hand to stop them. 'Tonight, we need unity. We're here to stop the Lady and weaken her power. If you agree with that, then you ride with me. If you don't, then you stay here. All other disputes can wait until later. Do I have your word on that?'

Everyone watched Cador and Kay as they slowly nodded in

agreement.

'Right, let's saddle up and ride,' said Arthur. 'We've got a lot to do tonight.'

In the fading light, they galloped across Cador's lands, heading for the large farms in the west. Aurelius caught up with Arthur and matched Horse's pace. 'It's nearly dark now. How the hell are we going to find Merlin?' he shouted across.

'When we get there, I suspect Merlin will probably find us,' Arthur called back. At least I hope so, he added to himself.

At the edge of the first farm, Cador held up his hand and they drew to a halt, their horses breathing heavily in the cold evening air. 'The next farm after this is where my scouts saw them. We should travel quietly from here.'

'Shall we leave the horses here?' questioned Bane.

'I think so,' replied Arthur, dismounting. 'Post six soldiers with the horses, but get them stationed in pairs, away in the trees. If anyone hears the horses and creeps up, I want our sentries to have the advantage of surprise.'

Arthur patted Horse's neck and left her untied. Feeling slightly less daft talking to his horse, he whispered in her ear. 'Stay here and watch the other horses. If it's not us who returns first, then give them a good kick.'

Aurelius leaned over from tying up his stallion and spoke quietly. 'Are you talking to a horse? Have you lost your senses?'

Arthur grinned back at his uncle. 'That would certainly put paid to my reign before it's even begun. But no, I'm not going mad, there really is something special about this horse.'

'There certainly is,' said Merlin, stepping out from the shadows and making them flinch. 'Glad you could join me, Arthur, and very good of you to bring some friends. If you could all gather around, that would be most helpful.'

Merlin waited for them to get closer. 'I have found the Lady and Gallow's forces at the next farm. Unfortunately, she has already started gathering the raw magic from the central well. However, it is not yet too late. If we can take them by surprise, then she may not get it all.'

Cador raised his hand and pointed to the southwest then the northwest. 'I can divide my soldiers in two to show you the way, then we could attack from both sides at the same time. But be warned, the going will be slow as it's nearly dark.'

'I can help with that,' said Merlin. He touched their eyes briefly one by one, and after a moment everything became a little brighter, though somewhat blue in hue. 'It will not last long, so you must be quick. I will tackle the Lady; you handle the soldiers.'

'Good. Let's get into position, then we attack on Cador's signal,' ordered Arthur. 'And remember, this is not the tournament. You'll need to fight hard and only take prisoners if they lay down their weapons.'

Cador, Aurelius, Kay and Bane took half the soldiers and moved off towards the northwest side of the farm. Arthur and Lancelot took the rest and moved quietly through the trees to the southwest, with Merlin keeping step beside them. They crossed the farm boundary and crept through a field of wheat.

Stopping at the edge of the field, but still hidden by the high crops, they could see a large group of soldiers surrounding a hooded figure. The soldiers were turned outwards as sentries, and the figure was bent over a well. Arthur focused his eyes in the gloom and could see she was pulling on a rope. As he watched, she raised a bucket of water out of the well.

'Are you sure that's a powerful sorceress gathering magic?' asked Lancelot. 'Doesn't look very magical to me.'

'What do you think, Merlin?' asked Arthur turning around. But Merlin was no longer with them. He was striding towards the well and the soldiers. Powerful blue magic was forming in his hands as he got ready to fight.

'Bloody hell, there goes the plan,' said Lancelot.

'Yup,' said Arthur and he turned to the soldiers with them. 'You all fan out around Lancelot and me. We hit them quiet and hard right now.'

They charged across the field as quietly as possible, but they needn't have worried, none of Gallow's soldiers saw them. They were all staring at Merlin as he raised his hands and sent a huge fireball straight at the Lady. In one smooth movement she deflected the blazing blue magic with a red flash of her own, and the fireball blew up the farmhouse behind her. She unhurriedly tightened her hood and reached down to the bucket of water beside her. She brought out a dark red glowing mass in her grasp. As she held it in her hand, it dripped splashes of fire onto the grass.

'It's raw magic. Get down,' called out Merlin.

Arthur and Lancelot hit the dirt immediately. Some of their soldiers followed them to the ground, but others stood in fascination, just like their foe around the well.

The Lady squeezed the glowing ball of magic in her hands and a blast of red lightning flew out in a circle. It skimmed over Arthur's head with an intense heat that made his skin itch. Those who were still standing, friend and foe alike, just disappeared into ash. When the dust cleared, only their smoking boots remained.

Arthur looked up, and Merlin stepped out from behind his magical shield. 'Get everyone away,' he called out as he advanced on the Lady again, fire reigniting in his hands.

'You heard him,' said Arthur to Lancelot.

'And what about you?'

'She's far too dangerous already, this has to be stopped. And I've got an idea how to help Merlin.'

'That's what I was afraid of,' muttered Lancelot as he reluctantly carried out Arthur's orders.

The Lady separated the raw magic into two parts. Grasped in each hand, the magic changed shape like a living creature. It then moulded to her hands and burned bright red around its edges, all the time maintaining the dark heart at its core.

'Are you really sure you want this fight, old man?' she asked Merlin calmly, no real malice in her voice, just cold confidence of her superiority.

Not a word came from Merlin as he sent another blast of blue fire raging across the field. She raised her hands and caught it easily. Casually she crushed the fireball, then blew into her hand. Blue dust escaped in a puff of smoke and drifted slowly to the ground.

Merlin threw again and again. Blue magic erupting from his hands and tearing across the field towards the Lady. The heat was intense as wave after wave flew through the air, but she deflected or caught them with no apparent effort or concern.

When Merlin finally stopped, not a building or tree was left standing within two hundred paces. Everything around them had been turned to rubble or ash.

'Is that the best you can do, old man?'

'Yes,' replied Merlin, just loud enough for her to hear, 'but not the best we can do.'

Arthur rose from the ground behind her and plunged Excalibur towards the Lady's heart as she turned around. His sword grew hot as it pierced her cowl. Red and blue magic boiled into the air as the sword fought to continue its journey. The Lady grabbed hold of the blade with both hands to try to stop it, dark red magic flaring viciously, but Arthur pushed harder. The sword became hotter in his hands, but its power did not falter. With one final push, he drove it into her chest, almost to the hilt.

The Lady dropped to her knees and Arthur crouched down with her. 'I'm sorry,' he said, 'but I can't let you poison our lords against each other and destroy this land.'

She looked at him, red fire burning in her eyes from within the darkness of her hood. 'I'm not destroying the land you

101

stupid boy. The weak cannot help, and the best of us must start leading. This land you so love, I'm making it stronger.'

She raised a hand glowing with power and pushed him away. With her other hand, she squeezed harder and crushed Excalibur's blade right near the hilt. Disconnected, the handle fell to the ground and the magic in the sword went quiet. With that, the Lady brought her hands together and there was a blinding flash of red.

After his eyes had recovered, Arthur looked around. There was no sign of the Lady, only Merlin standing in their circle of destruction, and the two broken pieces of his sword lying on the ground. He patted himself down, not quite believing he was still alive and in one piece.

'Bloody hell, I'm not sure whether to give up right now or ask a hundred questions,' said Arthur, looking around at the devastation. 'What the hell just happened?'

'Sadly, I believe that was the start of another long and costly war.' Merlin carefully thread his way through the many fires still burning and placed his hand on Arthur's shoulder. 'I do hope you get to ask your questions, young Sire. I suspect you are going to need a very good answer to every single one of them.'

CHAPTER 9

On the ride back to the castle, Arthur had held the two pieces of Excalibur together to make it look intact. The hilt was cold in his hand and offered no comfort or strength. It was a hard ride, and that was the last straw for Arthur. By the time they returned, he felt completely exhausted. When they had stabled their horses and he was finally alone with Merlin, Arthur took the broken sword from its scabbard.

'I need to sleep before the last event tomorrow, but I can't turn up without Excalibur. What on earth am I going to do about my sword?' He looked down forlornly at the two pieces he held in his hands. 'And that's not even starting to think about where the Lady has gone and what she's up to.'

'Regarding the Lady, we shall just have to hope she has exhausted herself in escaping,' said Merlin. 'Healing and transporting takes an enormous amount of power. It could not have been easy for her, even with all the raw magic she took.'

'So, you know what she's capable of? Can you do the same?' asked Arthur.

'Yes and no, in that order,' replied Merlin as he paced the small room. 'She is certainly more powerful than me, and that's not something I am comfortable with.'

Then he stopped and aimed a quick smile at Arthur. 'However, she still seems rather inexperienced. Where she may use raw power to achieve her goals, we shall use more subtle means. Come with me, young man. There is one more thing you should see tonight. Oh, and bring your sword.'

Arthur dragged himself out of his seat and followed Merlin.

They walked through Gallow's castle and the gate to the private garden. With no one around at this late hour, they sat by the still pond near the rear wall in peace and quiet. For a few minutes, Merlin didn't say a word and Arthur listened to the light wind rippling the waters of the pond. The gentle noise began to relax him.

'Good grief,' he said standing up and shaking himself. 'We've got to move, or I'll fall asleep.'

'Too late for that,' giggled a voice beside him. 'I think you already are.'

'What!' Arthur looked across to see a young girl in white standing next to him. 'Oh, sorry young lady, I didn't see you there. Do your folks know you're out of bed in the garden? Hold on, what do you mean too late?'

'Look,' she said, pointing behind him.

Arthur turned and saw himself asleep on the bench. Merlin was still sitting beside him, also having a doze, hands crossed on his lap and a contented smile on his face.

'He looks a bit pleased with himself. Is this his magic?' asked Arthur.

'Oh no, it's all mine, just like the last time,' replied the girl. She held her arms out wide in a grand gesture. 'For I am the Lady of the Lake.'

Arthur stifled a chuckle. 'Sorry, I don't mean to be rude, but this is more of a pond and you can't be much older than six or seven.'

The girl looked a little embarrassed. 'All right, maybe we are a bit young. But I will be a lady one day and this will be a Lake,' she said determinedly.

'Well, I'm certainly grateful for the rest,' said Arthur, bowing a little. 'So I am in your debt already, young Lady of the Lake.'

'You are most welcome, young king,' she replied proudly, with a big smile on her face. 'I like you even more as a grownup. I think you can visit any time you want.'

Before Arthur could ask what she meant, she turned back to the pond and walked towards it. 'Oh, and don't forget your sword. The Lake and I are very tired after fixing it. We wouldn't want that to go to waste.'

'Sword?' said Arthur, waking up with a jolt and realising he was no longer holding Excalibur. *Must have slipped from my grasp while I was dreaming*, he thought. He looked around him on the ground, and just there at the edge of the pond was the hilt, poking out from the water. He walked over to it, looking for the broken blade as well.

Arthur picked up the hilt and felt the extra weight as he pulled it from the pond. Excalibur rose from the waters as he lifted it up, its blade now restored. The sword was whole, and he felt its familiar warmth return as he held it in his hand.

'Thank you,' whispered Arthur, looking towards the pond for the young girl but seeing only the dark still waters.

'Good, you have found what you required,' said Merlin, rising from his slumber.

'Who was she?' asked Arthur.

'Ah, you presume I have seen what you have seen, but I have not. This garden has good magic, I could feel it, so I brought you here to see what would happen.'

Arthur looked a little stunned. 'So, you didn't actually know what was here?'

'Indeed I did not. But these are difficult times, with harder ones to come. Sometimes bold action is required.' Then an unusually sly grin crossed Merlin's face. 'And with respect, young man, you are not the only person in this land to take a risk from time to time.'

'I can't believe I feel so refreshed. That snooze really was good for me,' said Arthur as they walked back across the gardens in the dark.

'Excellent. That is good preparation for your battle today,' replied Merlin.

'What! Today? Did we sleep all night?'

'I believe so,' said Merlin. 'It will be dawn very soon, and you need to find Morgan to discuss the plans for the day.'

'Good grief, do I ever get time to myself?' asked Arthur.

'The duty of a good king, or queen for that matter, is to their people and land first,' said Merlin. 'I rather think your wellbeing comes a distant second.'

'Ok, ok, I get it. Let's find the others. They'll probably be in Lady Anne's rooms discussing our tactics. Hopefully Lancelot too, if he's awake after last night.'

When they entered the castle, something else occurred to Arthur that had been bothering him. 'You know when Marcus' blood hit Excalibur it boiled away with your blue magic?' Merlin nodded in return. 'Well, after Lancelot and I were sparring, we tested a drop of his blood on the sword, and it boiled with blue and red magic. He thought this might be the Lady's dark magic influencing him, and I shouldn't trust him. I told Lancelot not to be stupid, that there is no one I trust more than him.'

Arthur looked at Merlin for reassurance.

'As much as I do not want to disappoint you, I am afraid there are two problems with what you just said,' stated Merlin. 'First, I do not believe that the magic belongs to me, the Lady, or anyone. The magic is ours to use, but not ours to own. Just because magic is red, it does not necessarily mean it is evil.'

'So, what is the difference between red and blue magic then? Does it even matter what colour Lancelot's blood turned into?'

Merlin stopped walking and looked at Arthur. 'It pains me to admit this twice in the space of one day, but honestly, I do not know. When I use magic, it is mostly blue in hue, but not always. Our observation of the Lady's magic has always been red, but again that may not be the case every time.'

Merlin sighed gently. 'What is the significance of the colour of magic? Unfortunately, I can only begin to guess. However, I would like to find out. I suspect the difference may be very important to us all.'

When Merlin didn't continue, Arthur prompted him further. 'And the second problem?'

'Oh yes,' said Merlin as he started to walk again. 'There should be someone you trust more than Lancelot.'

'Who?' said Arthur.

'I would have thought that would be obvious,' replied Merlin, as they arrived at Lady Anne's door. 'The person you must trust the most is yourself.'

Arthur and Merlin walked through the doorway and saw Lancelot pacing around the room.

'I think we're getting there,' he announced as they entered. 'My father has Lord Cador and Galahad on our side for the battle today. They have some excellent soldiers who are smart and can follow our tactics. They're also honest enough to fight fairly, and brave enough to fight hard. Lady Anne has even patched up Kane to fight with us.'

'Thank you, that's great,' said Arthur to his aunt. 'I have an idea for Geoffrey, so getting Kane as well is even better.'

'Lady Anne, how has your friend got on?' asked Merlin.

Arthur looked at his aunt again. 'I hope it's not something I'm going to regret later?'

'A little helping hand is all,' she replied. 'My friend is the head cook here in the castle. He and his family have been keeping an eye on the food. So far they have foiled three separate attempts to poison you, sire.'

'Ok, that I don't regret.'

'Although it must be said, none of those attempts were made by Lord Gallow,' she added. 'However, be that as it may, last night my instructions were to lace the meals with extra mead and some tainted meat for Gallow and his allies. Many of the opposing side today will have a fair bit of distraction with sore heads and disagreeable stomachs.'

She offered an uncharacteristically crafty smile. 'Oh, and don't touch the breakfast. A little fruit from your room might be best.'

Arthur returned the smile. 'Now that I can live with. Gallow deserves it for all his manipulation. Morgan, Marcus, what are our tactics for the field battle itself?'

'We have fewer trained knights than the other lords, so we need to balance foot soldier tactics with mounted strategy,' said Marcus, as he started to lay out their thinking. 'With arrows and spears banned, Gallow and his allies will probably go with one hundred mounted knights. We, on the other hand, only have about sixty knights with us.'

'Aye, your rule about no archers was a big disappointment for me, sire,' added Morgan. 'However, we can have Geoffrey lead the soldiers. That will increase their effectiveness, especially with Kane as well. We only need to knock the enemy off their horses. It's not like we actually need to kill them. Mores the pity.'

'A good plan, but just one change,' said Arthur. 'I want Geoffrey and Kane on horses with the knights.'

'I'm not sure about that, sire,' countered Morgan. 'Geoffrey's okay on a horse, but nothing compared to his skill on foot.'

'It's a distraction,' said Arthur. 'Our foes will be so wary of what Geoffrey might do on a horse, that they'll pay less attention to what I intend to do on the ground.'

'I'm intrigued,' said Marcus.

Lancelot rose from his seat. 'Woah, hold on. Don't tell me, you're going to lead the soldiers personally. You know you can't just cut people in half with Excalibur, it's against the tournament rules. And you'd be mad to lead a group of foot soldiers against mounted knights without your sword.'

Arthur grinned in reply to his friend. 'You're right, I would be mad to do that. That's why you'll be leading the soldiers. I'll just be there to help out a bit. Come on, walk with me and I'll show you my plan.'

The two armies lined up on the field at opposite ends. One large group of mounted knights followed Gallow. On the other side, two groups formed up. Lord Bane led their group of knights, with Geoffrey and Kane among them. Lancelot stood with Arthur and their smaller group of soldiers, with Morgan and Marcus bringing up the rear. Both sides were armed with training weapons. Only Arthur, as king, still had his sword strapped to his belt, though as he looked at the opposing knights on their war horses, he figured those blunted swords were backed with plenty of muscle.

'I hope you're right about this,' whispered Lancelot.

The Master of Ceremonies called out from the royal stand and introduced the two sides, then Lady Anne dropped a silk scarf to start the battle.

Gallow's forces immediately split into two, and most of the knights charged at full gallop towards Arthur and his group. As the foe thundered towards them, Arthur called to Lancelot. 'Told you they would go for the weaker group first, especially if I'm in it.'

'That gives me so much comfort,' Lancelot shouted back as nearly four score knights bore down upon them.

While Bane and his knights charged through the smaller group of Gallow's knights and quickly unseated them as expected, Lancelot held up his hand. Arthur's group remained where they were as the majority of Gallow's forces thundered towards them. Then, at the last instant, Lancelot dropped to the ground and his soldiers followed. Just as the first knights rode into them, Lancelot and the soldiers all rose from the ground and brought up lances with them.

Concealed in the grass before the battle, the blunted lances were dug into the ground at their rear. They then angled them up towards the charging knights at the last instant. But unlike the long spears used by pikemen, they did not aim for the horses but instead for the knights themselves.

Many of the soldiers were thrown to the ground as the horses crashed through their ranks, but every soldier unseated an enemy knight. By the time Gallow's forces had ridden through them, nearly half his knights were down.

Before Gallow could recover, Bane's knights rode through his ranks. More knights were unseated, and the remainder of each army manoeuvred to regroup.

Arthur scanned around him quickly. Of their company, about twenty soldiers were down, Morgan and Marcus among them. When Arthur sent him a quizzical look, Morgan just shrugged and winked in return.

'Just a precaution,' Morgan said quietly across the space between them. 'We get to keep an eye on things better from down here, undisturbed by the enemy. Nae reason you should be the only one to bend the rules a little.'

Arthur saw another twenty soldiers remained standing and behind them, nearly forty knights were still on their horses. Lord Gallow however, had lost over half his force. He still had more knights but fewer fighters overall.

'Let's force his hand. Keep the soldiers on the lances,' Arthur called to Lancelot, then he walked over to Bane. 'Dismount all the knights. Now let's see if we can force Gallow into a ground fight. I don't think he'll want to ride through our lances again.'

Bane and his knights dismounted, Geoffrey and Kane among them. Across the field, Arthur saw Gallow and his knights do the same, with the last to dismount being Kay. Arthur held Kay's gaze for an instant and gave him a nod, one

110

fighter to another. Kay touched his forehead in return. Arthur knew Kay would not hold back, but was glad to see some respect had been shown, and hopefully his tentative alliance not lost for the future.

Arthur watched the opposing army organise themselves into attacking rows, then suddenly twenty of their knights split off and ran to the side of the field. 'What the hell are you doing?' Gallow called out. 'Get back here you cowards. It's just a boy with a training sword.'

'Yes, what are they doing?' Bane said to Arthur, as their group spread out in a line, giving themselves space for hand-to-hand combat. 'Surely they're not running away. After all, it's only a tournament fight.'

Before Arthur could answer, the running group stopped and reached down into the grass. When they rose, they had bows in their hands and right in the middle of the group was Jon, the tall wiry archer. He sighted on Arthur and his bowstring glowed bright red. Then he let an arrow fly. Jon's arrow was followed by many more from the rest of his group.

'Move,' shouted Bane and Lancelot at the same time. There was no cover at all in the field, so everyone just dived away from the flying arrows as best they could.

Arthur leapt sideways as the first flight of arrows crashed into them. Pain lanced through his shoulder as one arrow grazed him. Miraculously, no other arrows hit him, and he drew Excalibur as he rose from the ground.

'No sword can stop an army of arrows, not even a magical one,' called out Jon as he drew back his bow again. 'Your reign of weakness ends now.'

'No,' shouted Gallow charging into the group of archers. 'You'll not fight without honour in my name.'

Jon turned and fired at point blank range, his bowstring still blazing red. The arrow hit Gallow straight on and passed right through him and into the knight behind. Both men went down, but from the distance between them Arthur couldn't see if they were dead or not.

Kay crashed through the archers to reach his father, and Jon took aim again. Not knowing what else to do, Arthur threw Excalibur at Jon, willing it to fly through his skull and finish him there and then. His sword flew straighter than any had a right to, but it only succeeded in distracting Jon. He stepped aside and the sword flew into the archer behind him. Jon's arrow went loose and tore into Kay's shoulder, catching on his armour. The sheer force of the arrow, shot at close range, spun Kay around violently and took him to the ground.

Surveying his work, Jon calmly turned to face Arthur again. He drew another arrow and pulled back his bow. Arthur saw Lancelot and others racing towards Jon, desperately trying to reach him before he let the arrow loose. Time slowed down for Arthur, and he watched the magical red fire dripping from the bowstring as Jon reached the end of his pull. Not even time to duck, thought Arthur as he closed his eyes.

He heard the twang and an almost instant thud. Strange, thought Arthur, dying's not as painful as I imagined. Then, in the continued absence of pain, he cautiously opened an eye.

Jon had an arrow straight through his chest, with Morgan striding across the field with another notched in his bow. Marcus followed behind, also with a bow, watching Morgan's back as they walked through the enemy's rear guard. Blue fire consumed their bows, burning fiercely as they walked towards the archers. 'Anyone else want to have a go,' Morgan shouted at the remaining archers. As one, they laid down their bows, whilst Jon slowly fell to the ground, stone dead.

Not for the first time, Arthur patted himself down, still not believing his luck. 'How am I not hit?' he said to himself, then he looked around and saw the soldiers on the ground. Every one of them had at least one arrow in him, and there at the front was Bane with three.

'Oh,' said Arthur. 'Damn!'

He reached down to Bane's side and carefully turned him over. Arthur called out for help.

Bane grunted as blood dripped from his mouth. 'Never been hit by a single arrow my whole life, never mind three. Bloody well hurts,' he gasped as Lancelot arrived too.

'Lady Anne must be able to help, just hold on,' said Arthur desperately to them both. He looked around and saw her running across the field. Lancelot looked grim but said nothing.

'No need to hide it,' grunted Bane. 'I know there's no coming back from this.'

Lady Anne reached them and bent over Bane. She listened to his chest and looked up at Lancelot and Arthur. The tear glistening in her eye said it all.

'I can give you a few minutes, but that is all,' she said as she touched her hand to his chest. There was a delicate blue flicker, and Bane's ragged breath calmed.

'A few moments with my king and my son would be good. Thank you, Anne,' he said. The others stepped back as Lancelot and Arthur crouched closer.

'My last words will be for my son, but first a few for my king,' said Bane. 'I've watched you grow from a boy to a man, and I'm as proud of you as I am of my own son. You both fight for what is right and for those who need it. I believe you can unite this land in peace, Arthur, and I think that your trust of the goodwill in people is key. Never lose your faith in the virtue of mankind.'

Bane glanced across at Lady Anne treating the other injured, friend and foe alike. 'Or the incredible power and generosity in womenfolk either,' he added. 'Now, if I can request your leave, sire, let me speak with my son.'

Not knowing what to say, Arthur just nodded and stood up. Looking around, he didn't know what to do. As he walked about aimlessly trying to help the injured where he could, he saw Cador signalling to him. He was running across the field with a striking young woman in tow, desperately calling for Arthur's attention.

'My ward Guinevere,' said Cador, out of breath and keeping it short. 'She can heal.'

'Over here,' said Arthur. 'Lord Bane is dying. Can you help?'

Without a word, Guinevere sat down next to Bane and placed both hands on his chest. A powerful blue glow surrounded her hands as she muttered quietly. All the while she held her eyes tight shut. When she'd finished, she lifted her hands and opened her eyes. A brief flash of blue remained for an instant, then her eyes returned to their bright green colour. 'A helping hand for me to stand, if you please,' she said, and Lancelot quickly reached out to assist her.

She held his gaze as he helped her up. 'If you take care of your father well, he should survive this day. After that, nature will take its course, one way or the other. He's strong though, so I think he will live.'

Before Lancelot could feel relieved or even say thanks, Kay broke through their numbers. Still dripping with blood from his shoulder, he spoke quickly. 'Good lady, can you help my father?'

Lancelot lunged forward and shoved Kay hard in the chest. Despite Kay's larger size, he nearly fell over. 'You'll get nothing from us,' shouted Lancelot drawing his sword. 'Your father has caused too many deaths already.'

'You are wrong about that,' replied Kay, drawing his own sword in response, 'but I'll personally make it one more if you stand in my way.'

'Stop it now, both of you. I'll not leave anyone else to die if we can help,' said Arthur. 'Guinevere, please heal Lord Gallow if you can. Lancelot, care for your father. There's been enough death for today.'

Dawn broke and Arthur rose early again, still tired from the day before. He stretched as he thought about what lay ahead. He was due to announce which lords and knights would join him at his round table. Seven lords and eights knights, and of course, all of them looking to him as their king. Even after these four long years, it still didn't seem real.

There was a knock at his door and Arthur let them in. Despite the small size of his quarters, the division was clear. Lancelot and his father on one side, with Lord Gallow and his son on the other. Both older men were leaning on canes, but other than that looked surprisingly well. Merlin quietly slipped in behind them and shut the door.

Here we go again, thought Arthur, time to grow up some more. If I keep on going like this, I'll be an old man before I'm twenty.

'Lord Gallow, explain your actions,' commanded Arthur as confidently as he could muster. Gallow raised an eyebrow, and Arthur clarified. 'The actions where you tried to fix the tournament. Oh, and the two times you tried to have me killed.'

'Alright, I'll admit to the former,' Gallow said. 'Even though I believed you too young and weak for the throne, you do have a legendary sword and a powerful sorcerer on your side. You must admit I'd be bloody stupid not to try to tip the balance in my favour.'

'However, the attempts on your life were not my doing. I don't really care if you believe me or not, it's the truth.' Gallow turned and saw the doubt and accusation in Lancelot's face. 'Seriously, how stupid do you think I am? If he was truly weak and I won the tournament, then he would not deserve to be king and I could have made my claim. However, I did not succeed, so possibly Arthur is not as weak as I thought, and maybe he should be given a chance to lead. Trying to kill him does not really fulfil any purpose in my view, it would just lead to more fighting.'

'Glad you value Arthur's life so highly,' said Lancelot, but he quietened as Lord Bane placed a hand on his son's shoulder.

'Well, I've called you here for a reason,' said Arthur. 'This evening at the feast I will announce my choices for my round table.'

'You will have your work cut out trying to prove to me that it's going to work,' interrupted Gallow, 'even if you do place my son on it.'

'Yes, I agree,' said Arthur, 'it's going to be very hard work. Which is why you're on it too.'

'What!' said Gallow.

'You've got to be joking!' protested Lancelot. From behind him, Bane squeezed his son's shoulder more forcefully to quieten him down again.

'No jesting here,' said Arthur. 'I'm going to unite the land and have peace, and it starts now. The first four lords will be Bane, Gallow, Cador and Galahad. I want you two to pick one further lord each. Someone you trust with your life.' Arthur looked at Bane, then Gallow.

'Who will be the seventh lord?' asked Kay.

'Not a lord, but a lady,' replied Arthur. 'New times, new rules. Lady Anne will be the seventh.'

'Highly unusual,' said Gallow.

'But not unwarranted,' countered Arthur. 'There're many men from yesterday owing their lives to a woman, you included.'

Gallow shrugged, reluctantly conceding the point.

'For the knights, the first six will be Aurelius, Lancelot, Morgan, Marcus, Kane and you, Kay. Those not knighted, I will knight them this evening. Lancelot and Kay, I would like you both to decide and agree on the last two knights. I want you to work together on that,' said Arthur.

Arthur paced to the door and opened it. 'Now I request your leave. Talk to your people and prepare for tonight. We shall meet later in the afternoon to finalise the arrangements and choices. Thank you.'

Arthur closed the door after they left and slumped down in his chair. 'I'm glad that's over,' he said to himself.

'I expect you are,' said Merlin, making Arthur jump. 'Though you played it very well, so you should be pleased.'

'Blimey Merlin, even though I knew you were there, you still blended into the background.'

Merlin didn't comment, he just waited quietly for Arthur to continue.

'Hmm, my speech was ok, but the Lady is still out there. We had hoped she was exhausted after getting away from us on Cador's lands, but she still had enough power left for Jon's bow. And she certainly had enough influence to convince him to use it no matter the cost.'

'Yes, indeed. The Lady continues to exceed my expectations,' said Merlin. 'Still, she is not the only one. Guinevere's healing powers are extraordinary. I must say, I have not seen the likes of them before.'

'Well, I'm grateful for that at least,' said Arthur rising from his seat, 'and Lancelot seems to have taken a shine to her. Nice to see him lighten up occasionally, especially after the close call with his father.'

'Yes, your friend is rather serious most of the time,' replied Merlin, 'but with good reason, I fear. We may have taken Gallow from the Lady's grasp, but I am sure she will not stop. In her own way, she is every bit as determined as you.'

Arthur stopped pacing and looked at Merlin. 'I'm just hoping my round table will help. If I can unite the land and the lords, then there's no one to stand with her. Surely then, with you and Excalibur, we can defeat her?'

'Your round table is a noble idea,' said Merlin, placing a hand on Arthur's shoulder, 'and we will need this table of lords, lady and knights to stop our foes. But do not underestimate your own contribution. This is a brave new land you are creating today. Never doubt your importance within it.'

PART 3 – THE BORDER

CHAPTER 10

'Have you asked her yet,' shouted Arthur over the clash of metal as he parried a sharp blow from Lancelot's sword.

'You know I haven't,' replied Lancelot, stepping across the large table and following up with a stab of his dagger.

Arthur knocked the arm aside and gave Lancelot's standing leg a kick to unbalance him. 'Don't wait too long, or I might ask her myself.'

'No, you won't,' stated Lancelot, adjusting his weight to his other leg and pushing forward with a fresh assault. 'I know you're not interested, though heaven knows why. She's the kindest, smartest, most beautiful young woman in the land. As king, you could ask her out in courtship, and she would likely say yes.'

Arthur parried the blows easily with Excalibur. He held its full power in check, using just enough to assist his defence. That had been one of the toughest lessons to learn in the last two years. The sword was always willing to give its power, but Merlin had taught him how to control it better. Consequently, he could now use the sword in training as well as battle. 'The sword should never leave you,' Merlin had said, 'lest you need it for the unexpected.'

Arthur stepped aside, avoiding the edge of the table by inches. 'She's a fine lady and a good friend, but she's more like a sister to me. I've never looked at her with the same love that you do.'

Lancelot kept advancing relentlessly, but Arthur still repelled him easily. 'Not sure I can beat you when you have your sword,' said Lancelot, breathing more heavily as their fight progressed.

'Don't change the subject,' said Arthur. He pushed back with blows of his own, allowing just a little power to flow into Excalibur as he pressured Lancelot. Magical sparks flew as he took tiny splinters out of Lancelot's sword.

'Hey, that's cheating.' Lancelot struggled to deflect the blows, and he retreated right to the curved edge of the table.

'No such thing as cheating in a fight, only winning or losing. Isn't that what Morgan always teaches us?' said Arthur with a final push.

'Yup,' replied Lancelot. Then he dropped his sword and stepped off the table. Arthur's blow sailed over Lancelot's head, and Lancelot reached out with both hands as he fell. Gripping Arthur's belt, he brought him crashing down onto the table, whilst Lancelot himself landed with his feet on the floor.

Winded when he landed, Arthur slowly looked up to see Lancelot's dagger at his throat. 'Wow, did you just cheat?' Arthur smiled and held out his hand in congratulations. 'Well done my friend.'

Lancelot pulled him up, and Arthur brushed himself down. 'Don't think I've forgotten what we were talking about. Guinevere may not wait for you forever, you know.'

'I'd be more concerned about the kingdom and yourself, sire,' said Lancelot. 'A good king needs a good queen, and one day an heir.'

'Bloody hell, Lancelot. I'm only eighteen. Give me a chance.'

The door crashed open, and Lord Bane strode in, followed by Morgan. 'We have trouble at the northern border, sire,' Bane started, then he looked at the table. 'Have you two been fighting on the Round Table?' he asked incredulously.

Arthur looked back at the table and saw his sword

embedded in its dark oak, right up to the hilt. 'Well yes, we might have been practicing a little. Fighting in and on Small Spaces was the original lesson I believe.' He pulled Excalibur from the table.

'One of your lessons no doubt,' said Bane to Morgan. The small Celt grinned in reply but said nothing.

'Never mind. Under your rule, Arthur, we've worked hard to make things peaceful these last two years. Strong alliances have been formed and treaties signed. It's been so successful that we've not seen a single case of the Lady's influence this last six months. Sadly, I fear, that's all about to change.'

They sat at the Round Table and Bane started to explain. 'There's trouble brewing in the north. Lord Salfor of Berwick has been in skirmishes with some of the Celtic lords north of the border.'

'I thought the trade agreement with our friends in the north had been holding strong. Is that not true anymore?' questioned Arthur.

'Aye, it has held,' replied Morgan, 'but it appears it's not my brethren starting the trouble. From what we hear, Salfor has been plotting to extend his lands further north, all under the guise of keeping the peace.'

'A classic case of one lord's word against another you might think, sire,' added Bane. 'However, Lady Anne despatched a spy and the news was not good. Sightings of the Lady have been reported near Berwick and the Celtic lords are adamant they're just holding their ground, not looking for trouble.'

'Do you know these lords? Can we trust them?' Arthur asked Morgan.

'I don't know them all, but some I do. There's no way they're lying, not to Lady Anne's man. Most value our trust too much. And contrary to common belief, the Celtic lords quite like these peaceful times.'

'What did my aunt's spy find out from Salfor?' asked Arthur.

'What is actually going on in Berwick Castle?'

Bane shifted in his seat. 'Now that's where it gets trickier. No more daily reports are making it back down here. The last one was two days ago, and then nothing. Lady Anne keeps her network widespread and her reports flowing fast. If we hear nothing by tomorrow, then she strongly suspects there's a serious problem.'

'I still can't quite get used to it,' said Lancelot. 'She has information flowing into Camelot every day from all around England. It's outstanding.'

'Yes indeed. I hear Kay is quite a fan as well. Lady Anne has been teaching him much of what she knows, and his network is improving too. Between them both, it's very impressive the amount we know.'

'Huh,' uttered Lancelot as his face darkened. 'Arthur might have made him a member of the Round Table, but I still have my doubts about that family.'

'King Arthur,' Bane corrected.

Arthur dismissed the lack of title with a wave. 'If the Lady has found a new ally up north, then we need to do something. She's been too quiet these resent months, that's a long time to plan and build up to something big. Send out the signal to the lords and knights of the Round Table. I want everyone here by tomorrow morning. I'll lead the discussion on what we should do. In the meantime, I'm going to find Merlin.'

'Hello Arthur,' said Merlin, without looking up from his writing desk.

'Still don't know how you do that,' said Arthur, giving up on his attempted stealth and slumping down in his usual chair. 'I'm guessing you also know why I'm here?'

'Yes and no,' replied Merlin, finally glancing up at Arthur. 'I heard about Berwick, so I suspect I know the reason why you are here. However, I do not yet know what you want from me.'

Arthur smiled, well used to Merlin's unusual methods of discussion and assistance. 'First, I think we need to know what's really going on in Berwick and what Salfor is doing.'

'Yes, I agree that is a good first step, but unfortunately I know little more than Lady Anne's reports.'

Merlin held up his hand to stop Arthur's impending questions. 'Yes, the Lady is there. I can sense the influence of her magic. No, I cannot transport you there. That is still beyond my power. So yes, we must travel there in person, even though it is a long journey. Not just to see for ourselves but also for you to resolve the situation.'

'I think we'll need to take knights and soldiers with us, to be fully prepared for what we might meet,' added Arthur. 'It's at least a week's hard travel, so there'll be no quick way to send for reinforcements. I'll need to persuade the Round Table tomorrow that it's a good idea to bring those forces with me.'

'You will indeed,' agreed Merlin, 'and probably best if you also decide who stays here in Camelot. As they often say, do not put all your eggs in one basket.'

'Hmm, I thought of that too. Berwick could just be a distraction. If there are problems up north now, then there could be plans in place for more trouble down here very soon. The difficulty is, which trouble should I address myself? I can't be in two places at once.'

'You certainly cannot.' Merlin nodded in agreement. 'Well, not yet anyway. That is another trick I have not figured out as yet. Nonetheless, I do have one piece of simple advice for today. It will be best if we are all well rested for tomorrow. Whatever you decide, it will likely be a very long day.'

Arthur turned to leave, then stopped. 'I think I know how you sensed me approaching. Just like you've learned to detect the Lady's magic, and sense where she is in our land, maybe you can track the magic in my sword?'

Merlin smiled for the first time. 'No, my boy, you just walk too loudly.'

In the morning, the Round Table was assembled. Eleven of its sixteen members were present and taking their seats.

'No Galahad or Kane?' Arthur asked Cador.

'Galahad sent word that they couldn't make it, even though he's only thirty miles away. Problems on his land too it seems. We're waiting to hear exactly what.'

'We're sending someone to see what's going on, and find out how we can help,' remarked Lady Anne as she took her seat, the final one of the eleven to arrive. 'It wouldn't do to resolve our problems in the north but ignore any trouble on our own doorstep.'

'Thank you,' replied Arthur.

Next to Lord Gallow, his son Kay spoke up. 'There's one more piece of information I received this morning. Unfortunately, it's not good. We hear Salfor has been building a new castle on the northern side of our border. Somehow, he's kept that quiet and the construction hidden until now. Clearly that should be impossible, but then so is the magic Merlin uses. We can only presume the Lady has had a big hand in the castle's concealment.'

'Well, that would explain why she's been so quiet. That must have taken a vast amount of magical power to keep it hidden.' Not for the first time, Arthur wondered just how much power the Lady had, but he kept his concerns to himself. 'Where exactly is this new castle of Salfor's?'

'It's outside his lands, just across the river in Caledonia. Word from one of his captains is that it's there to protect the border, but the feeling from the Celts is that he's preparing to invade and seize their land. Either way, it's not looking good. Our Celtic allies are very unhappy.'

'We need to go to Berwick to see for ourselves, but we also need to keep Camelot secure,' said Arthur. 'I see no other option than to divide our forces. I propose I take five battalions north with Merlin, Lancelot, my uncle and Lord Bane. The other battalions remain here under Gallow and Kay's command. Galahad, Cador and the others can support them as needed. Lady Anne will stay too, she can run her networks best from here. She can also send help to Galahad if needed.'

'Thoughts?' said Arthur as he looked around the table.

'As much as it pains me to be separated from my husband and his dreadful snoring, I agree it's a good split of our people,' said Lady Anne with a straight face. 'The fact that I may get a peaceful night's sleep is a coincidental bonus.'

'Thank you for that public display of affection, my dear,' countered Aurelius, though his eyes betrayed his love for her gentle humour. 'Yes, a good split. With Merlin to tip the balance of power up north, it still leaves a lot of strength down here for the unexpected.'

There were nods from around the table, then Arthur turned to Morgan.

'Aye, I wondered when you'd get to me,' he said. 'Nae doubt you'd like my help with a few of the northern lords, and most likely you've something dangerous in mind.'

'I think you'd be disappointed if I didn't,' replied Arthur, and Morgan grinned back at him. 'We'll discuss the details later. You'll need to get Geoffrey and Marcus too.'

Arthur looked around one last time. 'Any final points before we get ready?'

Lancelot shifted uncomfortably in his seat.

'Go on, say it,' said Kay.

'Alright, I don't like leaving you and your father in charge of Camelot. I didn't like you at the tournament, I still don't like you now. And I certainly don't trust either of you.'

Kay started to rise, going for his sword, but his father laid a hand on his arm. 'Let me speak, then you two can decide to fight if you want,' said Lord Gallow. 'Over the last two years, I've seen how much Arthur has done for this land and its people. I know I was very sceptical, to say the least, but he has proven beyond doubt his right to be king, sword or no sword. His kindness has strength, his use of force shows intelligence, and his loyalty inspires everyone. I will stand by Arthur until the day I die, as will my son.'

Lancelot stared at Gallow and Kay, then slowly nodded. 'Alright, I'll hold you to that.'

Arthur took in his Round Table. It contained friends old and new, but maybe now they were more united than they'd ever been. 'Right, let's gather our forces. I want to be on the road by midday. We have a long journey ahead and an uncertain future to face. Let's ride out and push that future in the right direction.'

The stables were peaceful whilst the others had lunch, and Arthur enjoyed the quiet time brushing down Horse. As he moved around, she watched him from the corner of each eye, occasionally taking a bite of hay from the feeding rack.

'I know you're watching me,' said Arthur. Horse turned away, then turned back, faking a surprised neigh.

'Very funny,' Arthur laughed. 'I'm not a baby playing hide and peek you know.'

Horse went quiet and Arthur looked around.

'Why are you laughing?' asked Guinevere, smiling brightly as she walked towards the stable door.

'Oh, just something Lancelot said earlier,' replied Arthur, now thinking of his friend's love for this beautiful woman and his lack of courage to tell her fully how he felt.

'That's odd,' she said thoughtfully. 'He's very kind and brave, but he does not ever strike me as particularly funny.'

Arthur grinned. 'You might be surprised, there's humour in there somewhere. Buried under the armour, valour and good hair of course.'

Now Guinevere laughed, and Arthur could really see why Lancelot loved her so much. Not only was she smart, but joyful as well.

'Anyway,' he said. 'What are you doing here? We're setting off this afternoon and it's going to get very busy in here soon.'

'I'm coming with you,' she stated. 'Sir Kay told me of your plan, and I'm here to offer my services as your finest magical healer.'

'Whilst I appreciate your offer, I'm not sure it's the safest thing.'

'We must all do our part,' she replied simply. 'Besides, do you have a better diplomat than me? I've gained quite the skill over these last two years, persuading people who don't want our help to let us help them.'

'You make a good point as always,' Arthur conceded. 'Thank you, Guinevere, we'll be grateful to have you along.'

She smiled and turned away. At the door, she met Lancelot coming the other way, and she stopped to put a hand on his shoulder. She looked him in the eye and rose to give him a kiss on the cheek.

'What just happened,' said Lancelot very slowly, after she had gone.

'I guess she got tired of waiting for you. Smart lady that one,' said Arthur with a smile. 'Anyway, you'll have plenty of time to ask her on the way to Berwick. She's coming with us.'

CHAPTER 11

On the eighth day of their journey, Arthur called a halt, and they slowed their horses to a stop. Down the hill lay Berwick Castle, and there across the river at the top of the next hill, was indeed another castle. Although not quite finished, its walls already loomed tall over the landscape and its keep dominated the skyline.

Aurelius whistled in appreciation as they rested their horses, and the soldiers jumped down from the carts. 'Very impressive. Wouldn't want to storm that one.'

'Looks like we have our answer already, sire,' said Bane. 'Salfor is clearly building across the border on Celtic land. He must be preparing to invade.'

'I don't want to jump to conclusions just yet. Berwick Castle lies open below. They certainly don't look like they're getting ready for war. Let's go take a closer look.'

'But carefully, yes?' added Lancelot.

'In this case, I'd very much agree with you, my friend. You and your father take two battalions to the west and the rest of us will approach the main gates from the east. Keep Guinevere with you and out of harm's way until we know what's going on. If we receive a friendly welcome, then we'll go inside with half our soldiers. The rest can hold outside the gates, just out of archer range.'

'And that lone arrow heading for you, young sire? You know, as you approach this castle we're so unsure about,' remarked Aurelius. 'Maybe you should also wait outside too?'

'I can take care of the occasional arrow,' stated Merlin.

'Good. Let's ride to the castle,' Arthur commanded. The soldiers climbed back on the carts and they spurred their horses down the hill.

Halfway down, they split into two groups, and Arthur approached Berwick Castle from the east. Its granite walls were weathered, but rose high before them and showed no signs of weakness. The main gate, however, was open and the portcullis up, no guards in sight. Arthur's group split up and one half rode through the gates, cautiously scanning the walls and courtyard as they entered.

They approached the central keep, and a knight appeared in the doorway. He waited impatiently until they got closer. 'You lot took your time. What the hell kept you?'

Aurelius started to speak, but Arthur held up a hand. 'Trouble with some roving Celts. You know how it is nowadays.'

'Bloody pain is what they are. Get in here now,' replied the knight, then he turned and disappeared back inside.

Arthur signalled for them to dismount and called Merlin over to join them. 'I'm pretty sure they don't know who we are,' he whispered. 'If we play this right, we'll learn more in the next few minutes than we would in days. Aurelius chose twenty soldiers and I'll meet you by the door. Merlin, you stay here with the rest. You would be too much of a giveaway.'

'I cannot help you, if I am not there,' observed Merlin.

'I know, but I think it's worth the risk,' replied Arthur. 'Wait here, and if trouble starts outside, make lots of noise and we'll come running.'

Merlin found a bench to sit down on. 'I shall wait here peacefully until the trouble begins,' he said firmly.

Arthur walked over to the entrance of the keep and met Aurelius by its large, fortified doors. 'Nice and subtle, ok? Let me do the talking and don't start any trouble unless we have to.'

'Not my strong point, but I'll follow your lead,' replied Aurelius. 'If it's not going well though, just give me a signal and I'll create a distraction to get us out.'

Arthur nodded and pushed open the doors.

Inside, they saw the keep was well maintained. The corridors they passed through were clear of dirt or obstruction, and what rooms they could see into were tidy and fit for purpose. Everything was normal for a working keep, except the eerie silence and apparent emptiness. Finally, when they passed an armoury, they saw a small squire. He was busy at work cleaning the swords, one by one.

Arthur stopped and held up his hand to the others. He ducked through the doorway and coughed to get the squire's attention. The squire nearly dropped the sword he was polishing in surprise.

'Hello boy, what's your name,' said Arthur.

'Err, Bedivere,' replied the squire quietly, then quickly adding. 'Sir.'

'Well, young Bedivere, we're the reinforcements,' said Arthur taking a gamble, 'and looks like we got here just in time. Hardly anyone left at the castle to guard it.'

'Err, it's Bevs, sir,' replied the squire.

'Pardon?'

'It's just that most people call me Bevs.'

'Not sure we've got time for this, sire,' interjected Aurelius.

But Arthur hushed him and waited patiently. Bedivere began to talk. 'Almost everyone is in Hillcastle getting ready to advance on the Celts, sir. They left me here because of my leg, so I thought I'd just check the last few weapons. Our knight is in the hall having dinner with his company, waiting for you before he leaves.'

'Thank you, young man,' said Arthur turning to leave. 'We

best go relieve them right now.'

Arthur led Aurelius out and Bedivere quietly watched them go. Once they were out of earshot, Arthur turned to Aurelius. 'Looks like our fears were well founded. If Salfor invades the Celts, our treaties will be torn up and much of the north will be plunged back into war. We need to stop this now, no more time to be subtle.'

'No argument from me, but you'll have a tough time of it,' replied Aurelius. 'We might take this castle, but even with it under our control, that new one at the top of the hill is a different matter. We don't have the forces for that, it's in a perfect defensive position, sire.'

'One problem at a time, my dear uncle,' said Arthur. 'Let's deal with this keep first. Suggestions?'

'Huh, you're the one who's been learning about fighting in confined spaces.' Aurelius turned to their soldiers. 'We have surprise on our side. We storm in with swords and bows drawn, then force them to surrender. Simple and quick. You four with Arthur and me, then the rest of you fan out into the room. They're eating in the hall, so there's likely tables. If they don't surrender and you spot archers, turn the tables over and use them as cover.'

They approached the end of the corridor and could hear noises from the hall. The sound of talking and laughing drifted towards them. Arthur counted down silently with his fingers, then they burst into the hall. 'Surrender or face the consequences,' shouted Aurelius.

The opposing soldiers were all facing the door with their swords and bows drawn, not a scrap of food on the tables. 'Down,' shouted Arthur as a volley of arrows sped towards them. Aurelius kicked over a table and they took cover behind it. Several of their soldiers joining them.

'Looks like they weren't fooled at all,' growled Aurelius. 'Now what?'

'Distraction time. Cover me.' Without waiting for a reply, Arthur ran towards the other side of the hall with its fireplace, while his soldiers let loose a volley of arrows to provide cover. Leaping across a table in front of the fire, he dragged it over with him and arrows thudded into it as he landed on the other side.

That was a bit too close, he thought. Arthur looked around and saw the ornamental drapes on either side of the fireplace. He tore down the drapes and threw them into the fire. When one caught alight, he skewered the burning cloth with Excalibur and pulled it back out of the fire. He waited until it was blazing fiercely, then he pulled power into his sword. The drape blazed hotter still, and he threw it high across the hall, right onto the table in front of the enemy. Immediately, he followed suit with the second drape. By the time Arthur glanced over the top of the table, half the hall was alight with flames.

The opposing soldiers began to flee through a rear door in the hall and Aurelius came running over. 'A bit too much distraction?' said Arthur.

'Maybe a bit. Let's get out of here.'

Their troops were already streaming out the main door, but the burning tables cut Arthur and Aurelius off. 'There, out the side door,' said Arthur, pointing to their left. But before they could leave, a small figure stepped into the doorway, sword drawn and blocking their exit.

The young squire stood in their way. 'I can't let you leave. I won't let you help the Celts take our land.'

'So, they told you who we are?' said Aurelius. 'Nice trap you laid for us.'

'No, they don't tell me anything,' replied Bedivere, 'but you called him sire in the armoury, and there's only one young man called sire in this country. Unfortunately, you're not as noble as people think, are you King Arthur?'

Arthur turned to Aurelius. 'No time?'

'No time,' Aurelius agreed.

'Sorry young man, but this is going to hurt.' Arthur swung Excalibur straight at the boy's head. Bedivere raised his sword to block the blow, his movement a perfectly timed defence, but Arthur's sword cut right through it. Even as Excalibur sped towards his head, Bedivere did not look away, just followed its path perfectly. Then, at the last instant, Arthur turned his sword flat and knocked the young squire out.

As the eves crashed down in flames, Arthur grabbed Bedivere round the waist and hoisted him over his shoulder. 'Let's go,' he shouted to Aurelius as he ran for the exit.

Merlin watched the keep burn, the flames reflecting in his pale eyes. Arthur and Aurelius burst out of the main doors, fire erupting behind them. They staggered forward then collapsed to the ground coughing, a small form dropping by Arthur's side.

'I believe they might like a little water. Would you be so kind as to fetch some,' Merlin said to a soldier standing next to him, then he rose and walked over to his young king.

'You found the trouble you were looking for then,' said Merlin, more of a statement than a question as usual.

Arthur coughed until the soldier brought over the water. He gulped it down, then poured some over Bedivere's head. The young squire spluttered and sat up. Arthur handed him the rest of the water.

'And who might this be?' enquired Merlin.

'A rather brave and stubborn squire,' said Arthur.

'Ha, never seen one of those before have we,' muttered Aurelius, before he wandered off to account for their soldiers and organise a search of the castle.

Bedivere looked around as he finished the water. 'Why am I still alive?' he asked. 'I don't actually know anything, so you can't even torture information out of me.'

'Contrary to what you may have been told, I don't torture and kill innocent people,' replied Arthur. 'I'm here to restore the peace. We have treaties with our friends in the north. The Celts are not about to take your lands, it's more like your Lord is meaning to take theirs.'

'How do I know you're telling the truth?' said Bedivere.

'By my actions,' answered Arthur. 'I could easily have killed you in the keep. No one but Aurelius and me would have known. But I saved your life instead.'

'Ok,' replied the young squire after thinking it through. 'So now what? I can't go back to my knight.'

'Then you need another knight,' said Arthur. 'You're smart, and good with a sword, and I am in need of a squire today. How would you like to be my squire young Bedivere?'

The boy thought again and then answered. 'Just one condition.'

'Brave indeed,' said Merlin, still observing from the side.

'And what would that be?' asked Arthur.

'Call me Bevs.'

'Well, young Bevs, you have a deal,' said Arthur smiling. 'Now go show some of our soldiers where the kitchen is. Everyone must be hungry by now, and no doubt you are too.'

'Sorry, sire, but you burnt the castle kitchen down,' said Bevs looking at the still smouldering keep, 'but I suppose there's the stable hand's larder. That might do.' He stood up and limped off towards the nearest group of soldiers.

Merlin raised an eyebrow. 'An interesting young man you have acquired there, Arthur.'

'For sure. Now let's get the rest of us into the castle. We have a lot to do.'

The stone walls of the keep were still standing but its insides were burnt to ashes, so Arthur gathered people in the stables to discuss their plans and get some food.

'Not a lot of options, I would say,' said Bane. 'This castle is defensible for a day or two, but we have no supplies for a siege or anywhere to safely sleep all our troops. Hillcastle isn't quite finished, but it's already impregnable to us. We have no siege weapons and too small an army. The only option I can see, is to retreat south for now and send word for more forces.'

'There's also the small matter of how they knew we were coming,' added Lancelot. 'And also, why they didn't leave a larger force here in Berwick Castle? It was far too easy to take this place.'

'You may have a spy on the Round Table,' commented Merlin. 'As to why they did not defend this castle more heavily, I cannot say.'

Arthur finished wiping the soot from his face. 'I wouldn't say it was totally easy, but I take your point, this castle was weakly defended.'

'They could have just wanted to delay us,' said Bane. 'Maybe Hillcastle is not as ready as it looks, or they really are waiting for reinforcements to their army.'

'It's all a bit odd if you ask me.' Arthur rubbed his temples. 'A single day's delay just doesn't seem worth it. I think there's something we're missing, but I don't know what. And the possibility of a spy on the Round Table troubles me a lot. I want to have more of a think about our options.'

'Not much we can do until morning anyway,' stated Aurelius with some finality. 'Too tired to travel and too dark to attack anything.'

'There is one more option,' added Guinevere, breaking her silent observation. 'You could always try diplomacy. Lord Salfor might not be all he seems. Maybe the Lady's influence over him is not the only aspect at play here. If so, could he be reasoned with? As Arthur intimates, quite possibly we do not understand the full picture.'

'Building a bloody great castle on Celtic land seems pretty straightforward to me,' said Aurelius. 'Not much room for misunderstanding there.'

'Well, there's definitely something we're not seeing, so maybe Guinevere has a point,' said Arthur. 'Let's post some guards and get some rest. We'll see what opportunities tomorrow brings.'

CHAPTER 12

Arthur awoke with someone shaking his shoulder. A single candle illuminated the gloom. The candle moved and a face appeared.

'I was right. Lord Salfor is having doubts about the Lady's influence,' said Guinevere. 'If we go now, he has agreed to meet you in secret.'

'Humph, what?' said Arthur.

'A friend got me a message from Salfor,' explained Guinevere. 'He doesn't want to fight with you or the Round Table. But he'll only meet you, he's too worried about the Lady finding out. He confirmed what we suspected; you have a spy in your midst.'

Arthur rose quickly and started to get ready, picking up Excalibur as he did. 'Can you trust your friend?' he said. 'A secret meeting alone sounds very risky, even to me.'

'I trust them with my life. They want this resolved just as much as we do. I think we can get this whole mess sorted out tonight.'

'Ok,' said Arthur as he finished getting dressed in light armour. 'Where do we meet Salfor?'

'Either castle is too risky, so he suggested on top of the hill by the edge of the woods. I would agree it's a good place. There's plenty of cover to hide us from Hillcastle and with only the river to the south, we should be unseen. There's a bridge near there we can use to cross quickly.'

'No guards on the bridge?' asked Arthur.

'No. Hillcastle is their strong point. They don't seem to care about the bridge.'

'Right, let's get going then.'

They made their way out of the castle on foot, deliberately avoiding the noise their horses would make. As they crossed the bridge over the river, all was quiet, as Guinevere had predicted. Even the footpath up the hill on the other side was deserted. Arthur began to feel more at ease when he saw a lone figure in the moonlight. The man was standing by the edge of the woods, just a few paces away from the cliff top.

Arthur approached and held out his arm in greeting, the other hand resting on Excalibur. 'Lord Salfor?'

'That I am,' replied Salfor with an accent from the middle lands. He took Arthur's arm in return. 'Welcome to Caledonia.'

'Not sure we've had a great welcome,' said Arthur. 'Your soldiers tried to kill us a few hours ago. What's going on?'

But Salfor didn't seem to hear. 'I've spent the last six years preparing for this moment. When I started out, you were but a boy yet to be crowned. No one knew how much you could do. Meanwhile, up here in the north, the Celts were pushing harder and harder at our borders.'

'So, we started to build Hillcastle and slowly gather an army. Two things to bring order to our land. With the help of the Lady Morganna, I kept the Celts at bay and the construction of this new castle hidden. And now Hillcastle is nearly finished, ready to dominate the north and protect our lands.'

Arthur held his breath for an instant as he heard the name of the Lady for the first time, and he felt Guinevere's hand tighten on his arm as she paused too. But Salfor didn't even notice and just continued, lost in his reverie.

'Despite all that, things have not turned out as I expected. You see, now there's you, Arthur. Not so young, not so weak. Making successful treaties with the north. Maybe even able to unite our land in peace after all.'

'And me, I'm just old and tired. Not really in charge of my own lands anymore, just looking for an end to it all. Looking for someone to take care of the people.'

Salfor concentrated on Arthur, as if seeing him properly for the first time. 'I don't want to fight you. Take Berwick Castle if you wish, and Hillcastle too. Just promise me one thing, don't listen to Morganna should she find her way into your court. Nothing good lies down that road.'

Not knowing quite what to say, Arthur turned as he felt Guinevere's hand tug a little more on his arm.

'Times are certainly difficult,' she said to them both. 'Lord Salfor, with your leave may I speak with Arthur alone for a moment.'

Salfor absentmindedly waved her away, then turned towards the wood, lost in his own thoughts once more.

Guinevere led Arthur out of earshot. 'I'm not really sure how much use he can be,' she said. 'He's just a tired old man, no good to me now.'

'This has got to be a good sign though,' replied Arthur. 'He doesn't want to fight. Even if he can only persuade some of his troops to stand down, then we're halfway there. With your diplomacy skills, I'm sure we can win out with his people. Then we can preserve our treaties with the Celts and prevent more fighting.'

'Aargh,' shouted Guinevere in frustration. 'Why are you always so short sighted? Can't you see how dangerous the Celts are? Why are you never prepared for the next threat?'

'Pardon,' stammered Arthur, not quite believing what he'd just heard.

'You don't ever really control what you have, and you don't even know it,' Guinevere continued, her eyes blazing red in the darkness. 'Camelot could rule the south and Hillcastle the north, but you just don't see it do you. Together, we could have built the strongest kingdom in the land. You can win the hardest battles and I can persuade almost anyone to my way. I could even turn Lancelot's eye. But yours, oh no, yours won't be turned.'

Guinevere advanced on Arthur and her hands ignited with red flames. 'Not just a stupid boy,' she shouted in anger above the roar of the blazing magic, 'but a short-sighted senseless man too. You could have wielded Excalibur with me. We could have ruled the land together. But now I think I'll just have to do it all myself.'

Arthur drew his sword as she advanced on him, the raw magic now pouring unchecked from her hands. He felt Excalibur erupt in silent screams as she reached for it.

No Merlin, no army, no friends, thought Arthur, even my sword is terrified. So, he did the only thing he could think of, and he threw himself off the edge of the cliff. The last thing he saw as he fell was a tremendous explosion of red fire on the cliff top, then as the fire reached down for him, he hit the bottom and it all went black.

It was cold. Arthur opened his eyes and saw nothing but darkness. Then slowly a face appeared in the gloom, and finally the figure of a small girl. That's odd, thought Arthur, why's she swimming.

Arthur opened his mouth to speak, but the girl darted towards him and quickly put her hand over his mouth. 'Best if you don't talk,' she said brightly, 'you're not made for the water.'

Then Arthur realised it was cold, dark and wet. The sudden dread hit him that he was in the fast-flowing river and about to drown.

'Don't worry, you might not be made for the water, but I am.' She took hold of his arm and pulled him upwards. Just as Arthur thought he couldn't hold his breath anymore; they broke the surface and the girl dragged him over to the riverbank.

Arthur crawled weakly from the river, coughing water. 'Thank you,' he spluttered to the young girl standing calmly in the shallows.

'You are always welcome, Arthur,' she replied.

He patted himself down, then looked around in panic.

'Honestly silly,' sighed the girl, 'I think you would lose your own head if it wasn't sown onto your body.' She pointed to her left and Excalibur rose from the river's surface.

Arthur waded back in and grabbed hold of the sword by its hilt. It was warm in his hand, and its silent screaming now replaced by a feeling of comfort, a feeling echoed in his own heart. As he held the sword, and his strength began to return.

'Thank you again, young Lady of the Lake,' said Arthur gratefully, finally recognising the young girl from the garden in Gallow's castle from that last night of his tournament two years ago.

'Hope you don't mind us being here,' she said, splashing through the shallows. 'The Lake and I have always wanted to travel, but we've never known where to go. When we saw you were here in the river, we couldn't resist visiting. We like you a lot. You're true and honest, but also a little bit silly. It's always so much fun when you're around.'

She looked at him and waited. Arthur rewound the conversation in his head. 'Oh, of course I don't mind,' he said, after figuring out what she was waiting for. 'You're always welcome to travel any of the waterways in our land.'

She smiled back at him with a huge grin, then started playing with a stick, gently poking at the weeds, trying to push them back against the flow of the river.

'Err, is the Lake with you too?' Arthur asked, thinking there was something left unsaid, but not really knowing what it was.

'Of course. We always go everywhere together,' she replied. 'Does your hair follow you wherever you go?'

'Erm, yes,' replied Arthur, not seeing the connection at all.

'There you go then,' she said, bringing the matter to a close. 'We'll have to go soon though. The river is a bit fast, and it's really difficult to stay in one place.'

'Just one more question,' said Arthur quickly. 'Am I dreaming again.'

'No,' she answered simply. 'What a funny question.'

'But I was dreaming the last time I met you.'

'No, you weren't. You were just asleep in one place and awake in another. It's very useful to be in two places at once sometimes. Your friend over there should know that.' She pointed behind Arthur. 'When he's standing in the right place that is.'

He turned around quickly, but all he could see were the walls of Berwick Castle in the distance. 'Which friend?' he asked, but when he turned back, the young girl was gone.

Arthur trudged back to Berwick Castle. Power from Excalibur gently flowed into him, and he felt it refresh his body, but his mind was racing with all he had seen. Approaching the castle, the lookouts called out. He held Excalibur up and it glowed blue in the dark night, letting the soldiers know who he was.

The gates opened, and Lancelot ran out to meet him with a full company of soldiers. 'Are you ok, sire?' he asked. 'And are you mad?' He punched Arthur on the shoulder. 'You can't go out alone. What if Salfor's soldiers had caught you?'

'I wasn't alone,' said Arthur. 'Guinevere was with me.'

'What, where is she? Did Salfor capture her? We have to get her back.'

Arthur held up his hand as they walked back through the gates. 'Go get the others.'

'But we must…' started Lancelot.

'Now,' said Arthur firmly. 'I'll meet you in the stables.'

Arthur ruffled Horse's mane absentmindedly while the others arrived. The soft hair and the warm neck of his horse comforting him, calming his mind a little and focusing his thoughts. He waited until everyone was present and the doors closed, then he turned to face them all.

'I'm pretty sure Lord Salfor is dead,' he started.

'Well good,' stated Aurelius. 'That's one less problem.'

'But how can he be dead if he captured Guinevere?' asked Lancelot.

'He didn't take her. It's more like she killed him,' replied Arthur.

'But she's a healer,' said Bane. 'How could she kill him?'

'She's not just a healer, she is the Lady,' stated Arthur.

'What, that can't be right,' said Lancelot. 'I don't believe it.'

'Do you doubt my word?' demanded Arthur, his voice unusually raised, and a little anger flashing across his eyes.

Lancelot looked at his friend. 'No, never,' he said, after what seemed like an eternity. 'I just don't want to believe it.'

'I'm sorry.' Arthur's voice softened. 'I scarcely believe it myself, especially after all the times she's helped us, but I saw it with my own eyes. She raged about controlling the land, and her hands were on fire with raw magic. She reached for Excalibur and the sword was…' He paused for a second. 'Well, it was terrified of her is the only way I can describe it. She was just so powerful. I think it would take an entire army to stop her.'

'That's certainly it then, sire,' said Bane. 'We must start our return to Camelot immediately and raise our armies. We must fight the Lady with everything we have. That's the only way to give ourselves the best chance of victory.'

'No,' said Arthur. 'I'll not leave this mess here in the north, not even for a day. We must make a stand and fight for the land and its people. Both for ours and the Celts. If we leave her here, she'll take it all.'

Bane shifted a little uncomfortably. 'The least we can do is send word back to Camelot, sire. They need to know who the Lady is.'

'But what if Gallow and Kay are still in league with her? What if they're actually the ones controlling Guinevere and making her act as the Lady?' protested Lancelot. 'We'll be giving away what we know.'

'I'm sorry Lancelot, but I believe my judgement on this is correct,' said Arthur. 'Lord Bane, pick the fastest horse and the lightest person, and send them to Camelot with our message.'

'The fastest horse over that distance would be yours.'

'Ok, our second fastest horse then,' said Arthur, correcting himself. 'I think we'll need Horse for the battle ahead. Apart from anything else, her touch might help heal some of the casualties we take.' No one added the obvious, that Guinevere was not with them any more to do the healing.

'In the meantime, we need to stop the Lady's power from spreading further up here,' stated Arthur.

'I'm all for acts of courage,' said Aurelius, 'but not acts of suicide. From what you've said, she's too powerful. We can't win this one.'

'There's still a few hours until dawn. Time for us to come up with something. I think we just need to find a way to take Hillcastle, then the Lady's power in the north will be drastically cut.'

'Ok, just storm the impregnable castle, on top of a cliff, defended by an invincible sorceress,' said Aurelius. 'I'll just go and prepare the soldiers. I'm sure they'll be delighted.'

'An excellent idea,' said Merlin, patting Aurelius on the back. 'Get your troops ready. Arthur and I will have a plan for you by sunrise.'

After the others had left, Arthur joined Merlin and they sat on the hay bales. 'Aurelius does have a point you know. I've no idea how to defeat Guinevere, I mean Lady Morganna.'

'What did you say?' asked Merlin, rising out of deep thought.

'I said, I've no idea,' started Arthur.

'No, the name,' interrupted Merlin.

'Morganna. I think that's what Salfor called her,' said Arthur. 'Does it matter? It's probably as false as Guinevere.'

'Maybe or maybe not, but I am sure I know that name from somewhere,' replied Merlin. 'For the life of me though, I cannot place it right now. Something to research when we return to Camelot.'

'That reminds me,' interrupted Arthur. 'The Lady of the Lake told me you know about being in two places at once. Could you send half of yourself to Camelot to warn the others?'

'Unfortunately, that is one type of magic I still cannot perform. Not that I have not tried many a time, but something about it still eludes me. No doubt it would be very useful right now.'

'Well, to be exact, she said you should know about it,' lamented Arthur. 'I guess she didn't actually say that you could do it. There was something else as well. Something about standing in the right place.'

Merlin stared into space, then his eyes flashed with blue. 'My goodness, that might be the very thing I have been missing. I think your dream friend is onto something there. Give me two hours and we shall have our plan. That mission you sent Morgan on, will he accomplish all that you asked of him?'

'No idea,' replied Arthur, 'but I trust him to get it done or die trying.'

'Then that will have to do,' said Merlin. 'You can gather the soldiers and start getting them ready. It will be best if we advance at dawn.'

Arthur summoned the others back to the stables just before sunrise. A small table had been laid out and two rocks placed on it. With them was a length of rope, a piece of string, and various scatterings of stones.

'Let me guess,' said Aurelius. 'The two castles, the river, the bridge and all the woods. Correct?'

'Exactly. And here,' replied Arthur, placing two more sticks on either side of Hillcastle, 'are our armies.'

'Armies?' questioned Bane, emphasising the plural.

'Yes, I've just heard. Morgan has succeeded in rousing the local Celtic lords into joining him, and they're bringing an army to support us,' said Arthur. 'And more importantly, they have some siege weapons. We now have catapults and battering rams.'

'I like our odds a little better now,' said Aurelius. 'Not great, but less than disastrous.'

'How about some of the Celts attack the south side of the castle with their ballista, then we join the rest with their battering rams to storm the main gate in the north?' suggested Bane. 'That gives them two fronts to worry about and cover with their archers. Divides their firepower effectively in two.'

'We can use shield formations to counter the arrows reasonably well,' added Lancelot, 'but we'll still be very vulnerable to burning tar.'

'I can counter that,' said Merlin.

'You can't help with both attacks at the same time,' said Lancelot.

'Well, young sir, that is where you are mistaken,' said Merlin. He concentrated and muttered under his breath. He appeared to shimmer in the early light from the windows and then he disappeared completely.

'Bloody hell, he can travel like the Lady,' said Aurelius.

146

'Not quite,' said Merlin from the far side of the room. They looked over and saw him standing in the corner.

'Indeed,' said Merlin from behind them. They spun round and saw a second Merlin, completely identical, standing behind them on the opposite side of the room.

'Amazing,' said Lancelot. 'Now we have two sorcerers. That should even up the odds a bit.'

'Do not celebrate too much just yet,' said Merlin. 'There are a couple of drawbacks. Firstly, there is an element of luck in how evenly we split our power.'

'Indeed,' added the second Merlin, as he began to fade away to nothing. 'One of us might not last long enough to complete the task at hand.' Then he shimmered out of existence, and there was just one Merlin standing before them. 'So you see, I can help both sides of the attack because I can separate myself in two, but I do not know for how long we will be useful.'

'What's the second drawback?' asked Lancelot.

'That one is a little more difficult,' answered Merlin. 'I must be in the middle of the two places where I wish to split myself to. So, I am very much afraid for our plan to work, you need to get me into the centre of Hillcastle.'

'Ha, back to the impossible,' growled Aurelius, then it dawned on him and he looked at Arthur. 'And no doubt you'd like my help.'

'Of course,' grinned Arthur, 'and I've got just the plan to get us inside.'

147

CHAPTER 13

'You're not serious, are you? You want us to get in the river dressed in armour?' asked Lancelot as they stood looking at the fast-flowing waters. Aurelius looked equally disturbed but said nothing. Merlin and Bevs just waited.

'Yup,' said Arthur. 'Step in and have some faith in me.'

They wadded into the icy waters and looked around.

'I think I might be with Lancelot on this one,' said Aurelius. 'Bit on the mad plan side, even for you.'

'I agree too,' said a small voice to the side of them, 'but then Arthur always is a bit silly.'

They turned around and saw the young girl. The river rushed past her as she calmly walked towards them, her long hair not quite touching the water.

'Are you going to introduce us,' she said to Arthur. 'I'd like to meet your friends. Especially if they're as funny as you.'

'Lancelot, Aurelius and Merlin. Not particularly known for their humour,' said Arthur, receiving a grunt from Aurelius. 'And this is Bevs, our newest friend. He's going to guide us around Hillcastle.'

'He's very brave then,' she replied. 'It's really dangerous in there.'

'Oh good,' added Aurelius, as Bevs turned a little red.

'And this is the Lady of the Lake,' Arthur said to the rest. 'She tends to speak her mind. Usually whatever's on it at the time.'

'How do you know it's dangerous in there? Have you been

inside Hillcastle?' Lancelot asked the girl, a little suspicion creeping into his voice.

'The water feels wrong,' she said simply, not seeming to notice the accusation in his tone. 'I don't like it in there. Sorry Arthur, but I don't want to stay in the castle after I take you there. I hope you don't mind too much.'

'That's ok young lady. I'm very grateful for any help you can give us. And don't worry, we'll make our own way back out.'

The young girl smiled broadly at Arthur and walked closer to them.

'Hold on. What do you mean, take us there?' asked Lancelot.

'Great question, wrong time,' replied Arthur. 'You might want to hold your breath.' Before anyone could say another word, they were dragged under the water.

Arthur emerged onto the cold stone and coughed out water. He stood up and scanned the room. Sounds of running water came from one wall, but thankfully all else was quiet and they were the only people in the small room. Most of the others were still on the floor, all except Merlin who stood calmly beside him. The only wrinkle to his image was his soaking wet robes.

'As always, Arthur, you make the very best of friends,' said Merlin in perfect seriousness. 'I could not have done a better job myself. Well, to be completely correct, I could not have done that job at all.'

'Ugh,' coughed Aurelius as he spat out more water. 'I never want to do that again. And what the hell is that smell?'

'We're in the guards' restroom in the dungeons,' said Bevs, 'right in the middle of the castle.'

'Perfect,' said Merlin, ignoring the obvious answer to where the smell came from.

'So, what now?' asked Lancelot.

'Our positioning has turned out better than expected, so I can separate from here,' said Merlin. 'I do not need you to escort me through the castle after all.'

'But you might like us to open the main gates for our forces coming from the north?' ventured Arthur.

'Now that would be very useful,' replied Merlin. Then he shimmered for an instant and disappeared.

'Ok Bevs,' said Arthur, drawing Excalibur. 'Over to you to guide us to the front gates. Can we get there without too much attention?'

'Mostly yes, through the kitchen and stables,' he said as he started for the door. 'With your forces outside, they'll be manning the walls and gathering in the courtyard.'

'Lancelot, take point with me. Bevs, you stay just behind us and direct where we're going. Aurelius, protect our rear. Usual engagement, disarm them if you can, but put them down hard if you can't.'

The rest drew their swords, and Arthur opened the door. On the other side was a long corridor with archways leading off it. Bevs pointed left and they got going. Occasionally, they heard voices and the clang of armour, but the young squire either took another route or made them wait. By the time they reached the kitchen, everyone was on edge, but they had managed to avoid detection.

Arthur stopped outside a small door. Sounds of activity came from the kitchen on the other side. Bevs briefly held his finger to his lips. 'This is where we get to my point,' he said quietly to Arthur.

Arthur raised an eyebrow in question.

'Not too much attention, you said. But we can't avoid some attention here. We have to go through the kitchen and there's always people around.'

'Do knights ever come down here themselves?' asked Arthur quietly. 'Could we just walk through taking food and get past without arousing suspicion?'

Bevs considered the question. 'It might work. Depends on who's in the kitchen. It's risky, but I can't think of anything else.'

Aurelius sighed and sheathed his sword. 'Reluctantly I agree. I'll go first with Bevs and you two follow us quietly. Try not to look too noble or regal.'

Aurelius pushed through the door with Bevs, and Arthur followed Lancelot. Arthur ruffled Lancelot's hair, playing the role of young knights, and enjoying messing with his friend's good looks. Lancelot waved Arthur's hand away but managed a laugh in return. They looked away from each other when they nearly bumped into Bevs.

Aurelius was standing dead still, his hand resting on the hilt of his sword. In front of him was the Lady with twenty knights.

'Bevs,' hissed Lancelot. 'You led us into a trap.'

'Now, now, my dearest Lancelot, always so suspicious of the wrong people,' said Guinevere. 'Did you really think I wouldn't notice the second most powerful sorcerer in the land appearing in my own castle?'

Arthur drew Excalibur, willing forth all the power it had. The sword responded, igniting with blue flames, but they flickered, and Arthur felt that same terror in his sword as before. He looked deep into his heart and pulled forth all the courage he could muster. Without really knowing what he was doing, Arthur added that courage to the power flowing into Excalibur. The sword's fear of Guinevere did not lessen, but the courage gave it the strength to overcome the terror. Excalibur now blazed with searing blue flames, its power flowing freely again.

Arthur looked into the Lady's cold stare. 'It's not too late, Guinevere. Stop your blood-soaked quest for power and control. Come back to us and we can continue the good work we were doing. The land is so close to being united in peace.'

Annoyance crossed her face and her eyes lit up with red fire. 'Sorry Arthur, you had your chance, it's too late for you.' Guinevere stepped in front of her soldiers until she was level with Lancelot. 'But not for you, my dear Lancelot. I still hope to show you what I am creating, what we must fight for. I can see your passion for making the right choice still runs deep. Maybe you will still join me one day.'

'I'll never join the Lady,' he said, drawing his sword alongside Arthur. 'But this is not who you are, Guinevere, I know it. Whether it's Gallow or whoever, you must free yourself from their influence.'

'Hmm, Lord Gallow. I really must pay him a visit soon and catch up. But right now, I shall leave you boys to it. Please try not to burn down the entire castle.' Guinevere turned away shimmering, then just like Merlin, she disappeared.

With the Lady gone, the spell was broken, and twenty knights charged at them with swords drawn.

With all the power poured into Excalibur, Arthur swung at the nearest large cauldron. He turned the sword sideways at the last second and hoped for the best. The sword hit the cauldron like a giant hammer, and the whole thing, boiling soup and all, went flying towards the advancing knights.

Those who could not leap out of the way were slammed into the wall by the huge pot and did not get up. Others were splashed with boiling soup and they shouted desperately as they tried to remove their scorching armour.

Bevs limped left and drew his fighting daggers. Two knights on the edge separated and grinned in anticipation of an easy kill. As they got closer, Bevs accelerated towards them, much faster than they expected. He slid between their legs, stabbing them both in the back of the knee as he passed, right in between their armoured plates. The knights howled and went down. As they did, Bevs leapt on the back of one to crash his head into the ground. Before the other could turn, Bevs kicked his head hard and knocked him out cold. He then calmly retrieved his daggers from the back of their legs.

Arthur was holding his own against several knights, with Excalibur keeping them at bay, but Lancelot and Aurelius were struggling against six more. They were surrounded and standing back to back to defend each other. Bevs crept up quietly behind the opposing knights, grabbing a small pan as he went. Aurelius spotted him from the corner of his eye and shouted to Lancelot. 'We go to my right.'

Lancelot pushed off with his trailing leg and swung at the nearest knight. Aurelius did the same. The knights stepped back to avoid the clumsy blows easily, but then fell over the crouched form of Bevs. As they came crashing down, Bevs leapt to his feet and landed a blow from the frying pan on their heads.

'That's better odds,' said Aurelius, handing Bevs his short sword. The three of them started to push back the remaining knights with well-timed blows. Quickly the two groups of Hillcastle knights were forced into one as they battled Arthur and his companions.

Everyone paused for breath and Arthur took advantage. He held Excalibur to his side and let more power flow into the sword. As it glowed hotter still, he slowly took a deep gouge out of the floor. Molten stone dripped from the sword as he lifted it and pointed at the enemy.

'You've seen what I can do with this sword,' said Arthur with steel in his voice. 'Stop now and you will be spared. I will even consider your future employment in this castle. I am not here to destroy, I'm here to unite. But mark my words, if you continue to fight us, we will have to put you down hard.'

The knights held their ground, hardly seeming to hear the gravity of Arthur's words, so Bevs stepped forward. Lancelot moved to pull Bevs back, but Aurelius stopped him.

Bevs laid down Aurelius' short sword and his dagger. 'He speaks the truth. With the Lady gone and Lord Salfor dead, we can stop this fight. Lay down your weapons and you can join us.'

The largest knight snarled at Bevs. 'This is our land to take, not the Celts, and not this southern pretender.' Without another word, he swung his sword towards Bevs' head.

Bevs ducked and the blade sailed over him. He spun and brought his other dagger out, driving it into the knight's waist, between the leg and body plating. The knight screamed out, but was not put down, his large size ensuring the small dagger hadn't hit anything vital. The knight turned on Bevs and bore down on him, aiming to land a deadly blow. The knight swung his sword diagonally so Bevs could not duck under it this time, but before he could finish the attack, Aurelius hit him with a vicious swipe to the side of his head. The large knight came crashing down, and Aurelius stepped in to finish him with a fatal blow to his neck.

'Any knight who attacks a squire is not worth the armour they stand in,' he said coldly to the remaining men. 'Make your choice now.'

A couple of knights dropped their swords and fled, but the last five charged forward in a rush to bring down Arthur. Aurelius and Lancelot parried the blows and Arthur cut their enemies down without mercy, Excalibur slicing through their armour with ease. In less than a minute, the remaining Hillcastle knights were dead.

'What was that?' asked Lancelot. 'Surely they knew they couldn't win. Why did most of them still attack us anyway?'

'This must have been brewing here for years,' replied Arthur. 'It seems the Lady has far greater powers of influence than we ever suspected.' Arthur paused for a second. 'However, it does have its limits. I remember how tired Lord Salfor looked. He was ready to give it all up. Maybe there are others like that we can reason with.'

'As fascinating as these discussions are,' remarked Aurelius.

'We've only conquered the kitchen so far. We still have a whole castle to take, so I suggest we get on with it. What do we do now?'

'The plan remains the same. Open the gates if we can,' said Arthur. 'It just got a bit harder, that's all.'

'So, let me get this straight,' shouted Lancelot as they ran through the empty stables. 'We're in a hostile castle, full of fanatics who've been planning this for years, with just the four of us trying to open the gates, and our sorcerer is on the other side of the walls. Did I miss anything?'

'Sounds about right as usual,' grunted Aurelius under his breath.

'Got it in one,' Arthur called back. He stopped at the end of the stables, and they studied their options. In front of them was the door to the gatehouse stairs. To the left were the main doors out to the courtyard, sitting slightly ajar.

Arthur looked out through the courtyard doors. Soldiers and knights could be seen setting up another line of defence should their gates be breached. Hundreds more were on the walls or running equipment up and down the steps.

'Suggestions?' asked Arthur.

'Well, walking out into the courtyard is a bad idea,' replied Aurelius.

'Agreed,' Lancelot nodded. 'So, we take the gatehouse. The problem is, I've never met a gate crew that would give up easily. They're always trained hard to hold the main gate no matter what. With this lot, it's likely to be even worse. The only option I see is surprise and extreme force. Get in there, finish them off quickly. Then we open the gate and barricade ourselves in to keep it open.'

Arthur grimaced. 'I'm not happy about this much death, but I know if we don't finish this soon, there'll be war with the Celts for years.'

He looked at them all, and then the young squire in particular. 'I'm sorry Bevs, this is bad. Maybe a few will surrender or run, but many probably won't. There could be a lot of blood today in order to prevent a war.'

Bevs nodded grimly. 'I understand, sire. I won't give up on my countrymen completely, but I know we must fight to end this.'

'Good,' replied Arthur. 'Let's explore those stairs. Quietly.'

They crept up the stairs, Arthur taking the lead. He quietened the power in Excalibur, so it did not glow too brightly in the gloom and give them away. The stairs led up and around in the usual spiral. They stopped briefly after every flight to ease the dizziness. At the top was a closed oak door. Arthur put his ear to it and listened intently.

'Nothing. Totally silent.'

'Why don't I have a look?' said Bevs. 'I'm still dressed in Berwick colours. Who's going to worry about a young squire?'

Arthur gave him the go ahead and stepped aside. Bevs unlatched the door and went into the gate room. Arthur could hear Bevs walking around, but no other sounds came from within. Then the footsteps returned to the door a little more quickly than when they had left it.

'They're all dead,' said Bevs. 'Smells of tar too.'

'Trap,' stated Aurelius.

'Trap. Go!' yelled Arthur. He grabbed a wide eyed Bevs and ran. They raced down the stairs two at a time, not stopping at all. By the time he reached the bottom Arthur was dizzy, but instinctively he flung Bevs straight out in the courtyard's direction and leapt through the doors after him.

As they hit the ground outside, closely followed by Aurelius and Lancelot, Arthur heard a hollow boom and air rushed out of the stable doors. 'We need more distance,' he shouted, and this time Bevs was first away, not needing further prompting.

They ran straight at a surprised group of Hillcastle knights.

Some drew their weapons, but others shouted and pointed up at the gatehouse. Fire was already gouging out of the arrow slits in horizontal streams.

'Get away!' shouted Aurelius, hoping to distract them from Arthur and who they really were. With the blaze reflected in their armour, the knights started to turn and run.

Arthur ploughed into the group just behind Bevs, trying to push the knights onwards. 'Run,' he called out, adding to Aurelius' command. Suddenly, the wind increased and fire erupted from the stable doors. The force of the explosion blew the slower knights off their feet and the rest of them to the ground, Arthur included. He could feel the heat singe his hair as it washed over him. He covered his head with one arm and Bevs with the other.

The heat blazed on almost endlessly, and then just as suddenly as it started, it was gone. Arthur looked back at the gatehouse, and that was now gone. Half the stables lay in ruins and the walls around the gatehouse were non-existent. Archers on the remaining walls looked on in horror at the destruction just a few feet from them, a place where some of their colleagues had been standing only an instant before.

Arthur stood and was grabbed from behind. A powerful hand turned him around.

'I know who you are, Arthur. I've heard how you deal with your enemies without mercy, but I never would've dreamt of this,' said an older knight with burns on his face. 'But we'll not let you poison the north like you've poisoned the south. Maybe you will still destroy us today, but as commander of this castle I vow you'll pay for it dearly.'

The commander raised his sword, as did his knights around them. Arthur allowed the power back into Excalibur and it burned brightly in the centre of their circle. 'It's not us,' he said, holding back for a second. 'The Lady has twisted your minds. We're here for peace.'

'I've heard all about your silver tongue, pretender king,' replied the commander. 'You'll not talk your way out of this.' He swung his sword at Arthur and the surrounding knights leapt at their group, but before they reached them, the castle exploded.

Crashing to the ground again for a second time, Arthur looked up at the blaze of blue above their heads, followed by countless lumps of stone. The southern wall had been turned to rubble, to join the ruin of the gatehouse on the north side. The Hillcastle knights and soldiers were in disarray, and Arthur's forces and allies poured in from both sides. Through it all, both Merlins came striding in, blue fire crackling from their hands, the powerful magic waiting to be unleashed on their terrified enemy.

Arthur stood, shaking off the grasping hand of the Berwick commander. He could only think of one thing to say. 'Merlin,' he shouted as loud as he could over the sounds of fighting. 'Stop!'

The Merlins looked towards Arthur, easily brushing aside the soldiers battling around them. They turned to face themselves and tendrils of blue lightning exploded out from them both. As one strand of lightning reached Arthur's body, he heard a single word in his head, as if uttered from Merlin's lips. 'Sleep.'

Then everything went black.

CHAPTER 14

Arthur felt a hand on his shoulder. He rose as if from a long night's rest, rubbing his face to clear the grogginess. Merlin stepped back and let him get to his feet. Arthur stared at the sorcerer and rubbed his eyes some more. 'I must have taken a big hit there,' he said to Merlin, 'everything looks fuzzy.'

'Your eyes are fine,' said Merlin as he sat down wearily amongst the countless sleeping forms. 'It is me that is not.'

Arthur glanced about and back at Merlin. On closer examination, he saw it was just Merlin who was strangely shimmering. His entire form seemed faintly unreal on its surface.

'But the power you just used was incredible. How can you not be fine? If I hadn't stopped you, we could have devastated this entire castle and its army in no time.'

'Yes, why did you stop me?'

'I don't think it's them. They don't deserve to die like this. I think Guinevere has twisted their minds over the years,' said Arthur. 'Like a corrupt courtier slowly turning a lord's mind against his family and friends. The influence she's able to exert over people is extraordinary. No, not that, it's bloody scary. How does she do it? Is it more magic or something else?'

'I wish I knew,' sighed Merlin, his age showing in every line on his face. 'But however she does it, I believe you are correct in one thing. This has certainly been going on for a long time. As unbelievable as it may sound, I think the Lady has been planning this whole thing for many years, and we have fallen into her traps every single time.'

'How so?' said Arthur, pointing around him. 'We didn't get blown up in the gatehouse. We won the battle. The north can return to peace.'

Merlin raised a tired eyebrow. 'Did we really win?'

He slowly stood up and paced around. 'Sorting out all these people when they awake will take days, if not weeks. Presuming that we can stop them from carrying on and killing each other of course. Then there is the matter of this castle. Both sides will want to claim it for their own, and each will have good cause.'

'We can sort that out,' said Arthur. 'I'm sure I can think of something and broker peace.'

'And now I fear we come to the point of this whole plan,' said Merlin. 'You would be stuck here for weeks and I am nearly spent.' He raised his hand. Not only did it shimmer, but Arthur swore he could see outlines of the grey castle wall through it.

'Splitting myself in two gave me incredible power, and the ability to storm both sides of this castle at the same time, but sadly I discovered two important facts,' continued Merlin. 'First, the extra magic I used was not free, it took a lot out of me. There is now very little power left in me. I honestly do not know where that will lead.'

'Are you going to die?' asked Arthur, concern clear in his voice.

'I am afraid I do not know if I will live, but I do know I must rest very soon.'

'Do I even want to hear the second point?'

'Probably not,' lamented Merlin. 'The two spells of transportation and splitting oneself are very similar. So, I thought mastering one would give me access to the other, but it turns out they are rather incompatible. From now on, I will never be able to transport myself instantly as Guinevere does. Sadly, whilst she is free to roam the land, I am stuck here in the north to await my fate.'

Now it was Arthur's turn to sit down. 'That is bad.'

'Regrettably, it is likely far worse than you think,' said Merlin. 'I now suspect Guinevere knew all this from the very start. After all these years, I believe we are coming to the endgame of her many interweaving plans. I do not think the border is important to her at all. It is just a distraction. Something to keep us away.'

'I suspect her real goal is taking Camelot. With that, she must believe she can control the entire land. If she controls the land and all its lords, then she can take the sword from you by sheer weight of numbers. Quite possibly, killing you is just a side effect in her plans to get the sword. To be honest, I am not sure she actually cares whether you live or die.'

'Thanks,' said Arthur dryly, as he stood up and started pacing with Merlin. 'But I'm not finished yet. While I hold the sword, I will fight her. While I still breathe, I will do what's right.'

Merlin smiled, genuine warmth returning to his face. 'And that is maybe where Guinevere has just one minor flaw in her planning. You see, I now believe the key is not really about controlling Camelot. It is not even about the sword, it is about you, Arthur. Look at how differently the sword reacted to the Lady when you poured your courage into it. I could feel that very act, even from outside the castle walls.' Merlin held Arthur's gaze. 'You do the same with people too. You give them courage they did even know they had. You give them hope. You, Arthur, are the very thing that can make the difference in this fight for our land.'

'Ha, I wouldn't presume to be so important,' replied Arthur. 'I'm not exactly doing a great job right now, am I?'

'Time to fix that then,' said the other Merlin, as he came striding towards them through the sleeping bodies. 'One of us is nearly spent, but the other is not quite finished yet.'

'We cannot transport ourselves or anyone else across this

land, but I can help you reach Camelot quickly. Bring me your horse and I will show you.'

'What are you going to do?' asked Arthur, as he jumped up into the saddle.

'I am going to pour the remainder of my magic into Horse,' said Merlin. 'She is already somewhat magical, though in ways I do not fully understand, I must admit. But I hope this will give her the strength to take you to Camelot in one day.'

'Wow,' said Arthur. 'Half the country in one day, that's outstanding. I don't suppose I could take someone with me, could I?'

'Maybe someone light,' replied Merlin. 'Ironically Guinevere would have been ideal, especially with her healing powers.'

'Yes, a shame she's our mortal enemy,' noted Arthur dryly. 'What about Bevs?'

'He should be light enough,' admitted Merlin. 'Whether he is tactically advantageous, I shall leave up to you.'

'Let's wake him up then,' said Arthur. 'One friend is better than none at all.'

Merlin found Bevs asleep in a pile of soldiers and leaned down to lay a hand on his head. Little sparks of blue raced through Bevs' hair, then he slowly stirred and stood up. They walked back to Arthur, with Bevs a little unsteady on his feet.

'I need some help and you're my best option,' said Arthur.

'Your only option,' observed Bevs as he glanced at the mass of fallen figures around them. 'Is it dangerous?'

'I'm sorry, but yes, even more than today. Will you still help?'

'Of course,' replied Bevs and he jumped up on the back of Horse's saddle. 'I just like to know where I stand.'

'Right,' said Merlin, 'let us get you on your way.' He placed his hands-on Horse's neck and closed his eyes. Slowly, faint blue sparks began to crackle across her hair. Arthur reached down to pat her neck to reassure her, but he needn't have bothered, she remained perfectly calm.

'That should do it,' said Merlin.

'Now what?' asked Arthur as Horse stood there.

'Ride as normal, I would say,' answered Merlin. 'Just do not forget to hold on a little tighter than usual.'

Arthur turned his horse toward the huge gap in the wall and geed her on. She didn't need further encouragement and took off at a gallop.

As Arthur and Bevs rode into the distance, the two Merlins sat down to rest. 'Not sure I know what to do next,' said the first Merlin. 'How on earth do we re-join? We still have not figured that out yet.'

The second Merlin held up his hand and looked straight through it at his other self. Second by second, he continued to fade. 'I do not believe we need to work out that problem just yet. I have put too much of my power into Arthur's horse. There is not enough left to keep me alive.'

'Oh,' said the first, somewhat lost for words.

'Do not be concerned. While Arthur still lives, then I am content. But you know you must tell him one day, the secret he does not yet know.'

'Yes,' said Merlin sadly to himself, as he saw his other self fade away to nothing. 'I just do not want to destroy his hope.'

Arthur raced south, the journey a blur of galloping countryside. They stopped only briefly for food and water, keen to reach Camelot before dark. After endless miles, the sun got lower and exhaustion started to set in.

Arthur was finding it hard to hang on, and he thought he might even have to tie them both to Horse before one of them fell off. Then she slowed and eventually reached a walking pace. The fields looked familiar, but Arthur could not quite place them. Then they rounded the corner of a wood, and before them was Dunstan Castle, the home of Lord Gallow.

'Why are we here?' wondered Arthur. 'We need to get to Camelot.'

'What?' mumbled Bevs, slowly rising from his exhausted state.

Horse came to a halt and looked at the castle. Arthur geed her on gently, trying to turn her west towards Camelot, but she wouldn't budge.

'Why won't she move?' questioned Bevs, now more alert.

Without a word, Arthur dismounted and stood next to her head. He looked at the castle while his hand idly stroked her mane. 'What am I looking for?' he asked.

'Are you talking to me or the horse?' asked Bevs.

'Both I guess.' Arthur made to walk west, but Horse stood in silence, staring at the castle. He then walked forward towards Dunstan Castle and Horse quietly followed him, Bevs still on her back.

'Ok,' said Bevs, 'I think your horse knows more than I do.'

They stood at the edge of the woods and looked up at the castle. A dark red flag flew on top of its keep, no sign of Arthur's blue flag or Gallow's colours.

'Ok, we'll give it a few more minutes until dusk, then see if we can find a way in,' said Arthur, taking off Horse's bridle. Content that she had completed her mission, Horse lowered her head and started nibbling at the grass. Arthur watched her for a moment while Bevs dismounted. He swore he could see little green sparks as she grazed on the land.

'Ever more surprises in you, my faithful friend.' He gave her a final pat on the neck. 'Come on Bevs, let's storm another castle.'

They trudged towards the moat under cover of near darkness. They could see plenty of torches on top of the walls and a few guards, but in the gloom, no one noticed them. They stopped at the edge of the moat and Arthur looked down.

'Again?' said Bevs.

'Sorry, it's the only way I can think of getting in.' Arthur sat on the edge of the moat and put his legs in the water, gesturing for Bevs to do the same. They sat there for a while, with their feet slowly going cold.

'I don't think she's here,' said Bevs, then he noticed a little ripple in the moat near his legs.

Arthur caught the slight movement of the water too. 'Lady of the Lake?' questioned Arthur. They waited, but this time nothing happened.

'Lake?' said Bevs, and this time there was a much larger ripple by his legs.

'Is she ok?' asked Bevs. A small ripple greeted his question. He thought for a moment. 'Is she asleep?' he said, but nothing happened in reply.

'Oh no, is she captured?' he asked. A large ripple set out across the moat towards the castle. 'We've got to help her,' he said to Arthur.

'We will. Maybe that's why Horse brought us here, though how she knew I'll never know.'

'Lake, can you help get us inside,' asked Arthur. No ripples greeted his question this time, just a powerful wave that swept them into the moat.

Arthur and Bevs opened their eyes and coughed up water. 'Not sure I'll ever get used to that, but thank you,' said Arthur, patting the edge of the pond with his hand. Little ripples appeared all over the water in return.

Arthur looked around. It was quiet in the rear garden, the peace and beauty at odds with their situation. 'Is she in the dungeons?' he asked the Lake. Small ripples came towards him like arrows, pointing to the centre of the castle.

'I'll lead the way,' said Arthur, getting to his feet and drawing Excalibur. 'Bevs, you follow behind me.'

He avoided the main entrance to the castle and headed for the side, looking for any hidden door to the kitchens. 'Garden and kitchen are often linked,' he said quietly to Bevs. 'Sometimes convenience outweighs military sense.'

Searching at the edge of the wall, Arthur found a small but heavy wooden door tucked beyond casual view. He tried it quietly, but it was locked. He laid the point of Excalibur on the lock and told Bevs to stand back.

'Wait,' said Bevs urgently. 'If the Lady knew Merlin was in Hillcastle, then surely she'll sense the power of your sword being used.'

Arthur stopped and held back from allowing power to flow into Excalibur. 'Well observed, young Bevs. I suppose I could try kicking the door in, or we could wait for someone to come out.'

'I think I can do better than that.' Bevs picked some nearby plants and knocked on the door.

Scuffling came from inside and the door was unlocked. A face appeared in the narrow opening. 'What now?' said an impatient voice.

Bevs held out the plants.

'I thought I told you lot to go to bed,' said the woman, but she reached out to gently take the plants from Bevs' hand. 'What's this? No herbs here.'

Arthur took her arm and pulled her outside, whilst Bevs put his foot in the door to stop it from closing. Arthur put his hand over her mouth. 'Not a word please, do you understand?' The woman's eyes were wide with terror, but she nodded in return.

'Good.' Arthur slowly took his hand away, but no sooner had he done that than her expression changed and she kneed him hard in the groin. As Arthur dropped, gasping for breath, she drew a dagger from her dress and held it to his throat.

'Where were you, Arthur?' she spat. 'What was so important up north that you left us at the mercy of the Lady?'

'I'm sorry,' gasped Arthur, now recognising Lady Gallow. 'The Lady fooled us all. Didn't you get our message?'

'What? No message arrived.' She moved her dagger away from his neck.

Arthur stood up gingerly. 'Guinevere is the Lady. She's been planning this for years. Plot upon plot, layer upon layer. We think her real target was always Camelot and the sword.'

'Well, she certainly has one of those. Thanks to all you stupid men running up north, Camelot was taken,' she replied. 'And that would certainly explain the ease with which the Lady took it. My husband would have let Guinevere right in the front gate. If I see her first, the last thing that woman will feel, will be my dagger through her heart.'

'What happened here?'

'With Camelot taken, your allies fell quickly. The Lady's forces were too strong,' replied Lady Gallow, leaning back against the wall for support. 'My son led our defence here, but we were no match for her army and her magic.'

Arthur hardly dared ask, but knew he had to. 'What happened to everyone?'

'The other lords, I do not know. Captured or dead, I presume. My son lies in our dungeon, slowly dying from his wounds and awaiting his sentence. I work in the kitchen to feed the very soldiers who would finish him off.'

'And my husband, he fought the Lady hard. He stood by you to the bitter end. But for all his fight, she just clicked her fingers and he fell. No magic will save me from this pain. Lord Gallow, my husband, is dead.' She looked up to the stars and a single tear escaped down her cheek.

PART 4 – THE SIEGE

CHAPTER 15

Arthur held Lady Gallow's look. 'I'm sorry. I can't imagine how you feel. But we have to save our grieving for later. We need to fight back and that must start now.'

'Too bloody right,' she replied. 'Given even half a chance, I'm going to skewer that evil woman's heart with a roasting fork.'

She put her dagger away and pulled them into the kitchen. 'Get into those servant robes and keep your weapons hidden. You're here at just the right time.'

Bevs and Arthur did as they were told, somewhat stunned into silence.

'I'm not working in the kitchens for fun,' she continued. 'There's not many of them here now. The Lady's forces are stretched. Too far, in my opinion. So I'm going to take advantage of that. We're going to poison the guards in the dungeon, free our soldiers and my son, then take back this castle.'

'Great start,' said Arthur. 'I'd just like you to make one change to your plan, Lady Gallow.'

'Jane will do. Lady Gallow will be held for the future wife of my son. I have no need of that title now.' She took some ingredients from the shelf and walked over to the boiling pot. 'What do you want me to change, young man?'

'Don't kill them, just put them out of action. I want them in the dungeons, not dead. We can sort out the good from the bad later.'

She stopped mixing for a second. 'I have no sympathy for any of them, but very well, sire, I will do as you command. You earned my husband's respect the hard way. I will not dishonour his memory by doubting his judgement.'

She handed them a stack of bowls each. 'Take these out to the hall and do try to look a bit like common kitchen hands.'

'No problem,' replied Bevs, speaking for the first time. 'Just keep your eyes down and your shoulders hunched,' he told Arthur.

They paused at the door, and Arthur could hear the hum of chatter. He pushed open the door, looked down, and shuffled in. Along with Bevs, he placed bowls on the tables one by one. No one paid them much attention, except to push them along if they got in the way of their quiet conversation. Arthur noticed a lack of the normal banter and laughter. Maybe not so keen on their task after all, he thought.

When they returned to the kitchen, Jane was tucking a small glass bottle back into her dress. 'Don't worry, sire. Just enough to make their bellies ache and bring them down. Take the pot out and put it near the fire in the hall. Serve the knights but leave the soldiers to serve themselves.'

'What if someone's not hungry?' questioned Bevs.

'Smart lad you've got there,' said Jane. 'Maybe take them some extra wine. Once the food takes effect, Arthur must do what he does best, he must fight. We'll join him of course, no room for passengers in this endeavour. If we don't take them down now, there won't be a second chance.'

Bevs nodded his understanding, checking his daggers beneath his rough shirt. Arthur grabbed hold of the huge stew pot and carried it to the door. Bevs took ladles from the shelf and two serving bowls with handles. Then he pushed open the door.

There was a muted cheer as they walked out into the hall and began to serve the knights. Soldiers rushed up to the pot to take their food. Before Arthur had even made it to the last table, some were holding their stomachs and hobbling from the hall.

A hand appeared on his ladle and Arthur looked down into the eyes of a knight still dressed in the orange colours of Lord Galahad. Recognition flashed in the knights' eyes, but he took his hand away. 'Finish your serving,' he commanded. 'Then we'll sort out the clearing up before the next guard change.'

Maybe a friend there, thought Arthur as he moved along to the next knight. He returned to the pot and took more stew. By now, many more soldiers were running from the room or dropping to the floor. Unfortunately, the rest were turning their attention towards Arthur and drawing their swords.

Arthur drew Excalibur but didn't pull power into it. He knew they couldn't risk Guinevere detecting its magic and turning up herself. Without Merlin, they couldn't hope to fight her.

Jane came out of the kitchen to join him, her dagger in one hand and a large roasting fork in the other. Bevs drew his knives and stood by her side.

Near them, the orange knight stood and pushed over the two men sat next to him on the table. He then joined Arthur and the others. 'Ector,' he said. 'Commander of Galahad's personal guard. Well, ex-commander I suppose. Conscript or die, the Lady ordered, but I think I'll take this third option now and follow you.'

The soldiers continued to drop like flies, and soon all of them were too preoccupied to even hold their swords. 'Hungry bunch in the end,' said Jane turning to Arthur. 'Dungeons?'

'Dungeons,' he agreed. 'Just show us the way.'

They strode through the hall to the main doors. Ector and Arthur slapped away a few grasping hands as they went, but few of the occupying soldiers even bothered them. Most were too busy with their own pain.

Through the doors Jane pointed left and they headed down the stairs, their boots echoing on the stone floor. Before the bottom, she raised her hand and they stopped. 'They'll have heard us coming,' she said quietly, 'but they don't know who we are. Ector, you go first and buy us some time to get the advantage.'

'I've got a better idea,' said Ector. 'I'll bring them to you.'

Ector opened the door and walked in. 'All right lads,' he said. 'Early relief is here. Go get your grub.'

The soldiers got up and hurried out. As they came through the door, Arthur and Bevs knocked out the first two. The last one was knocked over from behind by Ector.

'Good job you didn't leave any for me,' said Jane, kicking a downed guard as she entered the dungeon. 'I would not have been so gentle. Now let's free our troops and find my son.'

'We'll tell your soldiers to search and clear the castle. Can you get them to bring the prisoners here and lock them up?' asked Arthur.

'If you don't want a bloodbath, then tell them hammer,' replied Jane. She saw Arthur's questioning look and sighed. 'Hammer is our code word to keep the fighting less fatal if possible. No guarantees, but I know you like to keep the death rate down, so that will help you get what you want.'

They worked their way through the dungeons, and by the time they reached the deepest cells, nearly one hundred soldiers and knights had been freed.

'Will that be enough?' Arthur asked.

'It should be from what I observed,' replied Jane. 'Ector, you might like to assist them. As for me, I want to find my son,'

The last few cells held no prisoners except the very end one. In it was a small girl standing in a puddle of water, with a deep look of concentration on her face. A man lay unconscious beside her, covered in bandages.

'The young Lady of the Lake, I almost forgot,' said Arthur.

'What's she doing? Why didn't she call out for help?' demanded Jane as she unlocked the cell and grabbed hold of the iron bars of the door. She pulled hard, but Arthur put out his hand to stop her.

'Wait,' he said. 'She's our friend. She wouldn't be doing this for no reason.'

Bevs saw a small ripple in the water. 'Look,' he said pointing. 'She's talking to us, just like the Lake.' At those words, a larger ripple appeared.

'Are you both mad,' said Jane, pulling harder on the door. 'Let me get in there to help my son.'

'You can't help,' said Arthur.

A dagger appeared at his side, steady in Jane's hand. 'I won't ask again.'

Arthur did not move, then there was a dull thud. Jane's eyes rolled up and she collapsed to the floor.

'Sorry,' said Bevs, holding his dagger in reverse where he had hit her on the back of her head. 'I couldn't see what else to do.'

'Thanks.' Arthur slowly opened the door. He carefully walked over to the young girl and Kay's sleeping form. Kay's head and right arm were completely covered in bandages. His armour had been removed and deep bruises coloured all the bare skin they could see.

'Is he dying?' he asked her.

A large ripple appeared in the pool.

'Not the 'yes' I wanted to see,' sighed Arthur. 'Can you make him better?'

The pool remained still. Not a single ripple appeared. The silent stillness practically echoed around the dark cell.

'What do we do?' asked Bevs, his voice trembling as his young courage finally ran out. 'Surely we can't let him die.'

'I'm not done yet,' said Arthur. 'Wait here and tell Jane what's going on when she wakes up.'

He turned to the Lady of the Lake. 'Can you take both Kay and me out of here and still keep him alive?'

The tiniest of ripples appeared in the middle of the pool.

'Maybe I can help our odds,' he said, willing some power into Excalibur. He dipped the sword into the pool and stepped in.

Water swirled around him and he was swept away with Kay in tow.

'Wow, the power from your sword is like eating ten sugar apples all at once,' said the girl as they sped through the water. 'I can do anything. Where do you want to go, Arthur? Berwick, Caledonia, Ireland, Rome. I think I could take us anywhere.'

'Just to the north side of the moat would be good,' replied Arthur. 'I want to get as close to my horse as I can.'

'Oh goody, I like your horse, she's really nice.' The girl paused, as if looking for something. 'I can get you closer than the moat. Right next to her if you want.'

'Yes, please do,' stated Arthur. Then the rush of water intensified, and they landed on the ground. Hardly pausing for breath, Arthur took Kay's hand and placed it on Horse's leg, hoping for the best. Horse looked around in surprise but held still when she recognised them. As Arthur started to cough up water, Kay weakly did the same. Horse lowered herself to the ground and turned her head to place it gently across Kay's back.

'Thank you so much, young lady,' said Arthur, standing up and brushing himself down. 'How did you get so close?'

'You may wish to have a bath soon,' said the young girl, wrinkling her nose as she still stood in the small puddle of yellow liquid.

'Oh.' Arthur looked down and realised the nature of what

they had emerged from. 'Well, I still owe you more than I can ever repay, young Lady of the Lake,'

'Ellie will do,' she replied, then clear water gushed from the puddle and she was gone.

Arthur sat down exhausted and waited quietly. Kay's breathing became stronger and he started to slowly stir. After a few more moments, he raised his head. 'Where am I?' he croaked.

'Outside your castle, safe for now,' said Arthur.

Kay slowly sat up, but Horse kept her head rested on his legs. The bandage on his head slipped and Arthur could see his right eye was missing.

'I'm sorry for the cost to you,' said Arthur. 'It's my fault for not seeing this coming, for leaving us unprepared.'

'Yes, a high cost for me.' Kay raised his right arm and showed his missing hand as well. 'But not as high as some. My father is gone, but what about my mother?'

'Alive and well, though currently knocked out in the dungeons,' replied Arthur. 'I'll explain while we wait.'

The thundering hooves could be heard first, then the knights came galloping around the edge of the castle. Jane was at their head, dress flapping in the wind. She sped towards them and only pulled up at the last instant.

'My son,' she said simply as she jumped down from the horse. She bent down to feel his forehead, then kissed him gently on the top of his head.

'Now do you trust me?' asked Arthur.

'Yes. But don't rub it in, young man.'

Arthur stood. 'We should be able to move Kay soon. Then I need a wash, and we need a plan.'

'No time for a wash,' said Jane. 'We've retaken the castle with few casualties. However, Lady Anne is here and has plenty of news. Unfortunately, most of it is bad.'

'My aunt is here, alive,' said Arthur, the relief evident in his voice.

'We know she's not your aunt, no need to keep up the pretence,' said Jane. 'Another farewell gift from the Lady when she told my husband and his forces. No doubt to sow further discord about your right to be king. But I can see you care for Lady Anne regardless, so rest assured, she is safe and well. And no sore head, which is more than I can say for me.'

'Sorry about that.'

'Ha, that's what your young squire said too,' she replied as she remounted.

Arthur helped Kay up and lifted him onto Horse. He led them back to the castle where several squires and the household doctor greeted them. 'Horse has done all she can,' said Arthur. 'Hopefully with rest and your good care, he should start to feel better in a couple of days.'

'Thank you,' said Kay, as the doctor examined him, 'but just bring some food and water to me. I will listen and stand with the rest of you.'

Arthur nodded and turned to the squires. 'Fetch Ector and the senior knights of Dunstan Castle. We'll talk with my aunt in the main hall. Bring food and drink for everyone, it's going to be a long night.'

As a couple of squires hurried off, Arthur strode into the keep and its main hall, with the doctor still fussing over Kay. In the middle, Lady Anne was waiting for them. Arthur walked up and put his arms around her. 'My favourite aunt,' he said simply.

'Your only aunt,' she smiled, kissing him on the cheek. 'Well, not even that really, now everyone knows.'

'You'll always be family to me,' said Arthur. 'But this isn't the time for us, it's time to regroup and fight back. What can you tell us?'

Lady Anne urged the knights to gather round too, and they sat at a large table.

'As Lady Gallow has probably indicated, the situation is very bad,' started Anne. 'Camelot has fallen. Cador and Galahad's castles were the first to be taken, then Camelot and finally Dunstan. Lord Cador is dead, Galahad and Kane are missing presumed dead.'

'I saw Galahad consumed by a blast of magic,' chipped in Ector. 'I don't see how anyone could have survived that.'

'Bad to worse then,' said Lady Anne. She placed a hand on Jane's arm and continued. 'Lord Gallow is dead, as you know, and most of his forces were killed with him at Camelot. We smuggled a few people out of there, but not much more than a handful to add to the soldiers you have here. All our other allies are either dead or imprisoned.'

'Not quite all,' Ector shifted a little uncomfortably. 'As we know, the Lady has stretched her forces a little thin in places, which meant she had to conscript. I'm ashamed to say I signed up, but the alternative was not pretty, as Sir Kay can attest. However, we might be able to use that to our advantage. Some of those soldiers will desert her as soon as they can, and many of them will probably fight with us given half a chance.'

'That is a ray of hope, but we have one last problem and quite a pressing one,' said Lady Anne. 'I still have someone in place within Camelot and even a couple of friendly eyes in the Lady's forces.'

'You can call her Guinevere,' said Arthur. 'We all know her true nature now.'

'I know, Arthur, but it feels wrong somehow. The Lady is what she shows us right now, but that might not be all that she is. The Guinevere we saw these last two years may still be in there too.'

'Don't interrupt, sire,' said Jane to Arthur before she turned back to Lady Anne. 'And please don't make excuses for that bitch.'

Anne held Jane's gaze. 'You're right, there are no excuses for the Lady's recent actions, but it's her next move that concerns me the most. I have just received news that she felt Arthur use Excalibur's power. I am very much afraid we don't have much time. She knows you're here, Arthur, and she's sending her forces to destroy you.'

'Can we defend this castle?' asked Arthur. 'Could we hold out for six or seven days while our mounted forces return from the north?'

'Against a siege, maybe, depending on how many troops she sends,' replied Kay, now wrapped in fresh bandages. 'But against a magical attack, I doubt that very much. Her use of power was enormous when she stormed this castle the first time. Even though we were fully forewarned and prepared, it made no difference, and they conquered us in less than an hour.'

'I'm sorry to say this to you, but that fact is good to hear,' said Arthur. 'You see, magic is not an endless supply for anyone who practices it. Merlin uses magic and it runs out, and it's just the same for the Lady. I'll wager she sends part of her army, but she still needs to stay at Camelot herself to rest and recover. I also imagine she won't want to leave Camelot completely unguarded.'

'And if she turns up?' said Jane.

'Then I will head out to meet her myself.' Arthur placed Excalibur on the table, and he looked around at them all. 'Go prepare the defences. Go through the armoury for weapons. I want anyone able to stand, to be working on our defence. Tell them we hold for one week.'

People left to get started, but Lady Anne remained at the table with Arthur. Whilst she waited for the hall to clear, she glanced sideways at Bevs. 'Are you staying to just listen in, young man? Or do you have something to add?'

'Most people tend to ignore me or think I'm not important,' he replied, 'so I suppose I stop and listen more than I should.'

'You have earned that right with me,' said Arthur, 'but listening is not enough I'm afraid, so I'm hoping you have something helpful to add. Heaven knows, we need all the good ideas we can get.'

'I suppose I do have something to say. I think most of your plan is based on complete guesswork,' stated Bevs. 'You have no idea if the Lady will turn up or not. Same goes for your friends returning from Berwick within seven days.'

Arthur grimaced. 'Ok, not exactly helpful, but you are essentially correct.'

'Despite all those problems though, you lead us anyway. You give us hope, maybe even a chance,' added Bevs. 'And if needed, you would stand in front of us all and face the greatest danger yourself.'

Bevs stood up. 'I think that's why you're the king. Whether or not you're Uther's son, I don't think it's important. Now please excuse me, sire, I should go help too.'

Arthur nodded, and the young squire left.

'Let me guess,' said Lady Anne. 'You met him yesterday and now he would follow you to the end of the land if you asked.'

'Maybe the day before yesterday, it's all a bit of a blur,' replied Arthur with a tired smile.

'You need some rest, young man. I'll make sure the others work in shifts and get some rest too. Remember what your uncle would say?' she asked with a knowing grin.

'Eat, sleep, think, fight,' Arthur raised a genuine smile. 'Blood or not, that's my uncle indeed.'

CHAPTER 16

Dawn broke over the castle as Arthur stood on its walls, looking out across the fields and woodland. The Lady's forces stretched far along the grassland. Row upon row of soldiers and war machines.

'I can't see any evidence of magic yet,' commented Arthur.

'Good,' said Kay.

'But there must be over two thousand soldiers out there, with nearly fifty catapults getting set up.'

'Bad,' stated Kay. 'Not sure our walls will hold for seven days against all those catapults.'

'They won't,' said Lady Jane. 'Simple as that. I give them two days at most, then they're through to our keep.'

'How many days can we hold the keep?' asked Arthur.

'One or two more maybe,' replied Kay. 'Difficult to hit the keep inside the castle with catapults. The range and trajectories are all wrong. They might hit it more easily with the smaller ballista, but they won't do that much damage. However, they probably have battering rams travelling here as we speak. They'd be pretty stupid if they didn't, and we know the Lady's not stupid.'

'We can't win,' said Arthur, and the others looked at him in surprise, 'but we can delay and frustrate them. Maybe even deplete their numbers a bit. As long as Guinevere is not here using her magic, we've got a chance.'

'So, what do you suggest, sire?' Jane folded her arms and gave him a demanding look. 'How do we frustrate an army that outnumbers us twenty to one?'

179

'First order of business is to slow down the construction of those catapults, or even sabotage them somewhat,' said Arthur. 'Fewer siege engines will give us longer lasting walls. Simple but effective.'

'Excellent,' snorted Jane. 'You just walk out there, avoid two thousand enemy troops, ask them nicely if they would not mind going slow, and maybe while they're at it could they miss out a few vital pegs on the way. I'll go get the mead organised for our celebrations.'

'Mother! Help us or shut up,' said Kay.

She glared at him, then relented. 'Ok, ok, maybe I do have one suggestion. Sneak Ector out there quietly and he can try to infiltrate the enemy. They might not know he's on our side yet.'

'And if you've noticed, some of the people working on those catapults have orange shirts. Either stolen from Galahad's stores or they might actually be Galahad's engineers. If they are, Ector could probably talk some of them round to our side, maybe even get the catapults sabotaged. And with a bit of luck they could sneak back in here after dark.'

'Blimey,' said Arthur. 'You can see their colours from here?'

'I might be somewhat older than you, young man, but I'm not past it yet,' she replied. 'Always had excellent eyesight. On a clear day you should see me with a bow.'

Arthur grinned. 'We should get you together with my aunt sometime. But that can wait for later. Bevs, go get Ector, let's get this plan moving.'

Ector had left an hour ago, quietly down a rope thrown over the back wall. They'd seen him run to the cover of the woods and then nothing, no sight nor sound of him.

Now they watched the activity by the catapults. The work appeared to be progressing as normal, but when they looked carefully, they could see the occasional engineer move from one siege engine to another.

'It might be working,' observed Kay, as his mother looked on with a self-satisfied expression on her face.

Then an entire group of orange engineers broke off from one catapult, and after a short delay, so did another. They watched this activity steadily grow, and as it did, the groups started to move in the castle's direction.

'Ok, this isn't what I expected.' Arthur watched the advancing engineers and thought for a moment. 'Get ready to open the gates.'

'Are you sure?' asked Kay.

'Yes, I'm sure.'

The groups of orange engineers breaking away grew, then bit by bit they were joined by some of the soldiers. Except for some pushing and shoving through the rest of the ranks, they reached the front of the enemy lines with little resistance, whereupon the mass of nearly one hundred figures suddenly broke into a run for the castle.

'When they get close, open up the gates,' commanded Arthur as he started for the steps down to the courtyard. 'Once they're inside, shut the gates as fast as you can.'

'Are you really sure you can trust Ector that much?' said Jane. 'You'll be letting in a hundred people, with many soldiers among them. If you get this wrong, we'll lose this castle and our last hope very quickly.'

'Yes, I'm sure. And I'll be down there to make sure it goes well. Get the archers ready and the hot tar. You can bet the enemy won't be confused for long, then they'll chase them down. We need to be ready to defend those engineers as much as we can.'

By the time Arthur got down to the gates, they were open already. A lot of nervous soldiers and knights surrounded him, looking at him anxiously. No time for half measures, thought Arthur, and he brought forth all the power he could into Excalibur. The sword ignited, responding to his request.

'We get this right and we double our numbers to defend this castle,' he called out. 'I'll run them in myself. When I'm back inside, close the gates and raise the drawbridge. We leave no one outside. Understood?'

There was a roar of assent, and Arthur strode through the gates onto the drawbridge. He waited and watched the running men and a few women coming towards them. Dressed in orange shirts, over a hundred engineers, soldiers and knights ran towards him. Most had discarded their weapons and heavy armour in return for speed. Arthur spotted one exception, Kane, fully dressed in battle armour, with his powerful physique allowing him to keep up with the others.

But it was not going all their own way. Archers were pursuing them and firing volleys of arrows. Most of the runners were fast enough to dodge the danger, but a few were not so lucky and they fell. In the distance there was activity by the catapults, then the first one fired.

The large rocks screamed through the air, then exploded into shards of stone as they hit the ground just to the side of the fleeing engineers. The impact missed them, but some were hit by shrapnel and stumbled. Their companions picked them up and kept everyone moving forward, but each person they helped slowed their progress even more.

'They're not going to make it,' muttered Arthur and he stepped forward. A hand appeared on his shoulder, halting his progress.

'Sire, wait just one more instant,' said Kay, now standing by his side with a group of Dunstan archers right behind him.

Another catapult swung its huge arm, but instead of launching its deadly payload, the shaft swung over completely and drove the rocks it contained into the ground right in front of it. Everything shattered, exploding into lumps of wood and rock. The blast threw the surrounding soldiers back.

Before the enemy could react, several other catapults were

fired with similar devastating effect. Arthur could hear the shouts to stop even from here. One final catapult let loose. It did not drive into the ground like the others, but its rocks fell way short and took out the enemy's own archers.

A cheer went up from behind him as Arthur shepherded the fleeing men and women towards the gates. Many thanked him and Kay as they passed gratefully into safety.

With the last of the runners through the gates, Kay and his archers turned back into the castle. Arthur stood for a moment and faced the enemy. He looked out without fear and raised his sword high. Excalibur burned bright, its blue flames reaching up to the morning sun. Silence was the only reply from the besieging army. Arthur shouted out across the field, no idea if they could even hear him. 'It's not too late to join us. The Lady will not triumph here today. We will not bow down to her control.'

His words echoed up to the hills, and finally Arthur lowered the sword. He turned his back on the enemy and walked slowly back through the gates. The drawbridge was raised behind him, and it closed with a defiant boom.

They stood on the walls again in the fading light of dusk.

'How're our friendly new engineers doing with building some catapults of our own?' asked Arthur.

'Slow going,' replied Ector, 'but what they lack in materials, they make up for in determination.'

'Bit of a challenge though,' commented Jane, listing the points out on her fingers. 'They are building war machines with wood from the stables, that need to throw huge rocks over our walls, from the inside no less. All without destroying our own castle if they get it wrong. I'll be impressed if they actually work.'

'Have some faith, mother,' said Kay, looking tired in the darkening evening sky.

'I'll feel happier about things when you're resting in your bed, young man, as our doctor keeps reminding me,' she cut back. 'Come on, no more arguing, you're going to your chambers.'

'On your way down, could you ask my aunt to come join me?' asked Arthur. 'Oh, and Kane too if you see him.'

Jane nodded and left with Kay in tow.

'They've been working on their own catapults all afternoon.' Ector pointed out across at the enemy ranks. 'It's impossible to see their progress from here. But unless we do something, I suspect they'll attack again tomorrow. And this time their catapults will work.'

'You're probably right,' mused Arthur. 'We've done well to delay them today, but we need to do more. I could wade out under cover of darkness with Excalibur and fight them, but I don't want to just kill them all. And anyway, Excalibur is powerful, but it's never made me invulnerable. Their archers would get me soon enough.'

'What if we could somehow cover you, why not just kill them all?' asked Ector. 'They'll probably do the same to us if they win.'

Arthur put his hand on his sword. 'Uther faced impossible numbers with this sword, and he used its power to the full to try to destroy his foe. But it didn't work out too well for him. However hard he pushed the sword; it didn't help him kill all his enemies. Slaughtering them all is not the way.'

Arthur felt comfort come from the sword, and he knew he was right. 'The sword is here to help us all live, not to help me kill. I'm convinced of that. Sometimes I have to fight, I know that, but I should never resort to slaughter. We'll find another way.'

'I hope you're right,' replied Ector.

'He will need to be, or this land's freedom will be no more, not to mention our lives.' Lady Anne climbed the last of the steps, closely followed by Bevs and Kane. She placed a hand on Arthur's shoulder and gave him a strained smile. 'I had one last message from my friend in Camelot. He tells me the Lady has started preparing. Her power may still be low, but it is rising faster each day. We should have a little time before she's ready for an all-out magical assault, but I doubt we have the week that we need.'

'Any good news in amongst all the bad?' Arthur asked in vague hope.

'Actually, yes,' she said. 'Your young squire here had an intriguing idea for our catapults.'

Bevs turned a little red as she smiled broadly at him. 'Just an observation really,' he mumbled.

When he noticed them all waiting patiently, he started to explain. 'I saw Lady Anne making a magical bowstring for one of our archers, and I asked her what it did. When she said it massively boosts the power of the archer and their arrows, I wondered what would happen if we wove some strands of the string around the tension ropes of the catapults.'

'Now that does sound like good news,' said Arthur. 'Has it been tried yet?'

'We are considering it,' said Kane. 'But Lady Anne warned us it could be very effective.'

'What do you mean, warned? Surely effective is good?' asked Arthur.

'There are still a lot of our people out there, conscripted from Galahad's forces. We didn't all get the opportunity to run today. We'd rather not kill them too,' cut in Kane. 'In fact, I'd like permission to go out tonight and try to sneak some more of our people back in. The more we can save, the smaller that army out there gets. It'll also make it harder for the Lady to carry out her threats.'

'What threats?'

Kane looked uncomfortable. 'Conscript or die was one

option we were given by the conquering soldiers. Many of us refused however, and that was when the Lady stepped in. Conscript or your family will die, she personally promised. But she can't kill all our families, can she? I mean, if we make sure there's too many of us deserting her, then there's too many to kill for no real gain. At least that's what I hope.'

Arthur thought for a moment, holding Kane's look. When he spoke, the conviction was clear in his voice. 'You've got a good plan there. I'll come with you tonight and we'll bring in as many as we can. Get your troops ready for later, we'll set out at one hour after midnight.'

'Sounds good,' Kane nodded in agreement. 'But why wait so long before we go?'

'While you get ready, I'll do something to help your families,' replied Arthur.

'Thank you,' said Kane gratefully, and he left with Ector to prepare the soldiers.

'What's the plan?' asked Bevs.

Lady Anne watched Arthur turn back to the walls. She saw him stare out at their foe in the distance, still busy by torch light. She returned her gaze to Bevs. 'He doesn't have a plan yet,' she told him gently. However, her expression showed the granite like determination beneath her soft voice. 'But, young man, you have my word on this. We will surely help him find one.'

Bevs sat with his feet in the pond at the back of the castle gardens. As he looked up at Arthur, he was excited and anxious at the same time.

'It's going to work,' said Arthur, with a confidence he didn't quite feel. An all too familiar feeling, he thought to himself.

Every woman and man who could read, and was not preparing for the raid, sat with them at the edge of the pond. Nearly fifty people were there, each one holding a small map with a list of names on it. Torches were mounted around them to provide light, and Kane paced between them, answering any questions.

'Can we really rescue all these families?' whispered Bevs, holding up his map to Arthur. 'There's over ten people on our list alone. There must be hundreds in total.'

'It's going to work,' repeated Arthur firmly.

Kane finished his rounds and walked over to Arthur. 'They're all ready. Thank you for this, sire,' he said. 'Even if we can only rescue some of the families, it will be worth it. While you're gone, I'll get the raiding party ready. We'll leave as planned when you return.'

'Good. One more thing before you go. What did happen to Lord Galahad?'

'Merlin gave him a small device for dire emergencies. Least that's what Galahad told me,' replied Kane. 'But when the enemy overran us and he tried to use it, it exploded in his hand. Maybe the Lady sabotaged it with her magic, or the device just didn't work. I'm sorry Arthur, I couldn't get to him in time. He was consumed by an explosion of magic. There was nothing left when I reached him.'

'What colour was the explosion?' asked Arthur.

Kane looked confused. 'A bit like fire really, though there was a flash of white now you ask. Does it make any difference?'

'Maybe all the difference in the land,' replied Arthur. 'Go get your people ready. We'll be back before you know it.'

Arthur watched Kane turn and leave, then he placed his feet in the water. Through the gloom he saw the young girl coming towards them, her feet gently rippling the water as she walked on its surface. Walking on top of the water, she looked a little taller than last time. Arthur heard people gasp quietly, but as instructed, everyone held still and did not speak.

'Hello Arthur,' she said. 'Wow, you have a lot of friends here today.'

'Lady of the Lake,' said Arthur, greeting her with a gentle bow of his head. 'Thank you for answering our call.'

'We could have a great game with all these people,' she said brightly. Then she frowned and became more serious. 'But we're not here to play are we?'

'I wish we were, but I fear there'll be no play for a while. We need to save the families on our lists. Every person here has people to find and bring back. Can you take us all to the different places on our maps? I know it's a lot to ask, but I can't think of another way.'

Ellie walked along the line and people held up their maps. From time to time, she asked a question and listened closely to the answer. When she returned to Arthur, she looked carefully at his map. 'The Lake and me can take all the others in one go, and bring them back, easy as pie,' she said. 'Yours is more difficult. I'm not sure I can go that close to the Lady again. I think she might be watching out for me.'

'Just take us as close as you can,' said Arthur. 'I don't want any harm to come to you. Are you ready to go now?'

'Oh yes. It will be quite tiring though, even if I borrow power from your sword. It is ok isn't it, if I borrow some power?' she asked.

'Of course,' replied Arthur, 'just say when.'

Ellie looked thoughtful, then she counted to five on her fingers. 'When.'

Arthur plunged Excalibur into the pond, letting power into the sword. This time there were no flames. Instead, the sword shone bright blue through the water. The Lake rose up and one by one it took people under its surface. Arthur and Bevs waited for the usual rush of water and as the last of the others disappeared, they shut their eyes and held their breath in preparation.

The pond gently lapped against Arthur's shins, and after a bit he cautiously opened his eyes. People began emerging from the pond, children and families in tow. Tears and laughter filled the garden as relieved families were told their loved ones were safe. Group by group, they all moved off into the castle to find their husbands and wives, fathers and mothers, until Arthur and Bevs were alone.

'Why didn't Ellie take us?' said Arthur, almost to himself.

'She needed time to prepare,' said the teenage girl sitting next to Bevs, her feet gently playing with the water.

'Prepare for what? Where's Ellie? Is she ok?' asked Arthur urgently.

'Yes, she's ok,' said Bevs, 'but I don't think she'll get to play those games she wanted.'

'What? What's that got to do with anything?' questioned Arthur, the confused expression growing on his face.

'I think your young friend knows,' replied the teenage girl, idly brushing her long hair with her fingers.

'I'm sorry you didn't get to play more Ellie,' said Bevs, the look of sadness genuine on his face. 'But thank you for saving everyone's families. I can see it made you tired, and I can see what you gave up to help us. I know it won't be the same now you're all grown up, but I'll still play games with you when this is over.'

'Thank you, Bevs,' she replied, and she mischievously flicked water at him with her hand. 'Never too old to play games,' she giggled.

Arthur looked on in wonder. 'Ellie? Is that you? What happened?'

'When I get tired, I don't sleep like you, I get older,' she said. 'Saving everyone made the Lake and me very tired, so now I have aged.'

'Hold on,' said Arthur, standing up. 'You missed your entire childhood for us? I can't let you work any more magic today.'

Bevs took hold of Arthur's arm and dragged him back down. 'You know that's not what she wants,' he said. 'We should finish what we started. Especially as it's Kane's family on our list.'

'That's perfectly right, Bevs. People have to make sacrifices all the time, and this one is mine.' said Ellie. 'Oh, and don't forget to hold your breath, Arthur, you always look so funny when you're coughing up water.' She grinned at them both and then they were under the water.

Arthur sat up, and for a change, his nose was not full of water. 'Well, that was easier than last time.'

'The advantages of growing up,' replied Ellie. 'I'll wait here for you. Now don't get Bevs killed, he owes me a game of stones.' Then she quietly slipped back under the water.

'Stones?' asked Arthur.

'Really? You never played stones when you were younger?' replied Bevs in surprise. Then he ignored his own question when he remembered where they were. 'Anyway, what's Kane's family doing near Camelot? Wouldn't they live near Lord Galahad's castle? That's miles away.'

'They were last seen here. Most likely a trap or some other strand of the Lady's plan,' said Arthur, getting to his feet. He patted himself down and was surprised to find his clothes completely dry. Definitely the advantages of growing up, he thought.

'Aren't you worried about that?' asked Bevs.

'Hmm?' said Arthur, looking around to get his bearings.

'The trap,' Bevs prompted him.

'Oh that. Yes certainly,' said Arthur. He glanced at his map in the moonlight and set out to the west. 'But if I stop to think too much about every evil deed people wanted to do to us, I'd never get out of bed in the morning. Anyway, we have Excalibur and the Lady's magic should still be weak. We'll be fine.'

'Thanks,' said Bevs, falling into step with Arthur. 'I know

that's probably not totally true, but it still makes me feel better when you say it.'

Arthur glanced at Bevs as they walked through the gloomy woods, the moonlight not quite reaching the ground. 'Why follow me into such danger then? I know why I ask you, it's because I need people to help me, but why do you still follow?'

Bevs pondered the question as he clambered over a dead tree laying across their path. 'Some people would say it's because you're the king. Others would say it's for the sake of the land and the people. That might be true, but mostly I follow you because you're my friend and you need my help.'

Arthur stopped and Bevs bumped into him.

'What's wrong?' asked Bevs quietly, crouching down beside another fallen tree.

'I think I might know why Kane's family is here. What the trap is,' said Arthur, noticing for the first time all the other trees felled around them. 'The trap is not for me; she knows she can't easily kill me right now. The trap is for you. Well, not you specifically, but the people I bring with me. Guinevere knows I'd only bring someone I trust, and therefore someone I care about. We've got to get you out of here right now.'

'Too late for that,' came a snigger from the darkness, and an arrow flew from the gloom. Bevs cried out as it hit him, pinning him to the fallen tree. 'Time to even my score with you, Arthur,' said Lord Falcon as he stepped out from the darkness at the edge of the clearing.

Arthur's head whirled as he watched Falcon stride towards them, the sword in his hand burning red with magical fire. From the corner of his eye, Arthur could see Bevs' blood pooling fast on the woodland floor.

But the echo of Ellie's words played in his head, 'don't get Bev's killed', and Arthur controlled his rage. He drew Excalibur and prayed that the Lady of the Lake would hear him, and that his vague idea of a plan might work.

He shut his eyes and pulled all the power he could into the sword. It glowed incandescent blue, then he drove the sword down through Bevs' foot and into the pool of blood on the floor. Seeing Arthur's guard down, Falcon swung at his head. Arthur ducked and dipped his hand into Bevs' blood. 'Take him to safety,' whispered Arthur, as Falcon's blade seared over the top of his head. Two delicate hands rushed up from the pool, with clear blue water streaming from them. They pulled Bevs, the arrow and Excalibur all down into the blood. Within a second they were gone, and Arthur stood alone in the clearing with Lord Falcon.

'Looks like both you and the Lady were wrong,' gloated Falcon. 'You're not as invincible as everyone thinks. Time for me to kill you, as I should have done all those years ago had you not cheated me with that damn sword of yours. Well, look who's got the magical sword now.' He dived in at Arthur again, his sword blazing hotter than ever.

Falcon swung blow after blow at Arthur, each one intended as a fatal strike. Falcon's technique was almost non-existent, but his attacks were immensely powerful. Arthur ducked and weaved to avoid them, and where Falcon's sword hit the fallen trees, it tore great chunks from them. Even the dampness of the ground couldn't resist the sword's magical heat, and fires started up wherever it struck.

Avoiding a cross handed sweep, Arthur backed away again. When Falcon overbalanced, Arthur kicked out and caught him on the hip, sending Falcon barrelling over a tree trunk and onto the ground. Arthur stood breathing hard and looked about, wondering what the hell to do next.

Falcon rose from the ground. 'Tiring isn't it. Funny thing is, I don't get tired anymore. Not since she brought me back. I could do this all day.'

To his left, Arthur noticed more broken branches leading up to a small hill.

Falcon climbed back over the fallen trunk and advanced on Arthur once more. 'Well, I can keep this up until you're dead, and those stupid friends of yours.' With an evil grin on his face, he leapt forward again.

Arthur ducked the blow and reached down to grab a branch. It was over six feet, and so fresh, it still had leaves on one end. He countered Falcon's next attack with the branch, but the sword hacked through it easily. A good three feet got sheared off.

'I thought you were smarter than that,' laughed Falcon. 'You can't beat a magical sword with a stick.'

Arthur feigned to the right with the branch and Falcon swung in fast. Arthur pivoted and brought his weapon down hard on Falcon's knee. There was a loud crack and Falcon looked down. There was no pain on his face, just surprise as he tried to make his leg work properly.

Falcon limped forward. 'No matter. She can fix me later after I've killed you.'

Arthur kept backing away towards the small hill, avoiding the flaming sword and keeping Falcon at bay with blows from the branch. By the time he reached the bottom of the mound, his lungs were aching and the muscles in his arms screamed in protest.

He stepped up the slope as Falcon followed, limping heavily, but advancing relentlessly. The hack and slash of Falcon's sword kept going until one final blow sliced the remains of Arthur's weapon in half and took a chunk of flesh from his shoulder. A small grunt escaped his lips as he bit down on the pain.

'Hurts, doesn't it?' said Falcon stepping in closer, his grin becoming wider than ever. 'Just a shame you won't live to see me kill everyone else.' And he brought his sword down on Arthur's unprotected head.

Arthur stepped inside the blow and grabbed Falcon's arm

with both hands, hoping that Falcon didn't have a dagger to draw with his other hand. The sword kept its momentum swinging down and plunged into the side of the hill.

Falcon over balanced but pulled Arthur down with him. Crashing to the earth so heavily, Arthur thought the very ground shook. Then a hand grasped his throat, cutting off his air. As the grip tightened, Arthur saw Falcon reach out for his sword.

'You are truly finished now,' Falcon said, pulling hard at the sword still stuck in the hill. But before he could free it, the small hill erupted up around them.

Huge tree trunks were sent flying, and the sky twisted above them. Arthur felt himself thrown into the air as the ground rose unbelievably. No sooner had he flown up, than he fell back down and hit the ground hard, no more breath left in him to be knocked out. He pushed with his arms to rise up, desperately sucking in air. Something landed with a thud beside him and Arthur realised it was Lord Falcon. Even with one leg twisted at an impossible angle, Falcon somehow still got to his feet.

'Even if it kills me, she'll just bring me back,' he laughed, staring right behind Arthur. 'You, on the other hand, are another matter.'

Before Arthur could even turn to look, a giant talon swept past him at lightning speed, striking Falcon head on. More bones cracked and Falcon went flying horizontally into a tree.

No one could survive that, thought Arthur, but Falcon rose once more, and with a final cackle limped off into the woods. The air became still and not a single creature could be heard. Silence filled the clearing.

The ground beneath his feet shifted again, and Arthur glanced down in alarm. It looked like he was standing on a giant tree trunk, but unlike any tree trunk he had ever seen, it rippled strangely with movement. Arthur just about held his balance and he turned around carefully.

The huge brown eye that stared at him had to be six feet in size, and the many teeth below it were almost as big. Covered in bark, with branches sprouting out everywhere, it looked like a giant creature made out of trees.

It held Arthur's gaze for a second, as if deciding what to do, then it moved about slowly, trying to remove Falcon's sword from its leg. But every time the creature touched the sword, another small fire started on its claws.

'Wait,' shouted Arthur and he jumped down off what might have been its tail. He ran to the huge leg, leapt up, and took hold of the sword. The creature roared in pain, but Arthur pulled hard and the sword came out and he flung it away. When he looked around, he saw the creature's claws had stopped inches from his head. Deadly talons paused in their fatal blow.

The creature lowered its head on its long neck, and a single word appeared in Arthur's mind.

'Why?'

Arthur slumped to the ground, truly exhausted. 'You were setting fire to yourself trying to get that sword out. Seemed like you needed some help.'

Arthur looked up at the creature's immense size. 'Anyway, I didn't see any point in fighting you. Friend or foe, you could kill me instantly if you wanted. So I thought, why not help you with that cursed sword.'

'Not Cursed. Bad Owner.'

'Well, I certainly agree with that,' said Arthur, looking in the direction Falcon had fled. He reluctantly got up and limped over to the sword. He picked it up and held it in his hand. It was now just an ordinary grey blade; the magical fire having gone out.

'Help?'

'Sorry, not sure I follow you,' said Arthur turning back.

The creature unfolded itself even more, gaining further in size, and it showed the chains holding its hind leg. Where the red chains held it down, the bark was stripped bare.

'Help Here?'

Arthur walked over and looked closely at the faintly glowing red iron around the creature's leg. 'Looks like Guinevere's work,' he observed. He swung the sword at the trailing chains, but it just bounced off with a dull clunk.

'Ok, I'm going to try something. Don't kill me.'

Arthur closed his eyes and reached out to the sword in his hand. It felt cold and somehow old, but just there at the edge of his mind was a spark of something. He brought the sword close to him and remembered the first time he held Excalibur. The warmth, power and respect all rolled into one.

Arthur opened an eye and the sword blazed gently in front of him. But this time not red, or even blue. The flames had a deep green hue. He swung the sword down at the chains, and the blade sliced through them with ease. The chains fell away from the creature's leg and it stretched to its full size. Its huge head rose over forty feet and its leafy wings spread out over the width of the clearing.

'Ah, now I see why the woods are flattened here,' observed Arthur. 'What are you, some kind of tree dragon? What are you doing here in these woods?'

'Not Tree. Not Dragon. Am Mordred.'

'Oh sorry. Why are you here, Mordred?' asked Arthur again.

Mordred turned and looked at the broken chain by its leg, then back at Arthur. It tilted its head as if to signify the redundancy of the question and the clearly obvious answer.

'Good point,' conceded Arthur. He paced a little as he thought out loud. 'I've heard tales from faraway places of magical creatures like you. Though come to think of it, most of those tales were not good. To be honest though, I thought they were just stories told to children to make them behave. I guess they're not children's tales after all.'

Arthur thought for a second, figuring out how to rephrase his original question. 'Okay, apart from being held captive by Guinevere, why are you here in England?'

'To Fight.'

'Fight who?' asked Arthur, not sure if he really wanted to hear the answer. 'Who's side are you on?'

'No Side. Only Land.'

Arthur slumped down and sat against what might have been Mordred's wrist. 'Well, if you're here to help the land, then that's good,' he said tiredly. 'Ok, what do we do now?'

The creature lifted a hand and gently touched its talon to Arthur's head.

'Rest.'

CHAPTER 17

Arthur awoke and saw his aunt leaning over him, her hand laid gently on his forehead. 'Thank goodness you've woken up. We didn't know what was wrong with you.'

'What happened?' croaked Arthur, as he reached for the jug of water beside his bed.

'Your friend brought Bevs back to the pond in the garden. Bevs just about managed to tell us about a huge knight and a flaming red sword. The description sounded strangely like Lord Gallow. Lady Jane was most upset,' she replied.

'It was Falcon,' said Arthur flatly.

Lady Anne looked at him, for once lost for words of wisdom or comfort.

'Yup, back from the dead it seems,' said Arthur. 'Where's Bevs? How is he?'

Lady Anne looked at him sadly. 'Mortally wounded, I fear. We brought Horse to him, but it made no difference. His wound would not heal, and he got worse. Something on that arrow I suspect, something poisonous from the Lady. All the time your friend stood on the water and watched us trying to save him. Then she shed a tear and took Bevs in her arms. They disappeared under the pond and that was it. She looked so very sad. I wish we could have done more.'

Arthur forced himself up, driving his fists into the bed. 'You did everything you could. It's not your fault. Guinevere, the Lady, whatever the hell she wants to call herself. She's the evil at work here, she's the one to blame, the one who has to pay.'

'No Arthur,' said Lady Anne, helping him up. 'You fight for

us; you fight for the land. But promise me something, never thirst for revenge.'

She looked at him intently, and the rage began to wash away. 'You're right,' he conceded eventually, 'not for revenge.'

'But we cannot stop.' He grabbed his shirt from the end of the bed. 'We need to raid the enemy camp tonight; we need to find more allies.'

'Already done. Kane went out last night,' said Anne. 'You are now waking up to the third day of the siege.'

'Kane,' said Arthur slapping his forehead. 'I didn't save his family. And how did I get back here anyway? Last thing I remember, Falcon was trying to strangle me, and he was succeeding.'

'That would be down to a detachment of your troops and myself,' said Merlin, as he quietly got up from his seat at the edge of the room.

'Am I glad to see you,' said Arthur, the relief clear in his voice. 'We need your power to fight back against the Lady. But hold on, how did you get back from Berwick so quickly. Actually, how did you get me here? Did you defeat Falcon?'

'Bevs told Lady Anne what happened and where you were before he slipped away and was taken by the Lady of the Lake. I am sorry about Bevs. He was a brave soul,' said Merlin. 'So, we rode out to find you, ready to fight. However, when we got there, you were alone, unconscious at the foot of a hill near where Bevs said. After that, we brought you back here.

'Kane's family is here as well, thankfully. When we returned without them, Lady Anne asked her friend in Camelot to go get them. How she got her message to her friend so quickly, I do not know. She still has one or two secrets from me.'

Anne gently nodded, but did not explain.

'Unfortunately, we no longer have anyone on the inside of Camelot, but I do agree the sacrifice was justified to save Kane's family,' continued Merlin. 'As for my journey from

Berwick. I thought if I could make it to the middle of our land, then I could split myself in two and send one of me here and the other to the far end of Caledonia, cutting my journey time in half. This clearly worked, though unfortunately my other self is quite possibly in the sea. My initial calculations were a little hurried.'

'Great, your magical power increased massively when you split in Berwick,' said Arthur. 'So now you've done that again, you should have plenty to fight Guinevere.'

'It seems not,' replied Merlin reluctantly. 'Something about the enormous distance travelled has negated that effect. I'm now no more magical than Lady Anne here. No offence intended, my good lady.'

'None taken, but that is a big problem,' she remarked.

'Be that as it may, we are not quite finished yet.' Merlin started pacing the room while he spoke. 'I have seen what Lady Anne has done to help with the catapults. Her magical weavings have given them extra power. Indeed, they should be able to clear the castle walls and surprise the enemy. I also see she has repeated her feat with more bowstrings. We now have many new recruits and we also have some powerful weapons to use. That is always a benefit in any situation, even one as dire as this.'

'Excellent,' said Arthur, fresh energy returning. 'How long until the others get here? How long do we need to hold out for?'

'Three more days,' stated Merlin. 'If we can hold for that long, then we will gain a chance to fight back.'

'Then we will hold,' said Arthur determinedly. 'I have a plan forming in my head. Now do I have time to eat before we fight?'

Lady Anne smiled at his choice of words, and they headed for the door.

'Your swords, sire,' said Kane, placing them on the table.

'Swords?' questioned Arthur in between hungry mouthfuls.

'Yup,' said Ector. 'You had a different sword in your hand when Merlin brought you back. We thought it was Excalibur at first, but we found that later by the pond. So here you are, two swords as he says.'

'Not sure I need two swords,' said Arthur.

'Well, that one seemed to disagree,' replied Kane. 'We couldn't prize it from your hand until we'd placed you in bed and you were sleeping soundly. Looks to me it's yours as well as Excalibur.'

'Falcon had a sword blazing with magic from Guinevere. He was trying to kill me with it, before he started to strangle me that is. I must have grabbed hold of it somehow.'

'From what I've heard over the last few days, I'm amazed you're still alive. Plot upon plot, that woman has to kill you,' said Ector. 'What if this sword is another trick from the Lady?'

Arthur picked up the sword and looked at it closely. In the dull light of the hall, the blade just a lifeless grey. 'Could the sword be evil?' he asked Merlin.

'I do not believe the swords have an actual nature or take any particular side as such,' explained Merlin. 'More likely they work for a particular master or mistress as instructed, albeit less willingly sometimes.'

'Swords? You knew there was more than one?' asked Arthur. 'You could have said. Might have been useful to know there was more than one magical weapon in the land.'

'It would have done you no good, just as it has not served the Lady,' replied Merlin. 'She seems to think she can control them like everything else, but just like everything else, that is not possible. The swords are very old. They come and go over time. As yet, I have identified no pattern as to when they turn up.'

Arthur held up the new sword and a familiar feeling flowed

into him, the same comfort he felt holding Excalibur. He reached out to the sword and it warmed in his hand. With an easy will, he pulled power into the sword and it flamed with dark green fire. 'Then how do you explain this?'

The others scattered back from the table, but Merlin remained seated, a quizzical look on his face. 'Maybe you are part of that pattern too,' he smiled.

'I stand corrected,' said Ector from a few feet away. 'It's definitely your sword.'

Arthur extinguished the fire and tucked both swords into his belt, sitting back down carefully as he did so. 'Think I'm going to need a special belt or something.'

Jane clicked her fingers and talked to a young squire. She then shooed him away and he ran off quickly. 'Something will be made for you,' she said curtly. 'Now what of this plan of yours? We have catapults to fire, enemies to crush, and a woman I wish to bury in the ground.'

Arthur put down his goblet and looked around the rapidly gathering crowd. Many anxious faces stared back at him, waiting quietly for him to speak. 'Like many sieges from history, we are outnumbered, and we need to hold out until our main forces arrive. Fortunately for us, we know exactly how long it will be until they get here. We need to hold for three days,' he announced. 'But, unlike any siege I've ever heard about, we have magic to help us, but also magic to contend against.'

'So, first things first, we need to make sure they cannot storm this castle with the aid of their siege weapons. Day one, we use our catapults to destroy their war machines and keep them unsettled. Day two, we use our archers to destroy their cover with flaming arrows.'

'What about day three? What about the Lady's magic?' someone asked.

'Then we have Merlin and our own magic,' said Arthur. He

drew Excalibur and held it high, letting its power flow free. The sword ignited in blue flames, and cheers erupted from the gathered crowd.

'Kane, get your people ready on the catapults. We start our counterattack this morning,' said Arthur. 'Let's get out there and defend our families, our castle and our land.'

'Getting to be a habit this,' said Arthur as he stood on the walls again, looking out over the enemy forces.

'I notice you did not tell them about my lack of magical power,' said Merlin.

'Not something they can help with, so not something for them to worry about.' Arthur turned to look at Merlin. 'Wish I could recall what happened at the end of my fight with Falcon, and I'd definitely like to know why I can't remember.'

'I'd also like to know the story of this sword,' Arthur mused further, turning his new sword in his hand. 'In fact, forget that. What I'd really like to know is, are there any more swords?'

A catapult thudded from the central courtyard and a huge lump of rock sailed up and out over their heads. 'You want to know now?' asked Merlin, as he watched their missile crash into a large battering ram in the field outside. Enemy soldiers scattered, and many made for their own catapults to return fire. Merlin looked back to Arthur and saw the determination on his face. 'Yes, of course you do.'

'I can tell you what I know and what I suspect,' said Merlin, flinching ever so slightly as an enemy boulder smashed into the wall below them. 'There were three ancient sorcerers and they made three magical swords many hundreds of years ago. These three swords were made over the course of time. Kingdoms rose and fell in between their making. I do not know the first sword at all, unfortunately. The second sword was called Clarent, and a powerful sorcerer called Mordred made it, just before the Alexandrian Empire was born.'

Arthur stood dead still, even as all five catapults fired from the courtyard. Rocks sailed into the enemy forces and smashed several more war machines as they found their range. 'I've met Mordred,' he stated. 'I remember now, the creature saved me from Lord Falcon.'

'Creature?' prompted Merlin.

'Yes, a kind of dragon made from trees, but not that,' replied Arthur. 'It's hard to explain. I wonder why it was afraid of its own sword?'

Merlin looked at him questioningly.

'Sorry, just thinking aloud. We should probably come back to Mordred later,' continued Arthur, shaking his head to clear it. 'I presume the third sword is Excalibur. Who made it?'

'That would be me,' said Merlin. 'It is the reason I have known about the swords all along. The reason I could show Uther how to use this sword. The first sorcerer wrote a book and left it for Mordred. Mordred then made another sword and translated the book for me. I made the third sword to fight evil and keep this land safe.'

'What! You said the swords were made hundreds of years apart. How did Mordred translate a book specifically for you?' More missiles flew up from the courtyard and the enemy abandoned their own catapults, running for cover. Arthur briefly paused in his questioning to watch his plan unfold, but then further understanding dawned on his face. 'Wait a minute, you said all the swords were made hundreds of years ago. How old are you Merlin?'

'Very old,' said Merlin. He watched the soldiers in the courtyard load up another round of enormous boulders to be thrown at the enemy. 'Your plan is working well, Arthur. However, you best tell them to stop if you wish to keep the casualties to a minimum. Your catapults could kill every man and woman out there if you allowed it.'

Arthur started for the steps. 'This conversation isn't over,

Merlin. You are my most trusted ally and my friend, but I'm not a boy anymore. You need to explain yourself to me completely.'

Arthur ran down the steps and called out to hold fire. Kane raised his arm and waited for Arthur, the catapults standing still.

'Shouldn't we continue?' he asked. 'We have the advantage.'

'No, hold for now,' replied Arthur. 'I want to stall them until our forces arrive. I don't want to kill them all.'

Arthur looked out at the expectant faces around their own catapults. He raised his voice to call out. 'We have dealt our foes a hard blow today. They will need time to recover and regroup. But bear this in mind, I will not slaughter them all needlessly. Many are just like you and me. Many only fight because they have to, or to protect their families. We will win this battle, and then I will unite us all again.'

There was a chorus of agreement and nods. 'Kane, Ector, gather the others,' said Arthur, turning towards the keep. 'We plan the next stage right now.'

'What do you mean you ordered them to stop!' shouted Jane, slamming her fist on the table. 'Those bastards killed my husband and very nearly finished my son. Every last one of them deserves to be buried in the dirt.'

'Mother, please sit down. Arthur has a point,' said Kay, unconsciously rubbing the stump on his right wrist. 'Despite what they did to us, one day we will prevail and then we need peace. Do you really want an army of orphans growing up, hellbent on revenge in ten years' time?'

She looked at her son. 'No, you're right, I do not.' She finally sat at the table, the last one to take her seat, and stared at Arthur. 'But our next move better be a good one, sire.'

Arthur gathered his thoughts. 'The first stage of our plan was maybe a bit too successful. All their war machines are smashed and its only midday. We were going to save the archers for tomorrow, but if the enemy regroup this afternoon and try something else, then we might need those tar burning arrows today.'

'What can they even do without catapults and rams?' asked Ector.

'Oh, there are tunnels, grappling hook night raids, archers from camouflaged emplacements, wall sabotage and plenty more. Take your pick,' said Kane, listing the items off on his fingers. When they all turned to him in surprise, he explained a little more. 'I studied the siege of Uther's castle when I was a squire. Same enemy it turns out, who could have predicted that!'

'Well, that explains why you're so adept with the engineers and those catapults,' said Arthur. 'Good to know.'

'As much as this reminiscing is all lovely and heart-warming, what's the plan?' said Jane pointedly.

'Something for you actually,' replied Arthur. 'I had wanted our archers to aim for any points of cover with their fire arrows tomorrow. From what Kane says, we should probably bring that forward and seek out any hidden emplacements. I don't want the enemy firing ballista or even just arrows over the wall any time they want. We have too many people here now, including children running around.'

'I can do that,' said Jane. She turned to Lady Anne. 'Wouldn't mind your help with a few extra bowstrings.' Lady Anne nodded in return.

'If someone can fit me up with a hook on my right arm, then I'll join you,' said Kay rising from the table with them. 'I might not be able to swing a sword, but I can still fire a bow.'

'I can assist with that also,' said Lady Anne.

'Fantastic, get the archers ready,' said Arthur, 'and I'll join you on the walls as soon as I can.'

Jane walked out the door, and Arthur turned back to Kane,

Ector and Merlin. 'Your mention of tunnelling worries me,' he said to Kane. 'Is there anything we can do to stop them?'

'Depends on the purpose of the tunnel,' explained Kane. 'The most common use is to dig a mine shaft under a section of the wall and then collapse the part of the mine right under it. If done right, it brings down that part of the wall.'

'Did they do that at the siege of Uther's castle?' asked Ector.

'They did start a mine,' replied Kane. 'But as far as anyone knows, the gates were breached first. I guess they never finished digging the shaft. That's one disadvantage of trying that approach. You're digging a large tunnel and that takes a long time, even with many engineers working on it. Easier for the castle's defenders to spot too, as you've got to dispose of a lot of earth and rocks.'

'We haven't seen any evidence of that,' said Arthur. 'So, what about the other use?'

'That one's a bit more difficult to find. A small tunnel can be dug to gain entry to the castle. You dig one just big enough for a man to crawl through. Then you can get your soldiers inside the besieged castle to fight, cause damage, or most likely just open the gates.'

'You'd need a suitable location to surface at. But with all the conscripted soldiers in the Lady's army, there's bound to be plenty who know the layout of this castle. If they haven't started a tunnel like that already, they probably will now.'

'Then that's what we should concentrate on,' said Arthur. 'Merlin, can you use your magic to detect any tunnels getting close to the castle?'

'Only if they bring magical weapons with them,' answered Merlin. 'Or heaven forbid Guinevere comes through a tunnel. I will certainly sense her magic approaching.'

'Ok, great,' said Arthur. 'Kane and Ector, in case they don't bring any magic with them, you round up some people to watch over likely entry points. Use the children as runners to get more coverage, just don't let anyone be on their own.'

Ector and Kane departed, leaving Merlin and Arthur alone.

'Skilfully done, young sire,' said Merlin after a moment's silence. 'You have plans in motion. Everyone is busy with a purpose, and now you have me to question. You have grown up indeed.'

'I'm not quite on Guinevere's level,' said Arthur with a sigh, looking tired again despite it only being midday. 'But I'm learning that you sometimes need plans within plans to succeed. Wherever possible, each action should have multiple purposes and potential benefits.'

'Just beware you do not over plan or conspire,' said Merlin. 'The Lady thought she could kill your allies or maybe even you with Lord Falcon. And if that failed, then the creature would finish you off. But look where it has got her. The creature may not be a creature after all and certainly it cannot be controlled as she wanted. And you now have two powerful swords. Overlapping plans are all very well, right up until more than one of them goes wrong at the same time.'

'And what of you Merlin,' asked Arthur. 'Are your secrets part of some elaborate plan? I know you're my friend. I feel it to my core. But why do you have secrets from me?'

'For the very same reason you do not always share all your knowledge with your friends and allies,' said Merlin, then he gestured for Arthur to finish the train of thought.

Arthur considered this for a moment. 'Because to know your secrets would not help me?' he asked.

'Oh, it might help you in some small way. Maybe to plan a little more quickly or lose a few less people,' replied Merlin.

Arthur started to object. Merlin held up a hand. 'However,' he continued, 'it would not help you to win. That is why I hold secrets from you. This war you fight with the evil in our land, it is not fair or valiant, it will not respect your kindness or good intentions. This war is cruel, and our very existence depends on your victory. Sometimes I must help you make the most difficult choices by less than fair means. This is one of those times.'

Arthur rose from the table. 'Let me guess,' he said starting towards the door, 'there are more secrets to come?'

'Just one. However, it is a big one, and I am very much afraid you will not like it.' Merlin followed Arthur out into the corridor. 'But I can tell you this. We must hold for the next two days until the others join us. Otherwise, all the secrets in the land will not matter.'

Merlin stopped suddenly and he looked around the corridor. A boom erupted from outside and the walls about them shook. Dust drifted down from the low ceiling.

'Is this the secret I won't like?' shouted Arthur as he broke into a run.

'No, this is new,' called out Merlin. Seeming to look directly through the solid stone, he shouted a final warning. 'It is right in the middle of the courtyard. Something magical, something bad.'

Arthur burst into the sun and immediately ducked as a broken catapult shaft flew past his head. Pieces of what were once the base smashed into the wall to his left, soldiers leaping aside to save their lives.

In the middle of the yard was a single man. Covered in dirt, he wielded a huge hammer in one hand and a shield in the other. He stomped around the courtyard, smashing their catapults with unbelievably powerful blows. 'Bring me the pretender,' he shouted, 'or you'll be next.'

Arrows rained down on him from the walls. Most embedded in his shield, but some got through and pierced deep into his flesh. But they only seemed to make him more angry, more powerful. He aimed his next blow and sent pieces of a war machine crashing into the top of the wall and the archers above him. The lucky ones scattered, but some got caught by the flying machinery and were crushed or blown over the walls.

He stopped and pulled one of the flaming arrows from his back, then he turned to Arthur. 'There you are,' he sneered. 'I've come to get my sword back.'

Arthur peered at the man, then recognition dawned. 'I'll give you your sword,' he said to the advancing figure of Lord Falcon. 'Right through your cold black heart.'

Arthur drew both swords and let their power flow freely. They lit up with fire, Clarent no longer a dark green but shinning bright.

'You couldn't kill me before,' said Falcon as he raised his hammer. 'Not even that dragon thing could. What makes you think you could possibly kill me now?' And he threw the huge hammer at Arthur.

Arthur ducked, easily avoiding it, but the hammer hit the wall behind him, and stone exploded everywhere. Flying masonry hit him on the back of the head, and everything dimmed as he staggered away from Falcon's grasp.

Falcon kept going and seized his hammer from the ruined wall, more stones collapsing as he took it from the wreckage. In one smooth movement, he twisted back and swung it again at Arthur.

The blow was filled with power, but not that fast, and Arthur ducked it again. The hammer sailed over his head and Arthur counter attacked, slicing in at Falcon with Excalibur. The sword bit hard into Falcon's side and cut deep. A trail of black blood followed the sword's exit and the stench of decay filled the air.

'Can't even feel it,' laughed Falcon. He grabbed hold of another burning arrow from his back and used it to seal the wound with a searing hiss of flesh. 'Better than a bandage and twice as fast.'

Falcon hefted his hammer in his hand and his face darkened.

'The games are over now boy, this time you die.'

The hammer blow came from overhead, and Arthur only just stepped aside fast enough to avoid being flattened. The hammer buried itself a full foot into the ground and Arthur leapt in taking a swing at Falcon's outstretched arm. Falcon was too fast though, and he pulled the hammer from the ground and swung it at Arthur's sword in one lightning-fast move. The hammer crashed into Excalibur and the sword was wrenched painfully from Arthur's hand, flying away to bury itself in the castle wall.

'That's one sword for me,' said Falcon, throwing down his shield and walking over to the wall.

Arthur tried to hide the pain as his right hand hung by his side. He gritted his teeth and willed more power into Clarent, getting ready to defend them all from the rising power of this man monster.

Falcon took hold of Excalibur with one hand and pulled hard at the sword. Huge muscles showed in his shoulders through his tunic, black veins standing out on his massive arms. Arthur could swear he saw the whole wall get pulled slightly towards Falcon, but the sword would not budge from the stone of the castle.

'The sword can never be yours,' said Arthur as he retook his fighting stance, Clarent burning fiercely in his hand. 'You were not worthy all those years ago, and you are not worthy now. Lay down your arms and we will try to help you, try to undo the evil Guinevere has done to you.'

Falcon raised his head and laughed. He advanced towards Arthur, swinging his hammer in mocking blows. 'You think I want this undone? You still know nothing pretender king. No one can imagine the power she has put into me over the years. All for this eventuality. You could chop me into little pieces, and I would still come for you, still kill you. Then once you're gone, the land is mine.'

Falcon swung and Arthur stepped inside the blow. He powered in with Clarent and the sword cut through Falcon's arm. Both the hammer and the attached limb carried on their trajectory and flew across the yard. But Arthur's victory was short-lived as Falcon's left fist caught him in the chest. Arthur's chest plate armour crumpled, and he was knocked off his feet. His sword clattered away from his hand and landed in the mud, right by the tunnel exit that Falcon had appeared from.

Black blood dripped from the stump of his arm, and Falcon looked at it with annoyance. He walked over to the hammer and picked up the end of his severed forearm. Arthur coughed up some blood as he rose to his feet. He watched Falcon reattach his arm, the blackened blood flowing quickly over the cut until none was there. Archers cowered on the walls and soldiers backed away in fear.

Arthur limped towards his sword, holding his ribs. He saw Falcon striding across the yard towards him, and Arthur knew he wouldn't make it. Then he saw a stone bounce off the back of Falcon's head, making him turn.

'It's not just about him, you know,' said a solitary figure.

'What, you really think a few rocks can stop me?' shouted Falcon.

'No, but this might,' said Kane, and he pulled the leaver on the last remaining catapult.

The adjusted war machine threw its load of boulders straight at Falcon. They crashed into him and he disappeared in the mass of rocks as they hit the far wall.

The castle was dead silent as everyone watched the pile of boulders. Nothing moved for a second, then a pebble wobbled on the top and fell to the ground.

'Oh no,' said Arthur, and he started hobbling as fast as he could to the swords. He seized Clarent from the ground and pulled Excalibur from the stone of the wall. He turned just as Falcon's hand emerged and pushed a large rock out of the pile.

'Start getting people out,' he shouted to the soldiers around the walls.

'No,' called out Kane, appearing at his left side. 'We stand with you.'

'I can't beat him,' said Arthur, wincing as he hefted the two swords, pulling all the power they had into them.

'Yes, we can,' said Merlin on his other side.

'Yes, we can,' agreed Jane, with an arrow drawn in her bow, blue fire blazing from the bowstring and all along the arrow. Behind her, Ector and Lady Anne stood, weapons drawn. Lady Anne nodded to him in silent assent, faint blue sparks glittering in her long hair.

'How?' Arthur asked Merlin, watching the pile of rocks tumble down and Falcon emerge, cracking his joints back into place one by one.

'Just like anyone else,' whispered Merlin. 'Be still his beating heart.'

'Enough of this,' said Jane, and she let loose arrow after arrow at Falcon. The flaming blue arrows tore at his flesh until one speared him dead in the eye.

'Ow, that actually hurt you bitch,' he shouted out, more in surprise than pain, slowing only slightly as he pulled the arrow from his eye socket. 'I'll save you until last.'

'Any more bright ideas, old man?' she said to Merlin.

Arthur glared at her. 'He said his heart. Keep him distracted.'

Arthur ran straight at Falcon. Lady Anne levelled her bow and sprinted left with Jane. Together they rained arrows at Falcon. Ector and Kane stalked to the right and started to flank round his back.

Falcon recovered his hammer and shield from the ground. The arrows bounced off the shield as he angled it towards the women. The hammer he swung in wide arcs, keeping Ector and Kane at bay. 'Is that really the best that you can do?' he laughed at them all.

'No, this is,' said Merlin, appearing instantly right beside him, and he poked Falcon in his other eye.

Arthur leapt the last few feet and drove Clarent into Falcon's chest, pushing and shoving him to the floor. The sword screeched as it bit into the stone of the courtyard, pinning Falcon to the ground. Arthur raised Excalibur for one last strike, but Falcon batted him away like a fly.

At the same time, Falcon reached up with a hand and snapped the hilt from Clarent's blade. Then he raised himself off the floor, black blood oozing from the wound left by the sword. He discarded the hilt into the mud and advanced towards Arthur.

'Now do you see the true power she's given me!' bragged Falcon, his eye already healing from Jane's arrow. 'I don't even need the swords anymore.'

Arthur painfully got to his feet and raised Excalibur. His hand wavered with exhaustion, but he held a fighting stance again. Slowly he rotated around Falcon, hoping to keep him distracted and give the others time to get away.

Falcon swung his hammer and Arthur was too slow to avoid it completely. The glancing blow hit his shoulder and sent him crashing to the ground again, his sword clattering away.

'The end for you, little man,' sneered Falcon, and he brought the hammer down.

Arthur scrabbled desperately in the mud and grabbed hold of his sword. Time seemed to slow as he watched the hammer fall. Then the handle of his sword came into view, but there was no blade attached to it. His arm swung around with Clarent's blade-less hilt, and he realised he was done. He tried one last desperate kick with a leg. He knew the hammer would shatter it, but anything to delay the inevitable.

Then the sunlight cut out and the hammer stopped inches from his head. Arthur could see several talons gripping Falcon's arm. Falcon pushed harder, but there was no give. He turned to look up and saw Mordred, the immense creature a mass of bark and talons, branches and teeth. A clawed hand crashed down and pinned Falcon to the ground. A word appeared in Arthur's head.

'Evil.'

Falcon struggled hard, pulling bark and branches from the creature's hand, slowly but surely emerging from its grip. Arthur dragged himself to his feet, pain racking his body. He retrieved Excalibur and pulled power into it, igniting its bright blue fire, trying desperately to get ready to help, to do anything to stop Falcon. But Falcon just kept ripping away at Mordred's hand with ever more power.

'No,'

Then Mordred placed a claw over Falcon's heart and pushed.

'Stop.'

There was a final massive shudder and Falcon went still, pinned under the giant creature's hand with a branch like claw piercing right through the centre of his chest.

Arthur dropped to the ground, exhaustion taking over. The creature picked up Falcon's body and stared at it.

'What now?' asked Arthur, with a feeling of déjà vu.

Mordred looked into the distance and back at the body in its hand, then he opened his jaws wide and threw Falcon inside. He crunched twice and swallowed the pieces.

Ok, maybe not quite the same as last time, thought Arthur. He looked down at Excalibur gently burning in one hand and at Clarent's hilt in his other.

'Can you fix the sword?' asked Arthur, holding up the hilt.

'No. Don't Like.'

'I don't understand,' admitted Arthur. 'Why are you afraid of your own sword?'

'Wrong Question.'

Mordred looked at Excalibur gently blazing in Arthur's hand, then to Clarent's broken blade, and finally back to his own hide made of bark.

Arthur watched all this and thought for a moment. 'What made you vulnerable to your own sword? Or who?'

'Good Questions.'

'Can you answer them?' said Arthur.

'No.'

'Oh,' said Arthur.

'Can Change.'

'Change what, yourself?'

'No. The Sword.'

Arthur stared at the blade-less hilt of Clarent in his hand and raised it up to Mordred. The creature took it gently between two talons, then ripped a piece of bark from his hide and drove the hilt into it like a grip. Mordred lowered this down and gave it back to Arthur.

It looked like a crude shield, and Arthur held it before him. He felt a rush of wind and saw the creature's gaping jaws open wide. A spark of green caught at the back of Mordred's throat, then dark flames erupted from his jaws.

Arthur instinctively held up the crude shield, but knew there was no way it could stop all that fire. The grip heated and the shield started to melt around his arm, the intensity of the temperature making him cry out. Then a familiar feeling flowed from the hilt, and Arthur let it engulf him. Power gathered in the shield and it pushed the dark green fire away until the shield itself burned brightly with green flames of its own.

Mordred closed his jaws, and the jet of fire ceased. The creature looked at Arthur and the new shield he held.

'Clarent Good Now.'

Mordred unfurled his huge wings and padded in a tight

circle, like a dog preparing to sleep. As the creature's head passed close to Arthur, he swore he could see pride flicker cross its face. With that, two final words appeared in Arthur's mind.

'*Save Land.*'

Then instead of settling down, the creature took to the sky and in an instant was gone.

CHAPTER 18

Arthur awoke with the sun streaming in the stable window. He stayed resting against Horse, his ribs aching but slowly mending. Merlin sat on a stool nearby, looking as comfortable as ever, patiently watching over him.

Arthur yawned and looked at his old friend. 'Time for the truth?' he asked tiredly.

'Always the truth for you, Arthur. Just now it is time for more of it,' said Merlin. 'Though I do not necessarily have all the answers you seek.'

'Start at the beginning and we'll see how it goes.' Arthur shifted to ease the pressure on his ribs and patted Horse absentmindedly in gratitude.

'I was born during the Roman Empire, at the start of its occupation of this land. As a young lad, I discovered I had talents that no one understood, not even myself,' started Merlin. 'Then Mordred found me and took me in as his apprentice.'

'What was it like being trained by a dragon?' asked Arthur.

'If you continually interrupt me with your questions, we shall be here all day,' replied Merlin dryly, and Arthur waited in silence.

'He was not a creature back then, just a man, and no, I do not know how he became what we saw today,' added Merlin quickly, anticipating Arthur's next question. 'But he did teach me about magic and how to use it. He also translated a book for me. He said the book illustrated how to create weapons and fill them with magic. He told me that the weapons created could defeat any evil in the land. However, before teaching me all that was in the book, one morning he left and did not return. No word of goodbye, just there one day and gone the next.'

'After that, I studied the book for years, almost a century in fact. Then I eventually created Excalibur to protect this land and its people. After a few false starts, I gave the sword its power, or at least the start of it. Over the years, the sword has used far more magic than I ever gifted it. I like to think I brought it to life in some manner, but it is unlikely to be that simple.'

'However, contrary to Mordred's promise, the sword could not defeat all the evil in the land, as Uther found out to his cost,' added Merlin sadly. 'For some reason, Mordred lied to me. Maybe to protect me from the truth, that good people do not always prevail. Or more likely, to ensure I tried, no matter the odds against me.'

'I'll ask him next time I see him,' said Arthur, then something truly sunk in. 'Hold on, if you're over four centuries old, how have you stayed alive so long?'

'I would have thought that part was obvious, young sire,' replied Merlin. 'With the use of magic, of course. Even when I am weak, as I am now, my whole being is still filled with magic. It binds my body and mind together, prevents me from ageing any further.'

'So, you can't die,' commented Arthur. 'That's amazing. Hold on, Guinevere pulled Excalibur from her chest that last night of the tournament. Does she have the secret of immortality as well? In fact, how old is she?'

'No Arthur, it is not immortality. I can die, and I suspect so could the Lady. We are just very hard to kill. However, if my magic is lost, then I would simply fade away to dust,' explained Merlin, almost dispassionately. 'As to how old Guinevere is, that is harder to say. She organised the attack on Uther's castle, and very likely had infiltrated his court too. The number of children killed in the castle's nursery that last day of the battle, well that led me to believe she was there to ensure Uther's heir did not survive.'

'Why keep all this from me?' asked Arthur. 'You once told me you'd never lie to me.'

'Not lies, just secrets,' replied Merlin simply. 'A subtle but important difference. You were not ready then, but you are now. You have to be.'

'That's quite a lot of secrets,' said Arthur. He sighed and rubbed his face. 'But yes, you were probably right not to tell me everything when we first met. Not sure I would have believed it anyway, or even trusted you so much. But after all I have seen over these years, you're right, it is different now. I know you're telling the truth and I can trust you; I feel it.'

'That is one of the gifts you have, Arthur,' said Merlin, placing a hand on his shoulder. 'There is magic of sorts in you too, my boy.'

'Well, I wish it was the type of magic where I could throw fireballs around. That would be handy,' he replied. 'Or more importantly, have spotted Guinevere's duplicity.'

'I am afraid she is too powerful for that, my young friend,' said Merlin, his voice turning grave. 'She is by far the most powerful person I have ever encountered, and I have seen a few. And that brings me to the most terrible secret of all.'

'There's more?' was all Arthur could say. Horse tucked her head closer to him and he stroked her mane. With all he was hearing, he found her presence reassuring.

'You may rage against this. You may not even accept it. But since the Lady destroyed Uther and his castle, I have been convinced of this one fact.' Merlin shifted where he sat. 'Even with your magical weapons, your friends and allies. Even with your pure intentions, you cannot defeat the Lady in this war.'

Merlin shifted again and looked increasingly uncomfortable. 'My saddest secret to hold all these years is this. We cannot win, Arthur. The Lady, Guinevere, we just cannot beat her. And if we do not win, then our beautiful land and all its people will slowly perish under her domination.'

Arthur sat still for a full minute, looking in Merlin's direction but not really seeing him. When he broke the silence, his determination was like iron in his voice. 'You're right about one thing, I won't accept it.'

'Sire, I am afraid that you are not really being given the choice,' said Merlin. 'As much as I wish it was not so.'

'Nope, still not accepting it,' said Arthur, rising to his feet. 'We have just one more day to hold until our army returns. We will hold and we will plan. There's always a way, we just have to look hard enough to find it.'

He paced around the stable. 'Go get Lady Anne and Jane, then tell the others to start again with our last remaining catapult. Keep that army outside at bay no matter what.'

'For once, young sire,' said Merlin rising from his stool. 'I bow to the exuberance of youth.' And with a small nod of his head, he left the stables.

Arthur rubbed at his ribs and realised there was no more pain. 'You, my dear friend, are a lifesaver.' Arthur patted Horse once again on her neck. She lifted her head to lord over him, and Arthur grinned in return. 'And you are most modest too, young lady.'

'Do you think I'm mad?' he asked as he stood there with her. 'Should I just give in to the inevitable and let Guinevere win now? It might save many lives today.'

Horse shoved him hard on the shoulder.

'Good, I'm glad you don't like that idea. Will you stand too, when we fight the impossible?'

Horse nuzzled his shoulder this time, and Arthur rested his forehead on hers. 'Thank you, as always,' he said. 'I just hope I don't get everyone killed.'

'Who's getting killed?' asked Jane as she stormed into the stable. 'It had better be those devils out there, or even better still their mad bitch of a queen.'

Lady Anne followed her through the door, with Merlin bringing up the rear.

'That's what I like to hear,' said Arthur.

'What, no more being the nice guy then, trying to spare them, sort them out later?' questioned Jane.

'I won't slaughter the innocent, but yes, we're done being the good guys. The stakes are too high now,' replied Arthur. 'So, what do we have? If we can hold until Bane returns, what will the sum total of our forces be?'

'Seems to me you have plenty of magical things,' said Jane. 'Sword, shield, catapult, enhanced bows, a horse, Merlin, maybe that hammer of Falcon's and even a dragon. And when that army of yours does return, you'll have some of the best tactical commanders in the land. Don't see how you can possibly lose.'

Arthur sighed. 'If only it were that simple. For starters, I don't think Mordred is mine to command, but we can only hope he helps again if things get desperate enough. And as for our own sorcerer. Merlin, how much power do you have left?'

Merlin glanced at the others. 'Enough magic to split myself again, and over a short distance, that should enhance my power. For a time, I believe I could be a distraction to the Lady.'

'Will you have much magic left after that?' questioned Arthur.

'Some,' said Merlin.

Arthur didn't think that was entirely true, but he kept his doubts to himself.

'Hold on,' said Jane, interrupting Arthur's thoughts. 'Surely, if we survive until Lord Bane returns, with all that firepower we can take down the Lady. I thought we just needed to figure out how to keep them at bay for one more day, then we go kick her arse.'

Lady Anne put her hand on Jane's arm. 'I think what Arthur and Merlin are trying to protect us from, in their clumsy way, is that things are far worse than they appear. Am I right Arthur my dear?'

Arthur sighed and looked at his aunt. 'You're as observant as ever. How much should we tell them?' he asked Merlin.

'I'll answer that,' said Jane. 'You tell us everything, right down to the last grim detail.'

'Lady Anne is right,' said Merlin, sitting down once more. He gestured for them to join him. 'In short, we cannot win. The Lady is too powerful. In fact, I suspect she is letting us hold out, letting the others return. It would not surprise me if she wants us all to be here, just to witness her victory. Or more likely, to face her judgement.'

'You call what happened yesterday, letting us hold out?' exclaimed Jane. 'I can't imagine anything more powerful than that abomination, Falcon. You've reached a strange conclusion there, Merlin.'

'I don't care how powerful she is. I won't accept defeat,' said Arthur. 'There must be a way.'

'Too bloody right,' added Jane. 'Bugger Guinevere and her bloody magic, she's got to pay for what she's done.'

'Not quite the way I would put it, but I wholeheartedly agree,' said Lady Anne smiling at Jane. 'And I do have one further point to add.' She adjusted her position to look at Merlin. 'You gave something to Lord Galahad I hear. Is that right? A small magical device you were testing.'

'Well, I did do some testing with Galahad last year. He was very helpful, and a most inquisitive assistant. But how on earth did you know that?' asked Merlin, looking a little surprised.

'Kane told me about a magical device you gave to Galahad,' she answered, 'but sadly it did not work for him, or the Lady sabotaged it somehow. Galahad was consumed by magical fire when he tried to use it. Do you have any more of those? Could we use them against Guinevere?'

'Ah, this is interesting. Though I would not say I gave any of the devices to Galahad. He must have quietly taken one when we had finished testing one day. Sometimes a little too curious for his own good, that man.'

'He's not the only one with that particular trait,' said Lady Anne, gently goading Arthur.

'What colour was the fire?' asked Merlin.

'That's exactly what I asked,' interrupted Arthur. 'According to Kane, it had an edge of white.'

'Then maybe the device did work for him,' remarked Merlin, getting to his feet with renewed enthusiasm.

'Bloody hell, get to the point will you,' said Jane. 'What does it do? Do you have any more? And can we use them to kill the Lady?'

'That is multiple questions for multiple points, my dear woman, and far more complex than you might suspect.'

Jane just folded her arms, looking cross, but she waited for Merlin to explain.

'As you may or may not know, the Lady can transport herself across this land, whereas I cannot. At least not with my own magical power,' said Merlin. 'But I have been working on some magical devices to transport anything and anyone, though I started the tests with something a little safer than myself.'

'Not Galahad surely?' said Lady Anne.

'Indeed not, just an apple to start with. The first problem I had, was that all the tests took time.'

'What do you mean, took time?' asked Arthur.

'The apple would indeed move, but it took time to get to its new location,' replied Merlin. 'It would disappear from one side of the room, then reappear on the other side just fine. But for no reason I could discern, this would take several minutes.'

'Where was the apple during this time?' asked Lady Anne.

'I am afraid I have no idea,' said Merlin, 'and that is not something I enjoy admitting.'

'More to the point, why has Galahad not reappeared?' chipped in Arthur.

'Sorry Arthur, but right now who cares,' said Jane. 'Get another one of those devices, throw it at the Lady, and send her to the bottom of the sea. I don't really care where she is in the meantime or how long it takes her to get there.'

'Now we get to the second problem,' said Merlin. 'Their power source is an issue. On their own, they cannot move an object more than a few feet. They need to be connected to someone to move any real distance. Something about this type of magic needs the touch of a person.'

'Easy, one of us can sacrifice themselves and take that bitch to hell,' said Jane. 'I'll happily do it myself.'

'And so, we get to the third problem,' sighed Merlin. 'How to control the devices. The first and only time I tried one on myself, I ended up across the other side of the county. It was not where I wanted to go at all. And furthermore, an entire week was missing to me. On top of that, it took me quite a long time to hitch a ride back here.'

'Why not just use another device?' said Arthur, then he realised. 'Oh yes, lack of control.'

'I did think of that, Arthur,' said Merlin dryly. 'I took some more of them with me, before I learned about the control issue of course. Unfortunately, they did not survive the transportation themselves.'

'Ugh, we're going around in circles,' cursed Jane.

'Then let's stand still and look about, so to speak,' said Arthur. 'What's the most important thing? Stopping Guinevere. Everything else doesn't really matter. If we can send her far enough away or maybe even disappear for a long time, she can't hurt anyone.'

'Could we use more than one device and magnify the effect?' he asked Merlin.

'I do not know if that would work, but it might well do,' he replied. 'We do not have time to research it properly, but I could try some quick tests on an apple or two. However, if it does work, you would need multiple people willing to sacrifice themselves to a very uncertain future.'

'Right, let's get started. I'll lead the volunteers to use the devices,' said Arthur.

'Oh no you will not, young man,' interjected Lady Anne. 'This land needs you, and there's plenty of us older folk who can do what's necessary.'

'A little less of the old, if you please,' added Jane, grinning back at Lady Anne, then she turned to Arthur. 'But yes, what she said.'

'And now we get to the fourth and very last problem,' said Merlin. 'We will have to get past all of Guinevere's formidable defences and into the heart of Camelot somehow. All my devices are in my rooms there.'

'Of course,' said Jane. 'Where else would they be.'

Arthur found the others waiting outside, eating while their last remaining catapult lay still. The midday weather gently warmed him, but despite the sunlight, he felt no comfort. Lookouts and archers were taking turns on the walls, watching the fields.

'They upped and left this morning,' said Kane, indicating beyond the walls before Arthur could say a word. 'We thought they were retreating out of range, but no they just kept on going.'

'Surely they haven't given up?' questioned Ector. 'Why on earth would they leave? It makes little sense.'

'I agree,' replied Kane. 'I can understand them wanting to get out of our catapult's range, but retreating altogether is counterproductive. If they're so far away we can't see them,

226

then not only they can't attack us, but it also boosts the morale of everyone here. Definitely makes no sense.'

'Don't be fooled by their scarcity,' said Merlin. 'No doubt the Lady is preparing them for some plan or another.'

'Yup, Guinevere has never done anything without good reason,' added Arthur. 'We've found that to our cost too many times.'

He took some food off the makeshift table. 'Keep rotating the shifts. Anyone who hasn't eaten should be relieved. I want everyone full of energy and well rested. I suspect it will be a long day.'

'When we're all done eating here, I want us up on the walls too. Lady Anne, you're with me on the north side. Jane, you take the south. Ector, you look to the west, and Kay to the east. Any sign of activity, just raise your arms and shout. After that, we'll need to think on our feet. Kane, see if your engineers can finish repairing any of those other catapults. I suspect we'll need them.'

They headed for the steps to the walls, then Kay put a hand on Arthur's shoulder. 'Mind if I keep this?' he asked. He held out Falcon's battered hammer for Arthur to see. 'Merlin said there's a little bit of magic in it, probably to ensure it didn't shatter under the force of Falcon's blows. Anything without that would have disintegrated with the power he was putting into his swings.'

'Of course, that's fine,' replied Arthur. 'I don't have any right to all the magical weapons we find.'

'Thanks. My left hand hasn't got the skill for a sword, but I reckon I can swing a hammer easy enough. Sadly, I've not got half the strength Falcon had, but I'll wager I can dent a few skulls anyway.'

'Your determination will stand you in good stead,' said Arthur. He paused for a second and reached out for the hammer. Kay went to give it to him, but Arthur took Kay's hand and the hammer at the same time. 'No, don't let go.'

Arthur closed his eyes and reached out with his heart as he did with Excalibur. He felt Kay's burning need for vengeance, and he almost dropped Kay's hand from of the force of it. He'd never felt anything from a person before, just from the magical weapons. But he held on and felt something else too. There was a desire to protect in Kay, for the castle and its people. Arthur smiled at the warmth of that feeling. Then he reached out to the hammer. It was cold, unlike Excalibur and Clarent, it did not warm to him. But on the edge of the coolness, he felt something else. At first, he thought it was a sense of loss, but then he realised that was not right. It was the feeling of being lost.

With no real idea of what he was doing, Arthur pulled those feelings together. Kay's care for the people and the hammer's lost way. Then he let go of both and opened his eyes. 'Do you feel anything?' he asked.

Surprise crossed Kay's face. 'The hammer is warm in my hand. A second ago it was stone cold and now it's warm like a person's touch. What did you do?'

'No idea really,' replied Arthur, 'but I think that hammer is yours now. Just don't feed it your desire for revenge, Kay. Use it to protect the land and its people. I think it will respond better to that.'

Kay looked Arthur in the eyes. 'You saw those feelings in me?'

Arthur nodded.

'I won't apologise for rightful vengeance,' he said defiantly. 'That cursed woman deserves to die for what she's done to this land and my family.' Then his face softened, and a small laugh escaped him. 'Bloody hell, I sound like my mother.'

Kay slapped Arthur on the back. 'Okay, sire, I hear what you're saying. My thirst for vengeance remains, but I won't quench it in blood with this hammer. Despite everything, I fight with you because I believe in what you stand for. So, I won't use your good cause for my own purpose. You have my word on that.'

Kay turned and headed up the wall, the metal hammer light in his hand. Arthur watched him go, hoping he'd done the right thing. Then he shook his head clear and took the steps to the north side.

Lady Anne was waiting for him at the top. She stared out over the empty fields. 'So many different things they could be doing out of sight,' she said as Arthur approached, 'but to discuss that was not why you invited me up here, was it?'

'No. Merlin is off trying to create a simple magical device to shield us from detection, so we can get into Camelot. If we turn up at the castle unshielded, especially Merlin, then Guinevere will know we're there. But while he plays with magic, I want to ask you how you got messages to your man in Camelot so quickly? I don't know why you didn't tell Merlin, but I'm hoping you might tell me.'

'Oh, it's no great secret. I just like to tease Merlin a little sometimes,' laughed Lady Anne gently.

'What? Now? In the middle of this deadly siege?'

'We might not be related by blood,' she replied, 'but where do you think you get your cheeky sense of humour from? Your uncle?'

Arthur saw the playfulness in her eyes, and he couldn't help but grin. 'No, not quite Aurelius is it.'

Lady Anne turned away from the fields and looked at Arthur, a more serious expression crossing her face. 'You keep watch for the enemy and I will explain.'

'Ok.'

'Merlin will kick himself when he hears. Quite simple really, it's just homing pigeons with tiny scrolls tied to their legs. That's how I got my friend the message so fast and so easily.

229

Few people pay attention to the birds, they simply fly right over the walls and straight to their keeper.'

'I suspect Merlin and Guinevere both rarely think about the simpler, non-magical things in life. Guinevere seems especially guilty of this,' continued Lady Anne. 'She uses her power so skilfully, I think it genuinely doesn't occur to her to work in any other way.'

'Good to know, but how does that help us right now?' said Arthur. 'We need to get people into Camelot, not just messages. You'd need a hundred pigeons to carry a person over the walls. Would that even be remotely possible?'

'An interesting question, but you're missing the point,' replied Anne. 'As with many people, Guinevere's own view of the land taints what she thinks others see. Merlin too, though maybe to a lesser extent. After all, he's still trying to solve the problem with magic.'

She paused for a second and asked Arthur a question. 'What would Guinevere least expect us to do? What would she never suspect could lead to her downfall?'

'Something without magic, I guess,' replied Arthur. 'I don't know. Maybe a few of us walk in through Camelot's gates with woollen beards on.'

'Possibly it will come down to something as simple as that,' said Lady Anne. Arthur remained silent, and she turned to see what he was staring at.

'Hold those thoughts for later,' he said at last. He held up his arm to signal at the others. 'See there, just over the hill next to the trees, I can see the top of something slowly moving.'

Before Anne could reply, a shout came from the west wall and then the south. On the east wall, the highest of the four sides, Arthur heard Kay call out, the urgency clear in his voice.

'Get the catapults ready,' Kay shouted down. 'We have siege towers advancing on us. To the south looks closest, heading for our gates.'

Arthur found the nearest archer. 'Get every archer we have onto the walls, all four sides. When those towers get in range, I want fire arrows raining down on them, looking for any exposed timber.'

The archer ran off and Arthur hurried down the steps. He called to Lady Anne as he ran. 'Get the others to support the archers. I'll tell the soldiers to help bring up more burning tar. If they're coming from all four directions at once, then we're in real trouble.'

Arthur sped towards Kane, calling out orders for the burning tar as he sprinted across the courtyard. A bit breathless, he stopped when he got to their catapults. 'How many do we have working now?'

'We managed to get two more going from the remains,' replied Kane. 'But only just, not really a single bolt to spare. Did I hear right, four siege towers rolling our way?'

'Yup, and all from different directions.'

'Damn, we only have three catapults. We don't have enough firepower.'

'Could your engineers rig up something to turn a catapult quickly?' Arthur asked.

'Maybe,' pondered Kane, 'but that'll take time.'

'Ok, get some people working on that, and have the rest keep these catapults firing smoothly. We can't afford for anything to break.'

'What targets do we pick?' asked Kane.

'The north side has the largest tower approaching, but it seems furthest away, so leave that one for now. Concentrate on the other three smaller towers, one catapult to each. I want to test their strength and see if we can pick them off before they reach our walls. If we can at least stop those three before they reach us, then we only have one problem left on the north side.'

Kane got the engineers to begin leveraging the catapults around in the right directions.

'Start firing as soon as you're ready. And get spotters up onto the walls. They can guide you,' added Arthur. 'I want to keep the rest of us free as the towers get closer.'

'We'll get on that too,' said Kane.

Arthur walked away and left them to it. He collared a passing squire. 'Go find Merlin and ask him to join me on the south wall. That tower seems the closest.'

Arthur ran on to the gatehouse, then up to the top, where Jane had already been joined by her son Kay. 'The drawbridge is up, but the moat is narrowest here. Even a small siege tower can easily reach across. How long until we start firing?' she asked.

Suddenly, a whistling boulder passed over their heads.

'Now I guess,' answered Arthur.

The huge rock flew towards the tower, but fell short.

'Ten yards short. Adjust or wait?' called down the spotter standing next to them.

'Adjust. Thirty seconds. How much?' came the reply from the firing crew.

Having watched the speed of the tower's progression, the spotter quickly calculated in her head and called back. 'Five yards.'

Arthur waited as the tower advanced, then another boulder flew over their heads. It sailed towards the tower and found its mark, hitting dead centre and exploding into deadly shards of rock. But instead of shattering the tower's beams and crushing those within, a flash of red appeared at the point of impact, and the tower advanced unscathed.

'Direct hit. No damage,' called the spotter. She looked at Arthur questioningly.

'It must be shielded by Guinevere's magic. Keep at it

though, hit it again, but slow the rate of fire. Look for any weakness to the shields,' said Arthur.

'Remember, magic runs out eventually,' added Arthur, with more confidence than he felt. 'Let's keep up the bombardment as long as we can, then add in the archers when the tower is in range.'

While the spotter called down, relaying the orders, Arthur saw Merlin climb up the last few steps to the top of the gatehouse. Arthur walked over to join him.

'Siege towers on all sides, and it looks like they have magical shields,' he said to Merlin. 'Anything you can do about that?'

'Nothing magical, I am afraid. My reserves of power are still too low. However, there is nothing wrong with my brain. Look carefully at the base of the tower. Can you see the wheels?'

'Oh yes, I see them poking out. The panels on the sides don't quite reach the ground.'

'Exactly. That should be their weakness. The Lady cannot attach a magical shield to nothing, not without her being here. Unless she cast a shield over every single wheel, then we can destroy them,' said Merlin. 'Ask the catapults to aim low at the sides. It will be a very difficult shot, but if they hit the target just right, they will shatter a wheel or two. Broken wheels mean no movement, and that means no reaching our walls.'

Arthur turned to the spotter. 'Aim for the sides, right at the bottom,' he said. 'We want to hit under their shield and take out the wheels. Can you guide them to do that?'

'A tough shot,' she replied, 'but if it can be done, we'll do it.' She ran halfway down the steps and described the exact intention to the catapult crews.

Back on the wall, she calculated the fine angles in her head. 'Turn one finger left. Rewind two fingers shorter,' she called down.

Arthur watched the boulder as it left the catapult and sailed over the wall. It smacked into the ground just left of the advancing tower.

'Quarter finger back,' shouted the spotter.

The tower got closer still as the crew reloaded and adjusted their aim, but before they could fire again, Arthur caught movement in the corner of his eye and turned to see shutters open near the top of the tower. Without hesitation, he launched himself sideways, taking hold of the spotter and Merlin on the way. 'Take cover,' he shouted as loud as he could.

Arthur heard the distant thud of firing ballista, then a rain of huge arrows sped towards the top of the wall. Chunks of stone were blown apart by the giant iron tipped projectiles as they hit the wall. Some arrows passed over the top of the parapets, and he saw an unlucky archer get hit and instantly torn in two.

Before the dust had settled, Arthur leapt to his feet, dragging the spotter with him. 'Get our catapult shot off before they can reload,' he shouted at her, then he ran to the nearest archer.

'If that siege tower can shoot out through its magical shield, then we can shoot in,' he said. 'Set your arrows alight and fire through the tower's shutters next time they open. Show your squad what to do.'

'Yes, sire.'

'Warn us when they are about to fire again, and don't forget to take cover,' Arthur called out as he raced back over to Jane.

'Want me to keep an eye on our defence?' she asked.

'Yes. Try to take out the wheels with the catapult and set fire to the tower by aiming burning arrows through the shutters. Kay, you get a message to the east and west walls to do the same.'

'Will do. And you?'

'I'm going to see what they have in store for us on the north side with that larger tower,' Arthur answered. 'Knowing Guinevere, there'll be more to this than just one tactic.'

'Take cover!' shouted the archer.

Another set of thuds was followed by a rain of huge arrows, but this time they sailed over the south wall.

'Always more than one tactic,' observed Merlin, noticing these massive arrows were tipped with flaming tar. They fell near the far side of the castle and instantly set fire to anything flammable.

'Go to the north wall,' Merlin told Arthur as they both rose. 'I'll handle the fires.'

'Enough magic for that I hope,' said Arthur as he leapt down the steps.

'Sadly not,' said Merlin quietly to himself as he started down the steps as well. 'Just buckets of water carried from the well by many desperate people.'

On the north wall, Arthur arrived to see Lady Anne still watching the largest tower slowly advance. By now, the towers from the east and west were also close enough to fire, and huge arrows descended on the castle from three directions.

'Going for the wheels and shutter openings, I see,' said Anne, calm as always despite the surrounding terror. 'A good plan.'

'Thanks, but you know the odds are in favour of the siege towers, right? Three magically shielded siege towers, all firing giant arrows over our walls. If they take out our catapults, we're finished,' said Arthur. 'And then there is this one.'

He looked out at the tower to the north. It was easily twice the size of the other three. 'It must be in range now. Why haven't they started firing?'

'I am definitely too old for this,' said Merlin from behind them, his breath slow and slightly ragged. He flinched as one of the giant arrows from the south exploded against the inside of the wall below them. 'If you could kindly ask for them to attack from just one side at once, that would be nice. I am not built for running around anymore.'

'I thought you were putting out the fires,' said Arthur.

'That is in hand,' replied Merlin, indicating the many chains of people from the well to the various fires, each one passing buckets of water along as fast as they could.

'Thanks,' said Arthur, his expression betraying his concern for Merlin's tired state.

'No, I am not that low on magic. I am not going anywhere just yet,' he offered in reply. 'Unfortunately, I now need to save everything I have for when we confront the Lady. I have no more to spare for this fight.'

They heard another series of thuds and instinctively ducked. But no arrows flew over the walls and into the castle. Then they heard a cheer from their western wall.

Just over the top of the wall, Arthur could see the western siege tower start to topple sideways, fire engulfing its base. He looked down and their catapult below unleashed another huge rock covered in burning tar. It sailed through the air and hit the tower on its other side, exploding with burning fragments and accelerating the tower's fall.

He called down to Kane. 'Get that catapult turned to the north, let's see what damage we can do here. Keep going with the east and south, we might yet succeed.'

'Already on it, sire,' he called back up with a wicked grin on his face.

As the first flaming stone hurled over the north wall, a cheer went up from the east. Arthur spun around and saw the top of the eastern siege tower in flames, enemy soldiers sliding down its side trying to escape. Another volley of arrows flew up from their walls and rained down on the tower, its magical shield now broken. It caught alight wherever the arrows landed.

'Two down,' said Arthur, some relief edging into his voice. Then the sound he was waiting for erupted from the south. A cheer went up.

A second enormous stone was launched north from their

catapult and then was joined by a third from the second catapult they had turned around. The rocks smashing into the advancing tower, the magic shields flaring and fire splashing everywhere.

'I think we're starting to win,' said Arthur. 'If we can keep this up just a little longer, then we will hold Dunstan today.'

Suddenly, several thuds came from the roof of the tower to the north. Arthur glanced over the parapet before ducking down. 'What did they fire? I didn't see.'

Shaking heads came from all around him, then he heard a quiet whistling from above. As he looked up, the whistling got louder and louder. A group of huge iron arrows descended on the castle courtyard, like hawks attacking. But unlike diving birds, the arrows did not pull up and instead smashed into the catapults and their crews.

The screams reached Arthur's ears and he saw several engineers fall, Kane amongst them. Two of the catapults had metal arrows clean through their shafts, blocking them from launching their own deadly payloads. The third was miraculously untouched.

'No,' shouted Arthur. 'Kane, are you alright? Can you fire back?'

Lady Anne grabbed Arthur by the arm. 'Unfortunately, it's more than just Kane we need to worry about.'

Arthur followed her line of sight. The whole roof of the huge tower to the north was now stripped away, and on its wide top was row after row of ballista, all armed with iron arrows pointing at the sky.

'Get everyone into the corner towers and buildings as fast as you can,' he shouted, sprinting for the steps. But even as he called this out, he heard the thuds start up again from the north. Arthur counted down in his head as he ran towards the final catapult. He saw Kane was rearming it, blood pouring from a deep wound in his side. The remaining engineers were helping, getting the catapult ready to fire as fast as possible.

'Aim for the top of the tower, before they fire any more,' called out Arthur as he heard the whistling start from above. He counted full to twenty, and still the thudding had not ceased from the attacking tower. Salvo after salvo of metal death was being launched into the sky above them.

He looked at Kane as he helped the crew. 'We've got to get this catapult fired in the next five seconds,' he said. 'We won't survive that volley, but the others will have a chance if we take out the roof of that last tower before they can fire again.'

Kane lifted the huge stone onto the catapult with two others, his muscles straining and blood pouring faster from his wound. A fourth engineer poured burning tar onto missile, then leapt to the firing mechanism.

'We won't make it, but you must. Save my family, save our land,' said Kane, blood bubbling from his lips. As the catapult let rip, he grabbed Arthur, and with one last effort shoved him under the base of the firing catapult as it lifted off the ground with the recoil.

The last thing Arthur saw was the rain of deadly arrows smashing into everything around him. Then the catapult descended and knocked him out.

PART 5 – CAMELOT

CHAPTER 19

Arthur awoke slowly, his head aching. He opened one eye. Everything was blurry and he closed it again. He felt around, trying to remember where he was.

'I hear this is getting to be a habit,' a gruff voice announced.

'Uncle?'

'No, don't try to rise, Arthur,' said Lady Anne, scowling a little at her husband. 'Your head took a terrible blow.'

'Horse?' asked Arthur, sinking back into the soft pillow.

'She made it clear she couldn't help. Maybe your head is something she can't fix,' said Aurelius. 'Never seen a horse look so forlorn. Didn't even realise that was possible.'

Arthur opened an eye again, and his vision began to clear. Just his aunt and uncle were in the room with him. Memories of the catapult base rushing towards his head came back to him, and also the rain of arrows.

'Kane,' he said with a start.

Lady Anne shook her head. 'No Arthur. I'm sorry, he didn't make it.'

Arthur closed his eyes and a tear rolled down his cheek. 'Kane's family?' he asked as he wiped his face.

'Yes, they are well. Not everyone made it to cover, but they and many others did thanks to your warning,' said Anne. 'Then Kane's last shot from the catapult tore the top of the siege tower apart. After that it couldn't fire again.'

'By the time we arrived, there was not much left to do,' said Aurelius. 'Most of the remaining enemy had fled. Some were trying to salvage parts from the towers, and a few more regrouping around the entrance to a tunnel, but we made quick work of them all.'

Arthur opened both eyes. He looked from his uncle to his aunt. In his head, he knew they were not related by blood, but his heart did not care about that and he was glad they were here. 'How many didn't make it?' he asked.

'You can't save everyone,' stated Aurelius. 'You've had too many hard lessons to think that's possible.'

'I know,' replied Arthur. 'But I owe it to them to hear what our defence cost.'

'Over fifty souls have departed,' said Lady Anne, 'and twenty more may still leave us.'

'Are we treating any survivors from the other side?'

'Yes, another fourteen,' replied Lady Anne.

'Good. I want to question them,' said Arthur.

'That's not entirely why I kept them alive. But I expected you might like to do that.'

Arthur sat up and reached over to Excalibur. He picked up his sword and the shield lying next to it.

'I hope you will not use Excalibur to question the injured prisoners,' asked Lady Anne.

'No,' said Arthur, and he meant it. The warmth of the sword flowed into his body and sharpened his mind. 'I am going to tell them what I could do to them and then ask them to judge me by what I don't. Hopefully, someone will have some decency in their heart and give us useful information about Guinevere's defences.'

'And if they don't?' asked Aurelius, his expression hardening.

'I will cross that bridge when I come to it,' replied Arthur. 'Where are they?'

'In the dungeons,' said Lady Anne. 'We filled the stables with our own injured. The dungeon was the only place left to treat the rest.'

'Nothing they don't deserve,' added Aurelius. 'Maybe Morgan can scare some sense into them before you get there. Save you some trouble.'

'Anyway, they couldn't have stayed in the stables. I think your horse might have kicked them to death,' he added. 'She was definitely not happy when the enemy injured were taken past her to the dungeons. Especially that one who looked like Jon.'

'What?' said Lady Anne and Arthur together.

'Yes, strange that was,' said Aurelius. 'If I hadn't known he was dead, I would have sworn it was him. You know, Guinevere's man from the tournament?'

Arthur grabbed Aurelius by the shoulder. 'Where did you capture him? Was he by the tunnel?'

'Probably, most of them surrendered at its entrance.'

'We're in trouble,' said Arthur as he started for the door. 'Get everyone out of the castle. Right now!'

'Why? What the hell for?' questioned Aurelius.

'You thought he looked like Jon, it probably is Jon,' said Lady Anne. 'The dead don't always stay dead anymore it seems. And if Jon was trying to get back into the castle, despite their defeat, then that spells terrible trouble for us.'

'Guinevere's plans just keep getting ever more deadly,' stated Arthur as he paused at the archway. 'There's every chance this is her end game for us all, in the most literal sense.'

Arthur raced down to the courtyard and into the keep. People were streaming past all around him. Lancelot caught up with him just before he entered the stairway down to the dungeon.

'What the hell's going on? How can Jon be alive?' asked

Lancelot.

'No time to explain,' said Arthur, grabbing his friend and practically dragging him down the steps. 'Suffice to say it's dark magic and will probably go very bad, very fast.'

Lancelot drew his sword as they ran. He asked no more questions, just concentrated on his footing. They reached the end of the stairway and paused. 'Follow my lead,' whispered Arthur, and he walked calmly into the dungeons.

They rounded the corner, and Arthur saw Morgan standing in front of the bars to a cell. He was relieved, though not surprised, to see Morgan standing well back, out of reach from those inside.

'What do we have here?' said Arthur, approaching the cell and seeing the three prisoners inside as he got closer.

'Three lucky lads, I would wager,' replied Morgan, tapping the bars once with the end of his sword. 'They should be glad to see their king. A bit more tolerant he is, a bit more appreciative of help from his foes. Not like me, you see.'

Morgan tapped the bars again, a little harder this time to emphasise his point.

Arthur scanned the cell. None of the three men looked like Jon. 'Have you questioned any others yet?' asked Arthur.

'Naw, just this first bunch of idiots,' said Morgan. 'To be honest, I'm not convinced they have anything useful to say.'

Arthur held up a hand, then turned to the nearest guard on duty. 'I want the prisoners questioned quickly, so bring the other guards here for instruction.'

Morgan raised his eyebrow but remained quiet, waiting for a signal of some kind. Arthur lowered his hand to Excalibur. 'We'll have our answers soon.'

Morgan nodded and took his stand alongside Arthur and Lancelot.

Five guards appeared from deeper in the dungeon. Arthur beckoned them closer.

'What are your instructions, sire?' the returning guard asked.

Arthur leaned in and quietly whispered. 'Up the stairs. Run.'

The guard looked questioningly back at him.

'Now,' commanded Arthur a little more forcefully.

'What are you horrible men waiting for,' said Morgan. 'A personal invite? Do as your king commands!'

The guards nodded and walked past them just as Arthur heard the ping of a metal bar. It was followed by another, and then two more.

'Here it comes,' said Arthur pulling Clarent from his back. He held the shield before him, then with his other hand let power flow free into Excalibur, and blue fire erupted along its blade.

'Not it. He,' said a voice calmly from deep down the dungeon corridor. 'What kind of king cannot tell the difference?'

Footsteps approached, and they saw Jon walk around the corner. Four others followed him, all with eyes burning red.

'Excellent, I see Morgan and Lancelot are here too,' said Jon as he walked towards them. 'I shall be delighted to deal with you all in one go.'

Arthur stepped forward, bringing up his blazing sword and readying the shield.

Jon sighed at Arthur. 'Pretender king, you do not learn. Your sword did not stop me last time. Why would it now? You continue to disappoint me, but sadly not surprise me.'

'Big speech for you, no?' said Morgan, as he pulled the bow from his back and put a blazing blue arrow through Jon's left eye.

Jon teetered back, but did not fall. He slowly regained his balance and reached up to pull the arrow from his eye socket. 'To be fair to you,' he said to Morgan, staring at him with his remaining eye, 'you did miss Lord Falcon's encore. But really, your friends should keep you better informed.'

'Nae matter to me,' said Morgan as he drew his sword. 'Try that again once I've cut off both your arms.'

'Oh, we're not here to duel with you,' replied Jon shaking his head. 'You see, we've already died once for our queen. What's another time between friends?'

As he spoke, his eye blazed an even brighter red, as did those of the men behind him. They started to advance again, their movements strangely stiff but steady. Little by little, cracks of red fire began to glow in their veins. Arthur could feel the heat coming off them in waves.

'Plan?' said Lancelot.

'None,' replied Arthur.

'Run?' asked Morgan.

'Definitely,' said Arthur, and they turned for the stairs.

'You cannot run. You cannot hide,' Jon called after them. 'There is no stopping this firestorm.'

Arthur tore up the stairs. His legs burned, but he willed them on. The three of them breathed heavily as they climbed, the pounding of their feet echoing up the stone stairway.

They neared the top and heard a boom from below, followed by another. The surrounding air rushed past and up the remaining stairs. 'Run faster!' managed Arthur between his gasps.

He burst out from the stairway just after the others and the wind from the blast pushed them out the doorway. At the far end of the courtyard, the last of the people were running out of the castle gates in blind panic, Aurelius and Lady Anne among those ushering them out.

'Get out!' shouted Morgan as he sped for the gates, despite his extra years still having more breath than Arthur.

Arthur could feel the heat intensify as he heard another boom behind him. He saw Aurelius push his wife out of the gates, with Kay dragging Lady Jane and Ector not far behind them. His uncle turned to start back towards Arthur and then paused. The look on his face said it all as he held still in his tracks, caught between two impossible choices.

Arthur stopped as he ran out of breath, knowing he could not outrun what was coming. Lancelot saw his friend flag and backtracked to help him. Then he also halted in defeat.

'Keep going,' Arthur shouted to Morgan, who was still sprinting, nearly at the gates. 'Get Aurelius out of here.'

Arthur knelt down and drove Excalibur into the stone of the courtyard, as he watched the roaring red fire speed towards them.

'She'll not get the sword this easily,' he said. Then he held on to Excalibur's hilt and placed his shield facing the fire. Arthur poured power into the shield and it blazed bright green.

'Will that help?' said Lancelot, crouching down beside him, the advancing heat making him wince.

'Doubt it,' replied Arthur, 'but we're out of options.'

Sweat ran down Arthur's face as he pulled ever more power into Clarent, green fire erupting around the shield as he willed its magic to run free. Then the boiling red flames hit them.

The intense heat rushed past them, parted in two by the green magic around Arthur's shield. Another boom sounded from below the keep, and the fire intensified. Arthur willed more power into the shield, but no more came. The surrounding heat built further, getting through the shield's defence. Excalibur began to bend where they clung onto it.

'It's not going to hold,' shouted Arthur above the roaring flames.

Sweat flowed down Lancelot's face as he looked around and watched the edges of the magical green shield get pushed back by the raging fires. 'Can you bend the shield more?' he shouted back at Arthur.

'What?'

'Remember that pig's bladder you kicked around when you were a kid?'

A look of realisation dawned on Arthur's face, and he pulled the shield's magical protection around behind them. Another boom shook the ground, closer to them this time, and a jet of fire erupted from the courtyard just six feet away.

'All the way around,' shouted Lancelot, pointing at the stone ground.

Arthur looked down as another explosion from below shook the ground. Cracks appeared in the courtyard's stone, right under their feet. Arthur closed his eyes and thought of a perfect circle. His shield responded and drove its magical protection into the ground and right under them, just as another explosion rocked the castle.

Nothing happened for a second. Then jets of raging red magic hit them from below. Half the courtyard blew upward and they both went with it.

Hanging on to Excalibur and tumbling through the air, Arthur had no idea what was up or down. He concentrated on the protective shield from Clarent and just hoped Lancelot was on the inside with him. When he felt his friend's boot bounce off his back, he smiled despite the pain.

Through the green shield and the raging red fire, he saw a flash of blue. Is that the sky, he thought fleetingly. Then he saw a mass of green and brown. Ah, trees, he thought. Then they smashed into the forest to the south.

'At least you're awake for a change,' said Aurelius.

'Wish I wasn't,' replied Arthur, as he leaned against a tree, having finished throwing up. 'Flying through the air does not agree with me.'

'Did everyone get out ok?' asked Lancelot, grunting as Lady Anne popped his dislocated fingers back into place one by one.

'Most made it. Some got burns, but it could have been far

worse,' said Jane looking at Lancelot. 'Your darling Guinevere came close to finishing us all.'

'I don't think she's anyone's darling anymore,' replied Lancelot, 'least of all mine.'

'But are we safe for now?' Arthur asked Merlin. 'Here in the forest I mean.'

'As safe and hidden as we can be,' he replied. 'I have precious little magic left and your weapons lay quiet. Thankfully, our people are also concealed in this woodland. She may presume we have all finally perished in Jon's attack.'

'From what I've seen over these last two weeks, don't count your chickens,' said Jane. 'That woman leaves nothing to chance. She'll come to check or send someone. No doubt with a boatload of magical tricks and abominations.'

'Sadly, my good lady, I fear you are perfectly correct.'

'So, what do we do about it?' interjected Kay. 'I'm fed up with getting our arses kicked and our people killed. We've got to stop her somehow.'

'We need to get into Camelot to steal back something Merlin was working on,' said Arthur.

'Ah, this sounds strikingly familiar,' said Aurelius. 'Do I need to ask, or will you just tell us all the bad news in one go?'

'Merlin has some magical devices in Camelot that might transport Guinevere out of here, a long way away,' began Arthur.

'Not great, but I've heard worse,' said Morgan.

'Oh, you wait, there'll be more,' stated Aurelius dryly.

'We can't use magic to get into Camelot,' stated Arthur.

'Ah.'

'And I can't use Excalibur or Clarent, as Guinevere will see that as well.'

'Told you. Definitely getting worse.'

'The devices still need to be tested,' Arthur continued.

'Aye, that's not good either.'

'And they need multiple people to operate them at the same time. So, they will also be transported away too.'

'Where to?' asked Morgan.

'We don't know,' replied Arthur.

'Excellent. An all-round suicidal plan to take out Guinevere. I'm in,' said Kay, without a trace of sarcasm. 'How about you, mother?'

'Of course,' added Jane. 'I want to see the look on her face when we send her to hell.'

'I'll not order anyone to do something I won't do myself,' said Arthur. 'I will lead this.'

Lady Anne started to protest again, but Aurelius stepped in first. 'My wife told me all about this, sire, and I mean this with all due respect, but no, you will not be leading us. I concede we need you to come with us. We will need Excalibur to tip the balance once we finally confront the Lady, but the sacrifice must be ours alone. The land needs you, the people need you. A good king thinks of others first and not his own pride.'

Arthur went to object, but Aurelius talked over him. 'How many people do we need?' he asked Merlin.

'I have eleven devices. I need two for testing, so that leaves nine. That should be more than enough to send her far away, for a very long time.'

'Hold on, what do you mean for a long time?' asked Morgan.

'The further a device transports someone, the longer it takes,' explained Merlin. 'It is very likely everyone will not reappear at their destination for many months, or maybe even some years. If we are lucky, she will be at the bottom of the sea or frozen on a mountaintop. But if not, in the meantime, Arthur and I can prepare for her return.'

'Sounds like a dangerous plan. Count me in. One condition though,' said Morgan to Arthur.

'What's that?' Arthur asked.

'One day I will ask you for double payment for my services.'

'But you probably won't live to collect it?'

'That's my risk to take,' replied Morgan. 'As for Geoffrey, he should speak for himself on this.'

'Yes, me too,' said Geoffrey. 'You'll need my sword no doubt.'

Morgan grinned and slapped his friend on the back.

'And mine,' said Marcus, adding his name to the group.

'I'm in too,' stated Lancelot. 'After all, I'm the reason she got so close to us all. If I hadn't tried to court her for so long, then maybe someone would have spotted her deception.'

'But what of the Round Table?' countered Lady Anne. 'Arthur would need you more than ever, with the rest of us gone. You should help him build a new Round Table.'

'There won't be a Round Table if we don't defeat Guinevere,' replied Lancelot. 'This is what must be done to save the land and I must play my part. Maybe the Round Table should have new blood.' He glanced to Arthur and then down at Excalibur, remembering its mixed reaction to his blood boiling away with fiery red edges around the blue glow.

'Are you sure?' said Arthur, understanding Lancelot's look.

Lancelot simply nodded in reply.

'You'll need one more,' said Lord Bane. 'I will join my son.'

'Bloody hell, I've never seen so many people queue up so quickly for a one-way trip to oblivion,' said Jane. 'Either you truly are the greatest inspiration, Arthur, or we're all raving mad.'

'There are your nine volunteers,' concluded Ector. 'Can't say I'm disappointed to be staying and not get transported to who knows where. But I'll come along to help you get into Camelot. I've stayed there a lot in the past with Galahad, and he did like to investigate its secrets. There's a thing or two I know about that castle that's not widely known, not even to you, Arthur.'

Ector stood. 'Which returns me to the first problem you pointed out, sire. How the hell do we get in there without using any magic?'

'I've been thinking about that. I've got just the plan.'

'Are you sure you know what you're doing?' asked Morgan quietly as they walked towards Camelot's open gates. 'Not like this hasn't been tried many times in the past.'

'He's got a point, sire,' whispered Aurelius, hitching up his stolen uniform and looking around at the massed army outside the gates. 'Pretending to bring in prisoners is the oldest trick in the book, and it usually doesn't work. Only takes one of them to recognise us.'

'Stop whispering,' urged Arthur, scratching at his fake beard as they crossed the drawbridge. 'And give our prisoners a shove for the look of it. Those guards are watching.'

Aurelius gave his wife a push in the back, and she tripped over the chains round her ankles.

'Shove me like that and you'll feel my boot up your arse, you heathen,' shouted Jane, reaching down to help Lady Anne up, despite the chains attached to her own arms and legs.

They stopped in front of the guards at the gates. Jane still held up Lady Anne and spat at them all. 'I take that back. Worse than heathens the lot of you.'

'Prisoners for the Lady,' said Aurelius to the guards. 'Dunstan Castle has fallen, though the cost was high.'

Jane swiped a kick at him, but Aurelius shoved her back. 'Be still or you won't even make the dungeons.'

'Which way's the entrance?' he asked the guard as Morgan tightened his grip on the women's chains.

'First left, past the stables, into the smaller keep and go right,' replied the guard. 'Don't envy you seeing the Lady though. She's not happy about the losses.'

'At least she didn't have to send those lads outside,' chipped in the guard next to him, pointing at the assembled army. 'We're due to journey with them to the middle lands tomorrow. She'd have been really unhappy to delay that plan.'

'Ha, as long as we get an easy ride guarding women in the dungeon for a few days, and some food in our bellies, then I don't care,' said Morgan.

'Not if that woman finds the range of your arse,' replied the first guard, seeing Jane struggle against her chains. The other guards dutifully laughed at their sergeant's joke as he waved them through.

'Thanks,' said Aurelius, leading their party onwards.

'Bloody hell, that was easy. All you southerners really are a bit soft in the head,' said Morgan as they rounded the corner of the stables. 'You lot wouldn't last five minutes in the highlands. If you weren't eaten by wolves, then the neighbours would've sold you a herd of haggis by sundown.'

'Har bloody har,' said Geoffrey, as he pushed open the door and they entered the lower keep.

They moved to the side of the corridor as a few knights came running past them from the right. Instead of turning that way, Arthur and the others followed Ector to the left.

'Not far to the first hidden door,' he said. 'Just around this corner I think.'

'I hope so,' said Arthur. 'Someone will soon ask where we're taking these prisoners if we are not careful. We're going away from the dungeons, so we won't really have a good answer.'

Another group of knights ran past them. Arthur glanced at them as they turned the corner. He saw the last knight slow and look back at them curiously before he rounded the corner.

'Pick up the pace,' he said. 'Where's this door?'

Ector slid his hand down the wall, but nothing happened. Behind them, Arthur could hear heavily armoured footsteps start to get closer. Morgan stepped in front of him and drew his sword, Geoffrey moving alongside him instinctively.

Nothing happened and Ector moved along to the next join in the stonework, repeating his scan.

Arthur drew Excalibur to step up with Morgan, but Merlin placed a warning hand on his shoulder. 'If you use the sword, Guinevere will know we are here. We are not ready for that just yet.'

'He's right,' said Morgan. 'We'll hold them off while you take Merlin to his devices.'

'Lancelot, Marcus, Kay and I will stay with you,' said Bane. 'If we have to fight, we might as well take them on with some force and see if we can secure the keep's main door. That will give Merlin and Arthur time to find those devices.'

Aurelius unlocked Jane and his wife's chains so they could move freely. Jane pulled her concealed daggers from her belt. 'Count me in too,' she said to Bane. 'Oh, and Aurelius, don't get killed. I owe you for that shove.'

Lady Anne rubbed at her wrists before pulling the wickedly sharp needles from her hair. 'Maybe I shall distract him,' she suggested to her newfound friend, 'while you extract your revenge.'

They both grinned wickedly at Aurelius as he discarded their chains on the floor. 'Just make sure you put your daggers away first,' he replied.

Morgan and Geoffrey took their stance at the corner just as the first knight rushed around with his sword drawn. A split second after Geoffrey laid him out with one punch, Arthur heard a click from the wall near Ector. The five of them slipped through the hidden doorway in the wall, as Arthur heard the fighting in the corridor begin.

After the noise, the secret passage was deathly quiet. Small beams of light from tiny gaps in the walls crisscrossed each other in the gloom, giving just enough light to see.

'Follow me,' said Ector.

'How far to Merlin's quarters?' asked Arthur as they filed one by one through the narrow passageway.

'Not far,' replied Ector. 'I just hope they haven't discovered the hidden door and sealed it, or heaven forbid the Lady's in there.'

'I do not know unfortunately,' interjected Merlin, breathing a little more quickly in the confined space. 'I cannot tell where she is at the moment. Either she is not using any magic right now, or quite possibly, she has learnt how to hide its use from me.'

'That really doesn't help,' said Ector quietly as he came to a halt by a small door in the wall.

'I thought you said it was hidden?' questioned Aurelius.

'From the other side,' replied Ector simply. He steadied himself and drew his sword. The others did the same. 'Ready?'

Everyone nodded and he pushed open the door. They streamed in fast, covered by Lady Anne and the bow she'd received from Morgan.

Arthur breathed a sigh of relief at the sight of the empty chamber. He looked around and saw that everything appeared undisturbed. Even the lock on the room's door was still intact.

'Why's Guinevere left this room alone?' asked Arthur. 'Surely she'd have had it searched thoroughly.'

'She has,' said Merlin walking over to his cupboards. 'See that red book on my worktable? It is in the wrong order. It should be before the green one, not after it. I think she may have searched my room herself, then tidied up afterwards.'

'Why on earth would she bother trying to tidy up?' questioned Aurelius as he looked out the window, using the height of the second floor to scan out across the castle. Over the walls, he saw the large army still waiting. 'Surely she couldn't have expected to leave the room exactly the same?'

'I think that is precisely what the Lady wanted to do,' said Merlin, opening the cupboard and running his fingers down the hinges of its door. 'Notice those two books have no titles on their covers. Some people confuse certain reds and greens. I suspect she suffers from this condition and hence could not tell the difference. If not for that slight change, I would never have known she had been here.'

'More to the point, did Guinevere find your magical devices?' asked Arthur.

Merlin pressed down on a hinge and a hidden compartment at the back clicked open. 'I cannot say whether she found them, but thankfully she did not take them.' Merlin gathered the devices carefully and put them on the worktable one by one. 'However, we must consider the possibility that she knows of their existence, and maybe even their purpose, but left them here for some reason.'

Arthur brought his hand up to massage his forehead. 'Ah, always so complicated. It's like trying to predict which way the wind will blow next.'

'Don't look at me,' said Aurelius. 'We're way past my eat, sleep, think, fight advice. This complex intrigue is more my wife's area.' He shielded his eyes to observe the army outside in the bright sunlight. While he watched, distant shouts could be heard and the army started to manoeuvre towards the gates, heading inside. 'However, whatever you make of it, you'd better do it fast. I think they finally know we're here.'

Arthur moved over to Merlin at the worktable. 'How long to test two devices and get the rest ready?'

'Too long maybe. But I do have one last trick up my sleeve. Go help the others defend the keep. Buy me a little more time to work my magic.'

'Lady Anne and Aurelius, go see what you can do to help,' said Arthur. 'No doubt Lord Bane will have plans in place already. Ector, go with them and tell Bane I will lend my sword wherever is needed the most, then meet me back here and let me know.'

They rushed out, and Arthur quietly closed the door after them. 'Ok Merlin, tell me what you intend to do. How bad are things?'

'I am fairly sure Guinevere knows about these devices and just left them,' answered Merlin as he worked. 'Maybe she does not consider them a threat, or quite possibly she does not care if we use them. Worst-case scenario, she may actually want us to use these devices.'

'So why are you still working on them?'

'Two reasons really. One, we do not have any other options.'

'And two?' asked Arthur, starting to dread what was coming.

'I think I can prepare them to do something she does not expect,' said Merlin. He paused what he was doing for a second and looked at Arthur. 'But the cost to us will be high.'

'Higher than Guinevere bringing the entire land under her tyranny?' asked Arthur. 'Actually, do I even want to know?'

'This time, Arthur my boy, despite what I said before, I would like to spare you the burden.'

Merlin picked up two of the devices and they softly glowed in his hand. 'I know you do not have all the information you need, Arthur, and I will certainly never command you, but in this matter I would advise you let me proceed.'

'Do it,' said Arthur after an instant's consideration. 'The people and this land will only suffer more under her grip. I think we must pay our cost, whatever it is.'

'Go help the others,' said Merlin. 'I will bring you the devices very soon.'

Arthur left the room and closed the door behind him. Merlin took a deep breath and shimmered. A second later, he split in two. After a heartbeat, the two Merlins concentrated and split into four. They flexed their hands, blue magic shimmering around them, then once more they steeled themselves and spilt into eight.

'That is going to hurt in the morning,' said the first Merlin, breathing heavily despite the powerful magic radiating off him.

'You are not wrong,' said the second, massaging his temple.

'Well, it would if we lived that long,' commented the third. 'Our power has grown immensely, but I fear our time has very much shortened.'

'Morning is probably not something we need to worry about then,' added the fourth, as he held up his faded hand to reinforce the point.

'In which case, I suggest we best get to work,' said the fifth.

'To work indeed,' they all chimed in together.

CHAPTER 20

Halfway down the stairs, Arthur caught Ector running towards him. It was strangely quiet in the keep, no sound of fighting.

'Situation? Plan?' questioned Arthur quickly.

'This little keep was fairly empty, according to Bane. A few enemy knights slain or tied up. Doors barred, but they won't hold that long.'

'Where does Bane need me?'

'You, Kay and Geoffrey are to hold the stairs as long as possible,' said Ector. 'With Excalibur, Clarent and Kay's hammer, you have some powerful magical weapons. You should be able to slow their progress up this narrow stairway.'

'And the rest of you?' asked Arthur.

'They're up top already, bows at the ready. Morgan and Marcus are already exchanging ideas on how to cripple the enemy and slow everyone's progress. We might be able to slow the flow of soldiers into the keep, whilst you make it hard for them on the stairs. Hopefully, Merlin will be ready by the time you're pushed back up to the second floor. After that, retreat to the top via the ladder and we can seal the trapdoor after you. That will be the hardest place for them to breach. Though what we do after that, I've no idea.'

'If we survive the initial attack, we'll worry about that later. You help on the roof but run back to us if anything changes.'

Ector nodded and continued up the stairs while Arthur went down. He reached the bottom and saw Kay and Geoffrey getting ready. They had dragged tables from the keep's small hall and piled them up at the bottom of the stairs, almost blocking the entry to the stairwell completely.

'We've done the same at the door,' said Geoffrey. 'It won't stop them for long, but it will slow them down.'

Arthur nodded. 'Great. Once they breach the barricade, I'll shield us with power from Clarent. I should be able to block their arrows at least, if not all their swords. You and Kay take it in turns to return blows, but conserve your energy. We just need to slow them down to give Merlin some time. I don't want us getting drawn into a full battle.'

They heard the first crash from the main door and Arthur drew Excalibur, pulling power into the sword. He adjusted Clarent on his arm and let power flow freely into his shield too. It came alive with green fire and Arthur extended this across the whole of the stairway in front of them.

Another crash came from the door and then sounds of outside came rushing in with the enemies' charge. The roar of the soldiers hit them like a wave, and they saw their makeshift barricade get pulled quickly apart.

Arrows thudded into Arthur's shield, the magical green fire consuming them as they hit. Then the first of the soldiers reached them. Most of the blows from their swords glanced off his shield, but some got through.

They stepped up one stair whilst they parried the slashes from their enemies. Arthur sliced their weapons in two where he could, but the broken ones were replaced faster than he could swing Excalibur. The repeated clashing of iron echoed around the tight space, filling their ears.

'Up another step,' shouted Arthur, though he doubted they could even hear him. Arthur saw a shimmer from Kay's hammer as he launched a powerful blow at the two soldiers in front of them. The hammer glided through Arthur's shield and smashed into the soldiers one after the other. Even with all the noise, Arthur could hear the screams and breaking bones.

The two soldiers went down hard, but more replaced them

instantly, and the barrage of arrows increased its intensity in response. Arthur pulled more power into the shield. It responded to his call, but the effort was draining him fast. He could feel his legs begin to weaken.

Geoffrey stepped up another step, and Arthur felt himself pulled along by the big man. The large hand remained on his shoulder, keeping him steady as Geoffrey switched to single-handed blows, parrying more strikes from their enemy.

Kay hit out again with the hammer, blow after blow. But every time the downed soldiers were replaced with more. Arthur saw the strain start to show on Kay's face too, though his determination never faltered.

'We've got to do something, we can't keep this up much longer,' shouted Arthur into Geoffrey's ear.

'But what?'

'The last thing I ever wanted to do,' said Arthur almost to himself. He let enormous power into Excalibur. He wanted the sword to run free with magic like it had never before. With this, the sword burned painfully in his hand.

'No,' came a single word from Merlin as he appeared behind Arthur. The word echoed with power and the fighting ceased instantly. Merlin started down the stairs and another figure moved into view behind him.

They all watched, friend and foe alike, as two Merlins pushed past a surprised Geoffrey and thrust their fingers into Arthur's magical shield. The green fire hugged their hands and leapt between the two sorcerers as they made the shield their own.

'We can hold them briefly,' said one Merlin, already starting to fade. 'The devices are ready. Our brethren will follow you to the top of the keep. They will show you what must be done.'

Despite not fully understanding what he had seen, Geoffrey didn't hesitate and pulled Arthur up the stairs, Kay following close behind. Arthur stumbled as they ran, but he soon found the sword's warm comfort return and his strength began to restore. By the time they reached the top, Arthur was first up the ladder and burst into the fading light.

Most of the others were spread out around the edges of the keep, firing arrows from the parapets. Aurelius was ferrying arrows from a dwindling stack in the corner.

A few drops of rain started to fall, and Jane glanced up at the darkening clouds. 'That's not good. Do your magical bowstrings still work when they get wet?' she asked Lady Anne.

'Unlike common strings, they will still draw and fire quite well,' she replied. 'But their strength will be less. My magic amplifies the bowstring's power, but it cannot generate it completely.'

Jane looked over to Arthur after she loosed off another arrow. 'You'd better be bringing some good news, young man. When we run out of arrows, that stream of soldiers down there will become a flood.'

Before Arthur could reply, the remaining Merlins followed him out of the trapdoor, with Kay and Geoffrey emerging last. Ector shepherded them out as fast as he could and lowered the door. He rammed its huge bolts into place and stood back.

'Ok, I'll give you that one,' said Jane. 'Not just one, but six sorcerers, that's got to be some kind of good news.'

'Yes, it is,' said Merlin. 'The devices are setup and ready for you all. They just need to be activated.'

The Merlins pulled them from their pockets. Nine balls of magic in total. They handed them out quickly.

'Listen carefully,' said Merlin, as the others resumed shooting with the few remaining arrows. 'Each device obeys your will. Just decide when to activate it in your mind and the device will trigger instantly.'

'You will have to be close to the Lady, but you do not need to physically touch her. However, it will be best if you do surround her. There is no direction of fire for these devices, their effect will just radiate out. With that, Guinevere must be in the middle to be transported the furthest away.'

'Do they need to be triggered at exactly the same time?' asked Lancelot.

'Fortunately, they do not. I have made sure the effect will last for a few seconds,' replied Merlin. 'When you see the first one fire, then activate your own. That will be close enough.'

'Excellent plan,' said Aurelius. 'One minor detail. They know we're here. They're going to overrun us soon and then presumably kill us all. How the hell do we beat them, get to the Lady, and trap her all alone?'

The small keep suddenly shook, and Marcus grabbed hold of the parapet whilst he peered over the side. He stared in disbelief as the building shuddered again.

'Don't think you need to worry about all that, Aurelius,' Marcus shouted above the noise. 'I think it's going to be a challenge living past the next few minutes.'

'What the hell is it?' Arthur ran over, nearly losing his footing as the building shook.

'You remember when we first met, where you spared my life? You know, all those big rocks with deep red quartz running through them. Well, I think the biggest rock has grown arms and legs, and it's climbing up the wall.'

Arthur snatched a glance over the edge and ducked back quickly as a long boulder shattered the edge of the parapet and shards of rock went sailing over his head.

'It just threw its bloody finger at me,' he shouted.

'Ha, only nine more and it won't be able to grab you,' stated Aurelius with dry sarcasm.

'More like nineteen,' added Marcus. 'It's got four arms.'

'We're nearly out of arrows,' called out Jane.

'They've reached the trapdoor,' shouted Geoffrey, as he

stood on it with Kay, trying to keep it closed. Even with their weight and the huge bolts, it shuddered against the heavy blows from below. Around their feet, bits of wood began to splinter.

'I don't know what they've got down there,' screamed Kay above the noise, 'but this door won't hold for long.'

Arthur watched his friends in their desperate battle. Jane and Lady Anne running out of arrows as a volley from the enemy passed just over their heads, Lancelot and Bane throwing the last remaining defensive rocks over the edge, Morgan and Marcus slowing down and firing single arrows at the advancing rock creature searching for a weak point, and finally the others looking to him for instruction, for anything.

'The Lady has too many plans within plans,' he whispered to himself. 'It's time I really started using that against her.

He stepped back to the opposite edge from Marcus. 'Everyone, retreat to me,' he shouted.

One by one they moved from their positions, the Merlins coming with them. Then Arthur steadied himself. He reached out with his heart and felt the power in his weapons, just waiting to be called, waiting to be set free.

Out of the corner of his eye, he saw Jane caught by a volley of arrows. Ector stopped and returned to drag her with him as she bled onto the roof. But Arthur put it all out of his mind. He felt the power rising as he let it flow into his sword and shield, each one igniting with magical fire. He pulled at the power, kept it building, not caring where it was coming from.

The sky was almost dark, and rain poured down. Puddles of water gathered as the trapdoor shattered from its hinges and soldiers streamed out. From over the side of the wall, a giant hand made of rock appeared and smashed down on the top of the keep. The creature climbed over the parapets, not caring what was in its way, hand after hand smashing down on the roof. It finally crashed through the top of the wall and crushed enemy soldiers as it brought its legs up. Then it stood on the roof of the keep and adjusted its stance to face them, one foot stomping on the open trapdoor and sending the soldiers below tumbling back down the ladder.

The remaining soldiers on the roof looked around in fear, unsure of what to do. The rock creature ignored them completely and just strode through them as if they were confetti in the wind. Some fled back down the ladder as the trapdoor became clear again, while others cowered on the opposite side.

'That takes care of the soldiers,' shouted Lancelot. 'But what about that thing?'

'Leave it to me,' called out Arthur. He let the enormous power in his sword and shield cross over. The green fire around the shield became laced with shards of blue, and it spread out across their whole group. The creature punched down into the shield and its hand just disintegrated. Splinters of rock flew out, and the last few soldiers on the roof were torn to shreds by the stone shrapnel.

'Can you hold this shield?' Arthur shouted at Merlin.

Merlin looked at the shield, and he reached out to it with one hand. Veins of green and blue magic licked at his fingers, and his hand faded even more.

'We can, but not for long,' he replied. His expression hardened with concentration. Then all the Merlins plunged their hands into the magic streaming from Arthur's shield, taking it on as their own and separating it from Clarent.

Another massive hand smashed into the magical fire to their right. Arthur took his chance and dived left to emerge outside the shield's protection. No sooner had he done this than the monster turned its full attention to him.

It flexed its arms and magic pulsed through the red veins of quartz. In return, Arthur let more power into both his sword and shield, and they burned in his hands, hotter than ever before. He did not know how much further he could push them before they stopped responding, but he couldn't see any other option.

A split appeared in the rock, where the creature's head might have been. The monster let out a roar and charged. With no technique, just raw power, it smashed two giant hands into Clarent. The shield held, shattering both the monster's hands, but Arthur felt his arm break as the force of the blow sent him crashing back into the wall at the edge of the keep.

Lancelot moved towards his friend. 'No!' shouted Arthur. 'You won't last a second.'

The monster advanced and Arthur rose painfully to his feet, his left arm hanging by his side. Power flowed through Excalibur, and he held it high before him. The monster crashed down with its last remaining fist and Arthur stepped aside. He brought Excalibur down, and the burning blade sliced through the rock, severing the monster's remaining hand at the wrist.

It roared in almost animal like pain, but undeterred it started stamping down on the ground, trying to crush Arthur with its feet. Powerful but slow, Arthur avoided its blows despite the pain in his arm. Bit by bit, he sliced pieces from the creature as he ducked and weaved between its stomping feet.

Cut by cut, Excalibur tore away chunks of rock, until finally Arthur sliced a foot from the monster's body and it came crashing down. It lay on the floor, red veins throbbing slowly like a fading heartbeat.

'What are you?' questioned Arthur as he approached. 'What do you want?'

The monster crawled towards him. It extended what was left of an arm and reached out to the sword.

'Does Excalibur mean something to you?'

The monster tried to reach out further, but the red veins became dull and it lowered its head. After an instant, it became totally still and the glowing red quartz finally went dark.

Arthur sagged, and Lancelot ran over to help him. He lifted

Arthur to his feet. 'You did it. I don't really know how, but you kept us alive.'

Arthur looked at the still form and back to the burning sword in his hand. 'Something's not right,' he said to his friend.

'What?'

'Do you trust me?' said Arthur.

Lancelot nodded.

'Help me over to where its heart might be,' he requested.

Lancelot looked doubtful, but he did as Arthur asked.

Arthur sheathed the sword and reached out to touch his hand to the monster's centre. Under his hand, a slight flash of red pulsed where he touched.

'She filled it full of rage,' he said.

'What?' said Lancelot again.

'Guinevere. She filled it full of rage, when all it wanted to do was to come home.' Arthur drew Excalibur again and plunged it into the monster's heart.

Like drawing new breath, red fire flooded through the veins of quartz in its body. A forearm crashed to the floor, then another, and the monster rose up again. Hands and limbs of stone regrew as the mass of rock rose. Lancelot and Arthur staggered back as one of the Merlins strode over, blue magic crackling from his hands.

'No, wait!' shouted Arthur, and Merlin stopped.

The creature looked down at them, and then at the sword in its heart. It brought an arm round as the fingers finished regrowing on its hand. The creature touched the sword and fire pulsed stronger from its centre. Slowly, the fire was turning purple. As Arthur approached again, he could see blue flecks running through the red quartz.

Arthur looked up at what might have been its face. The creature knelt down and lightly touched his shoulder.

'It missed the sword,' said Arthur, feeling it in his bones.

'They became. I don't know what the word is or even if there is a word for this. I guess the closest is maybe friends or family. The sword was part of it for nearly twelve years.'

'Bloody hell,' said Aurelius, with the rain dripping down his face. 'Well, I hope it's your friend too.'

A quiet grunt came from behind them, and Arthur saw Jane struggling to rise. Even with Ector's help, she couldn't stand.

He placed his hand on the creature again. He pictured Jane in his mind and then Horse. Hoping it could understand, Arthur walked over to Jane and the monster followed. When it reached her, the rocky creature held out a hand.

Arthur bent over Jane as she clutched her bleeding side. 'Look at me,' he said to her. 'You have to live; do you hear me?'

She spat out some blood. 'Not dead yet,' she replied.

'Promise me you'll look after the land if I don't return?' said Arthur. 'Someone has to carry on the fight for the people.'

'What, you'd risk leaving the kingdom to an old bitch like me?' she replied through gritted teeth.

'Ah, you're not so old,' said Arthur, and she grinned weakly at his reply.

'I'll make sure she lives, or I'll die trying,' added Ector, as he helped her up into the huge rocky palm. 'I'm not losing two commanders in one lifetime.'

'Ha, what makes you think I want a failed bodyguard?' she said, but looked grateful for his strength nevertheless.

The creature gently closed its hand around them. Before Arthur could say another word, it leapt off the keep and into the mass of soldiers below. It strode through ranks of troops as if they weren't there, arrows bouncing off it as harmlessly as the rain. Smashing through the gatehouse, it left them all in its wake.

'Aye. You don't see that every day,' said Morgan.

'Why'd you let Ector go?' asked Lancelot. 'We needed him to take Jane's place. Now you'll have to do it.'

'She wouldn't make it without him,' replied Arthur, sagging to the ground and clutching his injured arm.

'What if one of us has two devices?' Marcus asked Merlin, then he noticed there was only one. 'Hold on, where're the rest of you?'

'All gone, I am afraid. Not enough power left.' Merlin put his hands into the pockets of his robe. 'But that is not our biggest concern. To answer your question, no you cannot use two devices. You would be torn apart as they triggered.'

'Sacrifices have to be made in war sometimes,' said Bane, stepping in to look at Arthur's arm.

'And then they would tear the rest of us apart, without taking the Lady anywhere,' added Merlin. 'Sorry, they are not very flexible in their use. Regrettably, I did not have enough time to give us more options. We could use less of them, but we risk the Lady returning too quickly.'

Arthur looked at Lancelot. 'Come on, we knew this might happen. Not a great surprise, is it? We're just lucky we're still standing.'

Arthur reached down with his good arm to steady himself, his hand splashing into the puddle, then he pushed to get up. But instead of rising to his feet, he went the opposite way and fell into the water. He held his breath instinctively as the water rushed by him.

Just when he couldn't hold it any longer, Arthur broke the surface and sucked in a lungful of air. A hand reached down to help him, and he was pulled onto the bank by a powerful grip.

'Good to see you again, sire,' said the young man.

Arthur looked at him in equal measures of disbelief and happiness. 'Bevs, is that you?' he said cautiously. 'You're old. Well, older.'

'Not so old as you,' said Ellie, as she touched Arthur on the shoulder to dry him.

'It's so good to see you both,' he said, 'but I've got to get back to the others. There's not much time.'

'You're right, there is not,' said Ellie, moving her hand to Arthur's broken arm. 'But I have just enough.'

She looked at Bevs. 'Are you sure?' he asked.

She nodded and closed her eyes. Arthur felt the warmth in his arm, and he looked down to see it straighten, just a tingle where the bones rejoined and healed themselves. Arthur flexed his muscles, the arm completely healed. 'Wow, thank you,'

Ellie removed her hand. A tired sigh escaped from her lips, and Bevs stepped in closer to support her.

'Wait, what just happened?' asked Arthur, looking at the tiredness in her face, then spotting a tiny streak of grey in her long hair.

Bevs took Ellie's hand. 'She healed you, but it took a lot of effort and a little time.'

Arthur stared at them both.

'It took her time. Healing is no different from any other time she uses great power, she uses up some of her own lifetime,' explained Bevs.

Arthur got up. 'No, you can't keep doing that.'

'Already done silly,' said Ellie, smiling. She played with the small grey streak in her hair. 'Suits me, don't you think? Makes me into a real lady now.'

Then her mood turned serious, and she placed a hand gently on Arthur's face. 'You have a lot to do, young king, and you know you always need my help. The Lake and I might have grown up now, but you're still my friend, same as always.'

She turned to Bevs, the beginnings of a small tear in the corner of her eye. 'You know what you must do.' Not a command or question, merely a statement of fact.

'Yes. I wish I could stay, but I have to go with him,' he replied. 'You're right, he needs all the help he can get, and you should rest after fixing his arm.'

She nodded and rose up to gently kiss Bevs on the lips. 'The Lake will take you where you need to go.'

Before Arthur could protest further, the water reached out for him and Bevs. Then, in an instant, they were gone.

Ellie sat down tiredly with her feet in the shallows. She felt the sadness of the Lake too, the pain of their friends having to leave to face an uncertain future. Ripples played gently with her feet. 'I don't know if we'll see them again,' she answered.

The Lake lapped at her feet some more, pushing a little harder, and she sat thoughtfully for a moment. Then an expression of determination appeared on her face as she seemed to make up her mind. 'You know what, you're right, I'm not having this. It's taken me a hundred years to grow up and find a nice boy. Bevs has been nothing but loyal and strong for his friends. If that lady thinks she can just disintegrate him or whatever for helping Arthur, then she can jolly well think again.'

Ellie scooped a handful of water from the Lake and rose to her feet. She smiled and let power gather in her hand. A ripple appeared in the Lake, but instead of spreading out, it strangely contracted to a point right under her hand. When the ripple disappeared, a drop of water rose from the Lake and floated up to join the water in her hand. It was followed by another ripple and another drop.

Soon the drops became a stream and then a torrent, all flowing into her hand. Ellie held her arm steady until the entire lake was empty. She felt the weight of it in her hand, untold tonnes of water, and she grinned from ear to ear. 'Ready to go help the boys?'

In her hand, tiny waves rippled with the power of an ocean.

'Good. It may take us a little longer to get there, what with me carrying a whole lake and everything.' She adjusted her stance and got ready. 'But you know what, we'll show that woman who's the real lady around here.'

CHAPTER 21

Arthur rose, spluttering from the drain at the base of the main keep, back in Camelot once more.

'You'd think I'd get used to that,' he said, spitting out water.

'Better than flying through the air though?' grinned Bevs, already on his feet and helping the others out.

'Oh yes, definitely better than flying,' agreed Arthur.

'Bevs, is that you? You're all grown up,' said Lady Anne, gratefully taking his hand as he helped her out of the dirty water. 'I'm so glad you're alive, but what happened?'

'Short version please,' said Aurelius, looking around them quickly for the entrance to the large keep, trying to get his bearings. Bane stood beside him, watching in case any of the soldiers rushing to the main gate stopped to pay closer attention to them. 'They must be after that creature still,' he observed.

Lady Anne patted Bevs on the shoulder. 'It's ok dear, just the highlights would be lovely.'

'Ellie and the Lake took me to their kingdom and spent years nursing me back to health. A lot of time passed there, but not much here.' Bevs cautiously walked around the wall with the others. 'I've no idea how it works. Not sure Ellie does either.'

'Great, that's all settled then,' said Aurelius. 'Love to hear the full story sometime, but right now we've got a woman to kill.'

'I know, we've been watching. Well, watching Arthur really,' said Bevs.

'How?' asked Arthur, but Bane whispered for them to hush. Around the corner, they could see the entrance to the keep. A small company of guards milled about outside its entrance.

Morgan hefted his sword in readiness. 'What now? Rush them and get inside before the others notice?'

'Simple,' said Aurelius.

'Effective?' questioned Geoffrey.

'Only one way to find out.' Morgan stepped around the corner and sprinted at the guards. Geoffrey and Marcus followed a split second later, correctly guessing what their friend would do. The others rushed in to support them and fanned out to surround the guards.

Without his sword, Arthur swapped his shield onto his right arm and worked with Kay. The large knight swung his hammer in powerful blows with his left hand, making quick work of the soldiers in front of them. Arthur blocked the counter swipes from their foes. Between them all, the guards were down in less than ten seconds.

Lady Anne stood by the door. Having despatched the guards inside with her bow, she waved them in. Once through the doorway, Aurelius and Lancelot closed the large doors and bolted them.

Morgan slapped Arthur on the back. 'Good to see you adapting, young sire, and I didn't even need to teach you that. But don't get cocky though. You and Kay side by side won't work so well in these small corridors. Not enough room.'

He handed Arthur his bow and a few remaining arrows. 'Use these and cover us as we advance. Now Bevs is here, he can take Jane's place and you can stay.'

'I can't let him do that,' said Arthur.

Aurelius held Arthur by the shoulders as if he were still his squire. 'No arguing, boy. We don't have the time. Do I really need to tell you again? A king must serve his people and the land, not himself or his friends.'

Arthur swapped his shield back to his left arm and drew an arrow ready to fire with Morgan's bow. 'With you to constantly remind me, how could I forget?' Arthur gestured forward before Aurelius could reply, and grinned. 'After you then, my good knight.'

'Very funny,' growled Aurelius as he scanned the walls. 'Where're all these secret passages Ector went on about? This will be the shortest surprise attack in history if we can't creep up on the Lady.'

Morgan lent on a stone in the wall, and a doorway clicked open. 'Not just a pretty face, huh? Main hall or courtroom chambers?'

'To run a battle campaign, I would pick the hall,' said Bane. 'Plenty of space for planning and a conveniently shaped table for discussion.'

'Round Table it is then,' replied Morgan, and he disappeared into the gloom.

Arthur brought up the rear just behind Merlin. 'I've changed my mind,' whispered Arthur. 'I do need to know the size of the cost I'm committing my friends to. What's your plan?'

Merlin trudged onwards. 'The last option of a reluctant sorcerer, I fear. I increased the power in the devices to as much as they can hold.'

'How far will it send Guinevere?'

'Very far away, for a long, long time. Maybe as good as forever,' said Merlin. 'She likely knows about the devices as I said. She may even be happy for us to use them. Sending her away could even fit into one of her many plans. But if I send her far enough, then I do not see how she could possibly use that to her advantage. The distance and time would be too great.'

'What does that mean for my friends?'

Merlin grimaced, his heavy footsteps matching his mood. 'I

am sad to say, all your friends will be gone as well. There is no conceivable way you will see them ever again. Nor they this land of ours.'

'Oh,' said Arthur, now fully understanding the implications of Merlin's intentions. He walked a little further, lost in thought, then he quietly broke the silence once more. 'And what of you, Merlin? I noticed you hiding your hands in your robe. How much magic do you have left?'

'Enough to see this day through.'

'And then?' asked Arthur.

'Never one to give up on your questioning were you, Arthur.' Merlin smiled. 'Whatever happens today, never lose that. Always seeking to understand is a valuable trait, young sire.'

Before he could push Merlin further, Arthur bumped into a stationary figure. Lancelot held his finger to his lips and gestured Arthur forward. They reached the front, and Bane pointed at a small beam of light coming from the wall. Arthur got close and shut one eye to look through the small hole into the main hall.

He saw soldiers and knights scattered in several groups. Many of the guards were concentrated around the two doorways. Most of the knights were in smaller groups around the big table. In the middle of it all was Guinevere, holding court and clearly leading the conversations around her. 'She's here.'

'What's the guard situation like?' whispered Aurelius.

Arthur scanned for a quick count. 'Probably two dozen knights and nearly three dozen guards.'

'Och, is that all?' Morgan rested on his sword. 'Just give me a minute for my breath and we'll get started.'

'Actually, there's also a dozen women over by the throne, just watching everyone,' said Arthur. 'Light armour, but with swords and bows. Looks like personal bodyguards to me.'

'Great. Maybe Geoffrey can find a nice wife finally.' Morgan grinned at his friend and picked up his sword, weighing it in his hand. 'If they don't chop you to pieces first that is.'

'I've never fought against women before.' Geoffrey shifted uncomfortably. 'Well, not knowingly anyway.'

'Most are not as strong as a man in a fight,' Aurelius slightly bowed his head to his wife, 'but underestimate them at your peril, they are no less deadly.'

'Another scheme of Guinevere's, I would think,' said Lady Anne. 'Most men still think twice before striking a woman down, and in that time you would be dead. The Lady plays for every advantage.'

Bane surveyed those around him and placed his hand on Arthur's shoulder. 'Sire, I'm sorry to say, but I just don't see a way to surround the Lady and activate these devices before most of us are dead. Maybe with the element of surprise, if we all rush her at once, a couple of us might just get through and hit her with a device or two.'

'I think even that option is now closed,' said Arthur gravely. 'Guinevere just looked right at me. I think she knows we're here.'

As if on cue, there was a click, and the door in the wall opened into the hall. Over sixty pairs of eyes moved around to look at them. The Lady raised her arms to beckon them in, a cold smile on her face. 'Lovely to see you, Arthur, but what took you so long? I've been waiting for you all week.'

Arthur stepped into the hall and raised his bow. He let power flow into the shield, and flickering green magic surrounded them as they slowly walked into the main hall. One by one, they raised their weapons. Lady Anne the last to draw her bow, the string quivering with blue fire, and she trained her arrow straight at the Lady.

'Well, well, you have learnt a trick or two since we last met.

Lovely shade of green you have there, Arthur,' Guinevere indicated to her bodyguards and they fanned out, returning the favour by drawing their bows as well. 'But you know you can't fire through a shield. Not much of a plan, is it Arthur?'

Arthur dropped the shield for an instant, long enough for his and Anne's arrows to let fly. But Guinevere was just as quick, and red fire erupted around her. Arthur's arrow disintegrated in the fire, but Lady Anne's sped through the shield in a blaze of blue. Guinevere raised a hand at the last second and the arrow deflected away into one of the bodyguards behind her. The gurgling scream was short, and the guard was dead before she hit the ground.

Surprise flickered briefly on Guinevere's face. Then her expression hardened. 'You take one of my friends, so I shall take yours. One, by, one.'

She snapped her fingers and behind him Arthur heard a quiet grunt, then the sound of armour hitting the floor. He turned and saw Lancelot bending over the fallen body of Lord Bane. Lancelot shook his father, then felt for a pulse. He looked up at Arthur. 'He's gone. She's killed him stone dead.'

Guinevere stepped forward, the fiery shield around her weaving as it moved with her, almost like a living creature. 'Drop your weapons and surrender, or I will end you all. It's not too late to join me. Stand by my side while I protect this land or be consigned to history.'

Lancelot stared at Guinevere. Sadness, love and hatred all vied for control on his face, his muscles getting ready to launch a suicidal attack. Kay reached down and placed a hand on his shoulder. 'That won't help the memory of our fathers. We can't beat magic like that. At least if we surrender, we may survive to fight another day.'

Arthur stopped midway towards his friends, and his mouth opened in realisation. He raised the intensity of his shield, and the green fire roared around them. 'She's tipped her hand too soon,' he said to them, under the cover of the noise.

'What?' said Kay.

'She can't actually kill us all just like that. She didn't kill Lord Bane or your father, she just took away the magic that was keeping them alive. Remember, it was her who saved them all those years ago.'

'Are you willing to bet our lives on that?' asked Kay.

'Yes,' said Arthur. 'Will you follow me?'

They looked at him and one by one they nodded. Lancelot gently laid his father down and held out his hand to Arthur. His father's device sat there, glowing in his palm. 'I guess you have to come with us after all.'

Arthur took it from Lancelot and helped him up.

'Don't tell me you've got a plan for this,' said Morgan, and Arthur nodded. 'How the hell do you think these things up?'

'I've had the best teachers,' he replied. 'Everyone get ready to surround Guinevere, you'll know when. Merlin, can you hold the magical shield and then push it out on my mark?'

'Yes, I believe I can,' replied the sorcerer. 'How far do you require?'

'As far as it will go.' He gestured Merlin to come with him as he advanced on Guinevere. 'You might want to be by my side for this one. You know, in the middle of it all.'

Arthur turned back to the waiting Guinevere and eased up on his shield.

'Well?' she said over the noise. 'Are you going to come to your senses finally? I really don't want to kill you all. That would be such a waste.'

'No, I don't think we will.' He tightened his grip on Merlin.

'He can't help you now.' Guinevere smiled coldly. 'I can see the magic in him has all but faded. You should have sided with me, not that weak old man.'

Arthur ignored her and let his heart wander out to Clarent. He felt the power flowing from it and into the green fire all around them. The shield was warm but wary in his grip, wary of the foe it faced. So Arthur balled up all his courage, all his belief in what was right, and he poured it into the shield. The stream of power from the shield became a raging torrent. Into this blazing green fire, Merlin split himself once more. Now standing east, west, north and south, the four Merlins pushed the shield out with all their magical might.

Guinevere screamed in pain as the raging green fire tore into her magic and the knights around her. The knights went flying and crashed into the walls around the hall. The expanding shield then caught the soldiers and bodyguards, sending them skating across the floor to be knocked unconscious with their comrades.

Merlin drew on the power he had gained and pushed the shield out until it finally crashed into the edge of the hall. Not a single enemy troop or guard was standing as the green fire faded into the castle walls.

Merlin's shoulders sagged and he turned to face Arthur. 'Not too bad for an old man.' Then all four Merlins sighed and faded to nothing.

'What a waste of time and magic,' said Guinevere, picking herself up from the floor, red fire already igniting again in her hands. 'It really looks like you will never learn.'

She glanced around at the nine of them surrounding her and laughed. 'You really think those devices can stop me. I've seen what they can do, it's pitiful. However far you send me, I'll just come right back.'

'Not that you'll even get as far as using them.' She opened her fingers and red magic shot out. The tendrils reached them and latched on to the devices, pulling them closer to her. 'I think I'll have those, thank you very much.'

Arthur fought to hold the device, even to trigger it, but it was wrenched from his hand in an instant. The others fared little better until only Geoffrey was left. His muscles bulged with the effort and sweat poured from him. Then his foot slipped on the floor and he came crashing down. The device finally wrenched from his hand.

'There, that wasn't so hard was it.' Guinevere held all nine devices in her hand. 'But just to be sure.'

She smashed the devices on the floor, and shards of glass shattered everywhere, glittering in the light. When she was done, red magic ripped from her hands again, and this time it grabbed them all by the throat. She dragged them slowly towards her.

'You were right of course,' she said to Arthur as she dragged him painfully across the floor. 'I did tip my hand a little early. I thought it worth a go though, just on the off chance you might finally realise how hopeless your fight is.'

'Your father was just the same. Well, not your actual father of course. King Uther never knew when to give up either.' She sighed once more. 'None of this would have been necessary if he'd just given me the sword and let me rule with him. I played the maid for years, gaining his trust, trying to gain his love. But just like you, Arthur, his head could not be turned. Moreover, he never let go of that sword. So, my army crushed him in his own castle, and I despatched all the children, finishing his bloodline.'

She looked Arthur in the eye. 'I didn't enjoy that, all those poor children, but it had to be done. And then, most annoyingly, it was all for nothing because you turned up.'

Her eyes glowed with anger as her voice rose. 'I couldn't believe it. It was like history repeating itself. A new king, but still too weak and shortsighted to rule properly, to control our land. Still too stupid to make the right choices, the right alliances.'

'You just don't realise what needs to be done to save this land. The sacrifices that have to be made.' Her eyes blazed red like a furnace. 'It just makes me so mad, all this wasted time. Well, no more.'

Another tendril of magic reached out and ripped the shield from Arthur's arm, bringing it back to Guinevere and dropping it by her side. 'I'll take that as well.'

Her magic reached back out and searched his scabbard, looking for Excalibur. Then Guinevere paused in surprise. 'Where is it? What have you done with it?'

She screamed again, all self-control gone, just pure anger in her voice. The grip around Arthur's throat tightened, and his vision began to dim. Guinevere walked towards him. Fiery magic dripped from her blazing eyes like tears of incandescent rage. 'Where. Is. The. Sword?'

Arthur pointed to his throat as his vision darkened further.

Guinevere regained some composure, let out an exasperated sigh, and dropped Arthur to the floor. He crashed down next to Geoffrey, who was still hanging in the air, desperately trying to break the hold on his throat. As Arthur reached out to cushion his fall, shards of the broken devices cut into both his hands. He watched as the blood mixed with Geoffrey's sweat.

'Tell me where the sword is right now, or your misguided companions will die so painfully they will wish they'd never been born.' Guinevere poured out power from her hands and into the magic holding his friends. Their screams reached him the instant the red fire pulsed angrily around their throats.

One last chance, thought Arthur as he watched the others losing their battle to stay alive. He reached out with a hand into the grimy mix of blood and sweat. 'Help,' he said.

The blood around his hand bubbled with streams of water. They spread out fast, heading for his friends. The streams became stronger and torrents of water rushed up to each person, crashing into the fiery red magic and extinguishing it.

Before Guinevere could react, Ellie emerged from the centre of the water. The Lake poured from both her hands, starting to fill the hall, crashing menacingly around Guinevere.

Ellie raised her hands, pulling the Lake up higher around Guinevere, trying to drown her in a column of water. 'You leave my friends alone, you evil witch.'

Ellie turned to Arthur. 'Get them out of here now.'

'I'm not leaving you against her.'

'Ha, I can handle that horrible woman no problem,' shouted Ellie against the roar of the Lake, and she increased the pressure of the water around Guinevere even further.

'I'm not so sure about that.' He looked into the rushing water around Guinevere and saw a bubble of red flare up. Then it pushed back the water bit by bit until the column collapsed around her.

'Is that the best you've got,' said Guinevere, the fire returning to her eyes and hands. Quickly, she shot out a blazing red fireball towards Ellie. The Lady of the Lake held up her hand and water poured forth, extinguishing the red fire instantly.

'No,' replied Ellie, and let loose another torrent of water at Guinevere. 'I've got a whole lake to play with.'

Exhausted, Arthur pushed himself to his feet. With fireballs blazing all around them and water crashing into the walls and ceiling, he lurched over to Aurelius and Lady Anne.

'If we don't get out of here soon, we'll drown.' Aurelius held onto his wife, supporting her in the choppy water that was already waist high.

'No, Arthur's right,' she said, exhaustion on her face but blue fire in her eyes. 'We must finish it now.'

Arthur stared at his aunt. 'I meant what I said to Ellie, but I just don't see what we can do. I'm all out of ideas.'

'Stop and feel the water,' she said. 'Can you sense them?'

Amongst the raging battle, Arthur closed his eyes and reached out into the water. Now up to his chest, he could feel the cold weight of the Lake and its desire to crush Guinevere. But there, just on the edge, he could feel Clarent, and faintly all around them the shards of the devices, scattered throughout the water.

He looked at Lady Anne as the water reached their heads. She nodded to him. 'Just bring them together,' she said.

And all of a sudden, Arthur saw what he had to do. He let power flow from his shield into the water and through the remains of the devices. He saw Guinevere's eyes open wide with realisation. She lashed out with unimaginable power, but he got there first and triggered the tiny shards of the devices with all the magic he could get from his shield.

White magic erupted in every drop of the Lake and Arthur felt he was burning and drowning at the same time. He saw the others contort in agony, as they were engulfed by the raging sea of power. Through the overpowering light he watched Guinevere, grim determination on her face despite the pain, still fighting the Lake and slowly losing. Ellie drifting past, with Bevs desperately reaching out to hold her. Lady Anne struggling through the boiling magic to help her stricken husband. Morgan, Geoffrey and Marcus already unconscious. Lancelot and Kay battling to reach the Lady and make her pay.

As all the magic from the shattered devices finally exploded with a blinding light, the past voice of Merlin echoed in Arthur's mind, drawn from his long lessons with the sorcerer.

'To sacrifice for the land, is the greatest deed.'

Then everything went dark.

EPILOGUE

Lady Gallow sat alone at the new table, its surface now beginning to show wear from all the meetings and negotiations it had hosted. A mixture of sadness and contentment played across her face as she gently rubbed her stomach. 'Not so old after all,' she said to herself as she felt the flutter of life inside.

'What's that, my dear?' asked Ector as he walked into the main hall.

Jane's expression straightened, and she placed her hands on the table, the usual stern look returning to her face. 'You'll see soon enough husband of mine.'

'You don't fool me.' He sat down next to her and placed his hand on hers. 'I know that look is reserved for tough negotiations and discipline. Of which I need neither. Something's up.'

She squeezed his hand back. Her face softened, and a touch of sadness crossed her features again. 'To the point, as ever. You are unique, my dear, and for that I love you dearly. But I must confess, I do still miss him. You can't replace him you know.'

'Wouldn't want to,' replied Ector in his straightforward manner. 'Lord Gallow was his own man. Myself, I never wanted to be a lord. Not interested in all that power.'

He rose to his feet and smiled back at her; the warmth in his face belying his short manner. 'Quite happy being the right-hand man, your right-hand man my dear.'

She glanced down at the life growing inside her. No need to scare him just yet, she smiled to herself.

'What?' he asked again.

'Oh, just wondering what happened to Arthur's horse. Did your scouts ever find her?'

Ector lowered his head a little. 'Sadly not. After she cared for you, she disappeared. We sent out word, but no sign at all unfortunately.'

Jane patted the seat beside her and Ector returned to sit next to his new wife. 'Never mind,' she said. 'I'm sure she'll find something useful to do.'

A look of concentration returned to her face. 'Now, down to business. With Lord Salfor long dead and the Lady gone, how do we restore peace with the north?'

*

The cold sea sat quiet and dark, the freezing wind blowing gentle waves onto the sand. The horse stood in the dunes, grazing on the occasional patch of grass. Every now and then it looked up and watched the ocean.

A ripple in the water caught its attention, and the horse walked down the dunes and onto the dark sand. Another ripple appeared, and then the top of a head. The old man slowly emerged from the water and placed a grateful hand on the horse's shoulder.

'Thank you, my friend,' said Merlin through chattering teeth as the healing power from Horse unfroze his old bones. 'That was a very long walk, and it is rather chilly down there.'

Horse neighed quietly, and Merlin closed his eyes in concentration. 'Oh dear. I could not tell while I was gone. But yes, Arthur has left us, has he not.'

Merlin kept his hand on Horse's shoulder, using her for support as she led him up the beach and onto the dunes.

'Well,' said Merlin, his energy returning, 'luckily you and I are rather good at waiting.' He patted Horse's neck once again. 'I propose we use the time wisely. You never know what might turn up.'

*

Arthur woke with a start, pain lancing through his whole body, every muscle screaming for attention. He opened an eye and saw Lancelot leaning over him.

'Hurts doesn't it?'

Arthur nodded, just hoping the pain would go away somehow.

'Drink this, it'll help.' Lancelot offered him a small cup of murky liquid and Arthur gulped it down. Immediately, the pain began to fade.

'Bloody hell, you weren't kidding,' said Arthur, sitting up. 'What on earth is it?'

'No idea. Found one next to me when I woke up.' Lancelot walked over to the thick curtains hanging on the stone wall.

'Is that wise?' Arthur put down the cup and looked at his friend in surprise. 'Not like you to throw caution to the wind.'

'Not my biggest concern.' replied Lancelot, and he threw open the drapes.

Arthur stared out of the window in wonder. Massive stone towers rose impossibly all around them in the busy sky, the huge granite constructions reaching up towards the clouds. However, he could barely wonder how they were possible before his eyes were drawn to something else.

'What are those?' he croaked, only just able to get the words out. He raised a hand and pointed to the hundreds of horseless chariots flying across the sky.

'Still not our biggest problem.' said Lancelot, and he nodded to the left.

Arthur followed his friend's gaze, scanning across the ever-rising towers until he saw the giant statue of a woman in the distance.

'Oh,' he said and sat back down.

'Yup,' replied Lancelot, slumping next to him.

'All our battles, all our sacrifices, all for nothing. Wherever we are, whenever we are, Guinevere just got here first and set up court as if nothing ever happened.'

'Yup,' said Lancelot again, having nothing more to add.

'The others?' asked Arthur.

'Don't know. I woke up next door, then I found you here.'

Arthur got to his feet, and his face hardened. 'Where there's you and me, there may be more. Somehow the Lady doesn't have total control.' Arthur grabbed some boots from the side of the bed. 'And if she doesn't have that, then maybe she doesn't have Excalibur or the shield either.'

Arthur made for the door.

'Where are you going?'

'I'm going to find our friends, then I'm going to get my sword. You coming with me?'

A grin appeared on Lancelot's face and hope returned as he rose. 'Too bloody right I am.'

'Good.' Arthur yanked opened the door, but stopped in his tracks when he saw the woman standing in front of him.

'Hello Arthur,' said Guinevere, her eyes blazing red. 'Welcome to my new world.'

*

To be continued in book 2

286

ACKNOWLEDGMENTS

A huge thank you to my wife Rosemarie McFadden for editing this book during its creation, for all her encouragement, and for her dry humour throughout the nine years it took me to write this story.

Many thanks to Pauline McFadden for detailed editing and lots of great suggestions. Thanks also to Lisa O'Connor, Rowland Furse and Miriam McMahon for many corrections and some interesting suggestions.

Thank you to Claire Charalambous, Pauline Cox, Kevin McFadden and Sue Stroobach for further read throughs and spotting typos.

A big thanks to Phil Tsang for painting an original and fantastic cover that brings the book to life.

And finally, thanks to Niamh Cox, Sam Cox and Robert Tremain. For different reasons, but you each know why.

Printed in Great Britain
by Amazon